Parallel Programming

Lou Baker and Bradley J. Smith

McGraw-Hill

New York San Francisco Washington, D.C. Auckland Bogotá
Caracas Lisbon London Madrid Mexico City Milan
Montreal New Delhi San Juan Singapore
Sydney Tokyo Toronto

McGraw-Hill

A Division of The **McGraw·Hill** *Companies*

Library of Congress Cataloging-in-Publication Data

Baker, Louis
  Parallel programming / by Lou Baker & Bradley J. Smith.
    p. cm.
  Includes index.
  ISBN 0-07-912259-0
  1. Parallel programming (Computer science) I. Smith, B. J.
  II. Title.
  QA76.642.B35   1996
  005.2—dc20   96-7182
                       CIP

1 2 3 4 5 6 7 8 9 0 DOC/DOC 9 0 0 9 8 7 6

ISBN 0-07-912259-0

*The sponsoring editor of this book was Jennifer Holt DiGiovanna, the
manuscript editor was Aaron Bittner, and the executive editor was
Robert Ostrander. The production supervisor was Katherine Brown.*

*Printed and bound by R.R. Donnelly & Sons Company, Crawfordsville,
Indiana.*

McGraw-Hill books are available at special quantity discounts to use as
premiums and sales promotions, or for use in corporate training programs. For
more information, please write to the Director of Special Sales, McGraw-Hill,
11 West 19th Street, New York, NY 10011. Or contact your local bookstore.

Product or brand names used in this book may be trade names or
trademarks. Where we believe that there may be proprietary claims to such
trade names or trademarks, the name has been used with an initial capital or
it has been capitalized in the style used by the name claimant. Regardless of
the capitalization used, all such names have been used in an editorial
manner without any intent to convey endorsement of or other affiliation
with the name claimant. Neither the author nor the publisher intends to
express any judgment as to the validity or legal status of any such
proprietary claims.

9122590
MH96

Table of Contents

Table of Contents

Foreword

Parallel computing has become a key component of high-performance computing in the 90's. But in order to exploit this technology, users must have a sound understanding of how to write portable parallel programs. In the past, an application written in FORTRAN or C could be compiled and executed on almost any computer available. This is not the case with today's parallel computers because, in general, compilers cannot create an efficient parallel programming from an existing serial program. Even if such compilers existed, programmers would still need to have knowledge about parallel programming because the most popular method of parallel computing is by using a network of workstations as a *virtual parallel supercomputer.*

Using a network of computers is called distributed computing. Distributed computing is the present trend for parallel computing and will continue for the foreseeable future, because it holds many cost advantages. By using existing resources there is no additional hardware cost; and the software (like PVM) to make a set of computers look like a single large computer is available free on the Internet. The aggregate power and memory of existing resources at a site can easily exceed that of a supercomputer. There are even cases where multiple supercomputers around the world have been combined for a few hours to create an immensely powerful machine. So distributed computing allows users to run their applications for the same cost and at supercomputer speeds, but there is a catch! These applications must be written as parallel programs. This requires that the scientist and engineers developing these applications understand the basic concepts of parallel computing, how to 'think' in parallel, and how to pass data between cooperating tasks. This book is written specifically for the scientist or engineer who wants to begin writing parallel programs.

Once the terminology and basic concepts are known, the next step is to learn how to write applications that can exploit parallelism and be portable. Portability used to be very difficult to achieve, but the recent development of the Parallel Virtual Machine (PVM) software package and the Message Passing Interface (MPI) specification has made this task much easier.

PVM is a freely available software package developed at Oak Ridge National Laboratory and the University of Tennessee that allows a network of computers to appear as a single virtual computer. PVM includes all the required functions to create a *virtual machine*, start up programs on this machine, and for programs to communicate and synchronize with each other. PVM is the de facto standard for distributed computing world wide. In a similar fashion, MPI is a standard message passing syntax that has been adopted by all parallel computer vendors. So an application developed on one parallel computer can be executed on another vendor's parallel computer with minimal source changes. Knowledge of both software packages is required to create portable applications. This book is based on PVM and MPI, and provides a wealth of information, examples, and tips on their use.

With a focus on scientists and engineers, this book assumes no prior knowledge of parallel computing and leads the reader by the hand through all of the basic concepts. There are chapters on identifying parallelism and on steps to convert an existing application to run in parallel. The main body of this book teaches the reader about message passing, which is the most portable and highest performance parallel programming paradigm. There are numerous examples to illustrate different parallel programming concepts. The final chapters of the book cover the difficult issues of debugging parallel programs and tips on optimizing parallel programs to run efficiently on particular parallel computers.

There has been a lack of books on parallel computing that are written specifically for the practical needs of scientists and engineers. This book is an attempt to fill this gap and open up the world of parallel computing to this group.

Al Geist
Oak Ridge National Labs

Introduction

This book is about real-world parallel programming. It is intended to "jump-start" development of parallel applications. It is based on experience the authors have gained struggling to produce parallel codes for the numerical simulation of real-world problems. It is hoped that this hard-won knowledge will be useful to others who plan to tread the same path. This book is intended as a guide book for such people. This book is not a survey of parallel architecture concepts; it is not about algorithms per se. It is not a collection of theoretical algorithms for formally-specified, abstract machines that do not exist.

Then just what is this book? It starts with two chapters that provide the background to understand the terminology and the basics of parallel programming. The third chapter discusses the basics of developing a parallel program. The fourth chapter discusses the details of partitioning a problem into tasks suitable for parallel processing. It surveys the classes of problems of interest to scientists and engineers and discusses strategies for each, with references to research papers for detailed examples. The fifth chapter provides guidelines for effective programming. It outlines the strategy we advocate, which is to first develop a working serial code, and then parallelize this code. The initial serial version of the code must be written with an eye to the ultimate parallel code, and how to do this effectively is discussed. The remaining chapters provide the specifics, including working code, for parallel programming. The parallel programming approach advocated by this book is called message passing. This is the most well-developed and general way to write parallel programs. We also advocate using the MPI standard for message passing, precisely because it is rapidly becoming the universal standard. Because this approach is still maturing, we cover the various options within MPI as well as around it; other approaches (such as PVM) are more mature and widespread, but are likely to be supplanted by MPI in the future. We discuss how to achieve the best of all possible worlds by layering MPI over PVM. This enables a single program to take the best advantage of systems with a native MPI implementation, as well as use systems (including heterogeneous networks) that are only supported by PVM. The sixth chapter is devoted to a discussion of message passing and the details of implementing message passing in a user's code, employing MPI and PVM. The next chapter provides an extensive set of code listings to implement the layered MPI/PVM interface, with examples of its use. The next chapter covers the debugging and performance tuning of a parallel program; code is provided to support the tracing of parallel programs. The final chapter presents a case study. This program, a parallel Poisson solver, is more than a toy code but obviously not a full-blown commercial application. Appendices give sources for more information, algorithms, etc. Appendices giving the location of more information, including both books and internet sites, close out the book.

We would like to thank Al Geist from Oak Ridge National Laboratory for providing a foreword for this book. We'd like to express our gratitude to the people at the Maui High Performance Computer Center, notably Brian Smith and Peggy Williams. We would also like to thank the MPICH development team at Argonne National Laboratories and PVM development team for providing examples and support for this book. Most especially, we would like to thank our families, friends and colleagues who provided assistance and support during the writing of this book.

We hope this book helps the reader to avoid some of the missteps and dead ends we did not.

Chapter 1

The Parallel Landscape

The first two chapters of this book are intended to give the reader the background necessary to read this and other works on parallel processing. If you have purchased this book, you are interested in the subject and have probably picked up at least some of what is contained in these chapters, so feel free to skim or skip sections as desired. Many reviews and/or views of this subject have been published, e. g., Bell 1992. In this fast-changing field, a review is probably obsolescent by the time it appears in print.

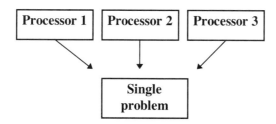

Figure 1.1: Parallel computing is using more than one processor to solve a single problem cooperatively.

What is Parallel Computing?

Parallel computing is the use of more than one Central Processing Unit (CPU) at the same time to solve a single problem. Today, parallel computing encompasses the entire spectrum of machines, from two personal computers connected via Ethernet to thousands of the worlds most powerful processors in a parallel supercomputer. The practical issues involved in parallel computing are much the same as those of a group of people attempting to work together on a single project. How should the work be divided up, and in what order? How will people communicate and coordinate work? How to accommodate workers completing tasks at different speeds? How can output from different workers be merged to form the final product? Who will oversee the overall project? These are the fundamental questions to be addressed.

Grand Challenges and the Gordon Bell Prize

A number of computationally difficult problems have been called "grand challenges." These are problems that would require teraflop computing rates; a flop is a "floating-point operation per second." A teraflop is a rate of 10^{12} flops (1 trillion flops). Here, floating-point operation is taken to mean an average of the addition and multiplication operations; divisions, which take significantly more time, are not used in assessing flops. On modern architectures, additions and multiplications are typically equally fast. Problems that are often called grand challenges include weather prediction, climate and ocean circulation modeling, and "numerical wind tunnels."

Gordon Bell, a principal architect of the DEC VAX, established a prize in 1987 to stimulate the development of parallel processing. There is an annual competition for the prize, with presentation of awards at the IEEE's annual Supercomputing Conference traditionally held in November or December. The principal criterion for judging is the flop rate.

Table 1.1: Recent Gordon Bell award winners.		
Year	**Organization and machine**	**Flop rate**
1994	Sandia Laboratory 1980-node Intel Paragon	~150 GFlops
1993	Los Alamos Laboratory 1024 node CM-5	~60 GFlops

Parallel Computing Models

Flynn Classifications: SISD, MISD, SIMD, and MIMD

In 1966 and 1972 Flynn published landmark studies of parallel architectures which established the customary terminology for discussing such systems. Due to technological advances over the intervening two decades, the relevance of his taxonomy has diminished, but the terminology is still widely used to describe parallel computers, and therefore is worth knowing.

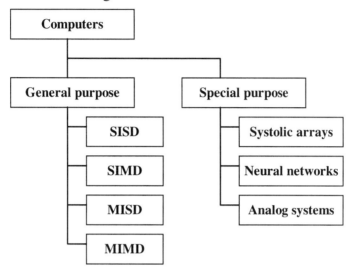

Figure 1.2: Diagram of computing taxonomy. The most common general purpose computer is the Single Instruction Single Data (SISD) processor.

The 1966 paper established the four classes of machine architectures: SISD, SIMD, MISD, MIMD. Single Instruction-Single Data (SISD) is the conventional, non-parallel architecture, e. g., that of the PC for example. The Multiple Instruction Single Data (MISD) architecture is a theoretical architecture proposed by Flynn, but not used for general purpose computing. The two major classes of parallel architectures he defined were Single Instruction Multiple Data (SIMD) and Multiple Instruction-Multiple Data (MIMD).

The SIMD architecture consists of a number of identical processors proceeding in lock step synchronism, doing the same things to different data. In the 1972 paper, Flynn defined three classes of SIMD machines: array processors, pipelined processors, and associative architectures. Conditionals are typically effected on such architectures by setting flags to exclude selected processors from sections of the code. Obviously, this can lead to a considerable fraction of the machine being idle at any moment. SIMD machines with an array architecture include the Thinking Machines CM-2, Goodyear (now Loral) Aerospace MPP (Massively Parallel Processor), the MasPar MP-1 and MP-2, the Active Memory Technology DAP (Distributed Array Processor) family, and the pioneering Illiac IV. So-called vertical processing systems (Fet 1995) are fine-grained SIMD machines with bit-slice architecture, and include the CM-1 and CM-2, the MPP, and the DAP.

Pipelined vector machines (such as the original Cray machines and Texas Instruments ASC) behave as SIMD machines in that the pipeline does the identical operation to the elements of a vector within a defined loop. Unlike the array architectures, these are not done simultaneously, but are "time-multiplexed" (in Flynn's phrase). The different data has different portions of the same instruction being done to it simultaneously. SIMD machines have limited flexibility, but attempt to make up for this by reduced cost of each processor node, resulting in many more affordable processors. The CM-2 was available with up to 65,536 processors, each being a relatively simple element. Despite the initial success of SIMD architectures, most vendors have discarded SIMD in favor of fewer but more powerful processors. The Thinking Machines CM-5, successor to the CM-2, was a MIMD machine. The CM-5 is no longer capable of holding massive numbers of processors, the largest (in existence) being the 1024 node CM-5 at Los Alamos National Laboratories. Each processor was a complete Sparc workstation microprocessor with two vector units, which are significantly more powerful than the CM-2's tiny processors. The move to fewer, more powerful processors in recent years reflects the fact that more powerful serial processors can be fully exploited, while a large number of less-powerful processors often cannot.

Associative architectures are typically forms of memory rather than full computational architectures. An associative memory is one that is "content addressable." When presented with a key, such as a user i.d. number, it returns the user's name or some other data. This is classed as parallel computing, because simultaneous comparisons of the key take place with many possible addresses. Cache memory simultaneously checks the desired address against the tags of all of the data lines cached, so (in some trivial sense) cache memories are SIMD parallel computers.

The MIMD model covers a wide range of interconnection schemes, processors, and architectures. The key point is that each processor operates independently of the others, potentially running entirely different programs. MIMD processors communicate using a high speed network. The network lets processors share data and synchronize calculations. Rare is the parallel problem that does not need any communication or synchronization between processors. (Such problems are called "embarrassingly parallel," and are typically only seen in benchmarks.) Most modern MIMD machines use an explicit message-passing paradigm to communicate between processors. One processor explicitly "sends" data to a destination processor, which "receives" the data. While this scheme puts a significant burden on the programmer to match sends and receives, it also gives the programmer the control needed to minimize communications and maximize performance.

Advances in computer design have rendered the Flynn taxonomy somewhat obsolete. The "superscalar" processor, which can perform a number of operations simultaneously, does not fit well into such a scheme. Even "simple" RISC processors have pipelines now, and so might be taken to be SIMD according to Flynn's taxonomy. Superpipelines employ long pipelines with very simple stages in order to maximize permissible clock speed. Very long instruction word (VLIW) machine architectures are beginning to appear, and their future is unclear; they too defy precise characterization as SIMD or MIMD. Systolic arrays were not envisioned in Flynn's scheme. Such arrays may be considered as SIMD arrays with a fixed communication pattern. Indeed, systolic arrays can be readily simulated by SIMD systems. Obviously, for some special purposes, a systolic array can be constructed more economically than an analogous SIMD array. Similarly, neural networks are a special-purpose architecture that involves a large number of identical processing units performing identical actions simultaneously. Such systems are often emulated on digital machines (serial or parallel), but are often implemented as analog rather than digital computational units. They therefore have some SIMD-like characteristics, although they should probably be in a class by themselves.

Because of the regular pattern of communication in systolic arrays, it can be useful to program SIMD or MIMD machines to emulate such an array (Gross et al. 1994). This is most appropriate for machines with their processors interconnected as a mesh (array).

Another approach to parallel computer design is "data flow." This is more of a programming model than a hardware architecture. In a data flow computer, computations are initiated by the arrival of data at a processor node. This can obviously be simulated on a MIMD architecture with a simple polling loop, or by generating and fielding interrupts on the arrival of data. See, for example, Denning and Dichy (1990) for more on data flow.

The PRAM Model; Shared Memory Models

Theoretical studies of parallel algorithms often assume that the machine is a Parallel Random Access Memory machine, or PRAM. This is a shared-memory machine. All processors have access to a presumably infinite, shared memory bank. All operations on memory, either local or remote, are assumed to have a theoretical cost of one unit. This is in contrast to real computers where the time to access a remote processor's memory location is often thousands of times greater than the time to access local memory. There are a number of versions of the PRAM model, such as the Concurrent Read Exclusive Write (CREW) PRAM. A CREW PRAM allows different processors to read the same location of memory simultaneously with no conflict or requirement to wait until the other has completed. If a write is attempted simultaneously to the same location, one processor must wait until the other has completed. If the attempted writes are simultaneous, one is randomly chosen and permitted to write, while the other must wait. Similarly, the Exclusive Read Exclusive Write (EREW) PRAM allows only one processor at a time to access a given memory location. In the Concurrent Read Concurrent Write (CRCW) PRAM , if two processors attempt to write different values simultaneously, the result is randomly chosen to be one of the values written.

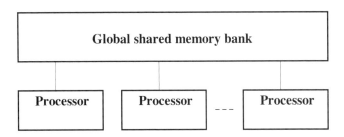

Figure 1.3: A Parallel Random Access Machine (PRAM) or global shared-memory machine. Processors share a global memory bank.

While shared-memory machines provide a convenient theoretical tool for developing parallel algorithms, shared memory is not yet a realistic model for high-performance parallel machines. The reason is that no one has yet designed a scaleable shared memory that allows large numbers of processors to simultaneously access different locations in constant time. The Kendall Square Research KSR-1 was a notable attempt to create a commercial shared-memory machine. It used a creative hand designed system of caches and global memory maps to simulate a globally shared memory. The hope was that the lion's share of the memory references would be localized, so that the additional cost of distant references would be negligible. Unfortunately, in practice some existing scientific codes performed poorly using KSR's "all-cache" memory architecture. In addition, the locally designed KSR microprocessor was quickly overtaken by a new generation of coarse grained MIMD machines from competitors using the latest commercial microprocessors. KSR was eventually forced to file for bankruptcy.

You will find remarks in the literature such as "The next wave of massively parallel computers will give the illusion of shared memory" (Zorpette 1992). This may be true in the limited sense that many machines will support languages such as Linda, which hide message passing from the programmer. Nevertheless, for the foreseeable future it will be dangerous to rely on such computing paradigms, in our opinion; memory access will be measured in nanoseconds for local memory and microseconds for global or shared memory. (The SP-2 claims a bisection bandwidth corresponding to 500 nanoseconds. This is still best expressed as 1/2 microsecond, and is two orders of magnitude larger than the local memory delay. It also does not include the initial latency.) If the programming model obscures this distinction, the result will be inefficient programs whose problems are hidden from the user.

One buzzword that seems to be establishing itself is "hierarchical memory." This is not really a new concept, merely a new term. Modern microprocessors typical have an on-chip cache or caches (typically separate caches for data and instructions, generally about 8 K for current technology). These processors often provide support for off-chip SRAM caches of greater size, which are typically on the order of 256 K. Then there is the slower DRAM memory, typically a few megabytes. "Hierarchical memory" merely extends this approach to additional levels. A global shared memory can be emulated, as on the Silicon Graphics Power Challenge (Nordwall 1993) where the final level memory is up to 16 gigabytes.

Bus-based shared memory systems become saturated when the number of processors is on the order of ten (Brooks 1992). Higher-cost interconnects become impractical. Brooks notes "CRI [Cray Research, Inc.] engineers often indicate that the memory interconnect in the C-90 consumes much more logic than the processors themselves, and that this situation has gotten worse each time CRI has increased the processor count in its machines." Brooks notes that using hardware routing and distributed memory (such as on the BBN Butterfly machine) substantially reduces costs while improving bandwidth. The moral is that shared memory, if used at all, will be emulated by distributed memory hardware.

Distributed Memory Machines: The Message-Passing Model

Most parallel computers are distributed-memory machines. These have memory associated with each processor (or sometimes a set of processors that share the block of memory). Conceptually, each can be viewed as an independent processor, with a high-speed network connecting all processors.

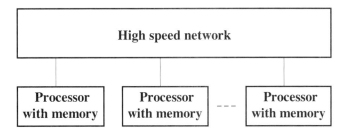

Figure 1.4: The message passing model for parallel
computing. Processors communicate by sending messages
across a high speed network link.

In such machines, processors have to explicitly send and receive data to communicate. Often, each processor node on the system consists of a number of microprocessors, some dedicated to housekeeping chores such as data transmission. The Intel Paragon is an example, in that each node is actually a pair of i860 microprocessors. In fact, one can use both processors for running programs under the SUNMOS operating system, but the original design intention was for one of the i860s to be dedicated to housekeeping. The message-passing model is the one we advocate for the user to employ. The reason is that it is closest to the behavior of the actual environments. By using a programming approach that reflects what the machine actually is doing, it is more likely that the programmer will understand what the machine is being asked to do, and consequently where the bottlenecks are and how they might be addressed. In addition, whatever is possible on the machine should be possible in the message-passing programming model, due to the close relationship of the two. A more abstract paradigm (e. g., that of shared memory) might be simpler and easier for some problems, but in general the performance penalty will be substantial.

In the message-passing paradigm, data is sent by one processor to an addressee or a set of addressees. The addressee processor will save the data in a buffer area, and will typically notify the appropriate task of the arrival of the data. Often, the receiving task is waiting for the data to arrive, but this is not necessary and it is more efficient if possible for it to await notification or to inquire whether the data has arrived.

Message passing can be either blocking or nonblocking. Blocking message passing calls will block, that is, wait, until the entire transaction (both send and receive) is complete. In contrast, nonblocking calls will return immediately after initiating a send or receive. A separate "wait" call is usually required to fully complete nonblocking sends and receives. Sends also come in synchronous and asynchronous versions. In a synchronous send, the send does not begin until a receive is posted. In an asynchronous send, the send may begin before a corresponding receive is posted. Inquiries to "probe" for data in the appropriate message class are provided by the message passing systems.

A Brief History of Parallel Computing

Parallel computing has been driven largely by government support for "number crunching" large problems. There was considerable interest in parallel processing of phased-array radar and sonar array data (see, e.g., Hobbs 1970). This led naturally to interest in array processors. There has also been interest in massive database query processing in real-time.

Early work focused on architecture development and on the design of algorithms developed specifically for an architecture. The hypercube architecture of machines from Thinking Machines Inc. and nCube resulted in much work focusing on algorithms for hypercubes. These approaches assumed that communicating information between adjacent processors was fastest, and routing information to other processors that were distant (in terms of the hypercube topology) would require proportionately more time.

More modern architectures are such that the time required to transmit information between any two processors is virtually identical. Often the overhead in making a call to the message passing system is longer than the network transit time for small messages. This is due to the use of VLSI technology for the switching and routing hardware, which enables relatively large numbers of processors to be connected dynamically, rapidly. So long as one processor is not the target of a number of other processors, routers have been developed that permit simultaneous communication between almost arbitrary pairs of all other processors. As a result, machine topology is no longer of great concern. Machines such as the IBM SP-2, Intel Paragon, and Cray T3D are of this character and are often called "meshes."

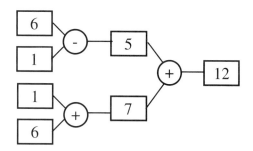

Figure 1.5: This parallel reduction is a fine-grained operation, because each processor only adds two integer values.

Fine-Grained Parallelism

Early parallel processing machines typically had a large number of relatively simple, often custom, processors, generally with a custom operating system. Fine-grained operations generally distribute the data as widely as possible, with each processor performing the simplest operations. A fine- grained example is shown in Figure 1.5, where each processor adds two numbers together to get a final result. One example of an early fine-grained machine is the Thinking Machines CM-2 (Hillis 1985). On the early TM machines, each processor was a custom bit-slice unit with a single-bit data path. Sixteen such processors were on a custom VLSI chip, along with a router unit and a single control unit (it was a SIMD architecture). Networks of INMOS Transputers were once popular, but are now harder to obtain. You can't get finer-grained than a single bit!

Fine-grained parallelism and much of current parallel algorithm theory were developed concurrently. If you pick up virtually any parallel computer science book, you will find a plethora of PRAM algorithms designed to divide a problem up as finely as possible, often using N processors to solve a problem of input size N. Unfortunately, in practice the overhead of processing a single floating-point value (or bit!) on each processor and then trying to merge results was found to be unacceptably large for real world problems. On the theoretical PRAM machine, where communications and calculations have identical cost, these algorithms were ideal. On real machines, where communications are thousands of times more expensive than calculations, performance was dismal. One of us (B. S.) has heard many programmers admit to getting worse performance running on thousands of fine grained processors than their desktop workstation. As a result, most modern parallel scientists are focusing on the development of new coarse grained parallel computers and algorithms.

Modern Message Passing Parallel Architectures

The number of message-passing systems is excessive. Among the protocols readily available are PVM, MPI, P4, PICL, Chameleon, pC++, ABC++, ESP, lparX, CHARM++,CC++,UC++,and μC++. This list does not include proprietary systems for specific machines, such as IBM's MPL or Intel's NX. There will undoubtedly be a shake-out. It is possible that features of such systems will find their way into later releases of other systems, so it is worthwhile to give a brief overview of the landscape. The potential number of actual hardware hosts for these systems is almost limitless, because virtually any network can be used as a distributed (parallel) computing host system with most of these messaging systems. This includes everything from the desktop PC to the largest special purpose architectures.

The Foreseeable Future

One key fact in the future of parallel hardware will clearly be the development of microprocessor technology. The speed of processors doubles almost every 18-24 months, and only the largest microprocessor vendors can afford the $1-billion plus price tag for a modern fabrication facility. Clearly, any competitive parallel computer must be based on off-the-shelf microprocessors, because the relatively tiny $200 million supercomputing market is not large enough to drive the multi-billion-dollar microprocessor market. (A reviewer commented that this was not clear to Cray Computer Corp. In reply we note that 1: they did so a number of years ago, and 2: they are now in Chapter 11.) This places severe limits on the future design of parallel computers. Any design based on a custom microprocessor will probably be obsolete by the time it reaches the market. Many parallel computers are obsolete by the time their operating systems reach a reliable state. Yet the cache hierarchy of current microprocessors makes it extremely difficult to implement some of the fast shared memory architectures envisioned by current designers. Further, message passing overhead could be significantly reduced by on-chip network interfaces. Manufacturers simply cannot afford to allocate scarce chip real estate to support features for this tiny market. However, as parallel computing enters the mainstream, such features will become more common.

What does all of this mean? For the near future, the fastest parallel computers will likely be based on off-the-shelf microprocessor technology, and in many cases off-the-shelf mini-supercomputer technology using a message-passing paradigm. Any other approach will likely be obsolete by the time it reaches the market and is stable. Until parallel computing escapes from the confined realms of scientists and engineers and enters the larger market for business and personal computing, we expect message- passing systems to dominate the field. We expect progress on other fronts, such as software and compiler technology, which will make parallel programs easier to write and debug. The general trend here will be away from explicit communications based on sends and receives toward compilers that perform some of this work for the programmer. For the moment, however, we expect to see message-passing hardware based on off-the-shelf microprocessors and a gradual evolution in parallel software tools toward less explicit programming models, including shared memory.

Distributed and Cluster Computing

Many people, when one speaks of parallel computing, think of large dedicated machines costing millions of dollars to operate. There are significant cost, developmental, and speed advantages to using existing clusters of workstations to develop, debug, and run parallel programs. The cost advantage is obvious. A typical workstation has a price tag in the $20K-$50K range, so even a dozen workstations cost an order of magnitude less than the cheapest parallel computer. Also, you likely already have all of the necessary hardware to operate your existing workstations as a parallel cluster. All that is required is one or more workstations or personal computers connected by a standard network, such as Ethernet. All of the necessary software can be obtained from public domain sources on the internet.

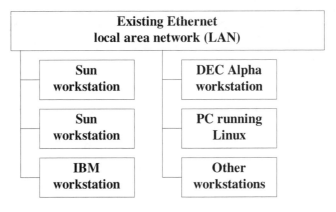

Figure 1.6: An example of a heterogeneous workstation cluster based on existing hardware. These clusters can be used in small numbers to develop and run parallel programs.

The advantages of developing code on a local workstation cluster are significant. First and foremost, the developer has complete control over the cluster. No special access to expensive parallel computers is required. No time is lost to temperamental parallel hardware, and you don't have to pay or beg someone else for the computing and disk resources needed to develop a parallel program. Second, it allows for easy progressive development. One can start by running serially on a single processor, move to running in parallel on multiple processors, and finally run in parallel on multiple workstations. Using simple portability techniques, which are the subject of this book, the program you develop on your workstation can easily be ported to a dedicated parallel machine after you have fully debugged it locally. Finally, one can work in a familiar development environment using existing compilers and debuggers, making the transition from serial development to parallel development easier for the programmer.

Used in small numbers over existing networks, clusters of workstations can attack problems much larger than any single workstation could, at a fraction of the cost. In many cases, problems that previously required Cray supercomputers to complete can now be done overnight on a workstation cluster. When one compares the turnaround time for a large problem running on a cluster to the total turnaround time for a large batch problem on a busy Cray supercomputer, one often finds it to be faster to complete the problem locally. Further, because disk resources are scarce and bandwidth to shared resource centers poor, data intensive-problems (such as creating movies) can often be done better on workstation clusters. This is not to say that workstation clusters are a panacea; clusters using traditional Ethernets are typically useful only in numbers smaller than a dozen. Larger problems, including all the so called "Grand Challenge" problems, require dedicated parallel supercomputers, though development may still be done on workstations.

Developing on the Cheap...

If you want to push the limits of what can be done on a budget, it is possible to develop and debug parallel programs on a single IBM style personal computer (PC). The minimum configuration is perhaps a 80486 computer with 16MB of RAM, and 300MB of disk space in a separate disk partition. The software to use is a UNIX operating system look-alike called Linux. The complete suite of Linux software is available for free on the Internet at sunsite.unc.edu using anonymous FTP. It is also available widely for less than $50 on CD-ROM from a number of vendors. We recommend purchasing a Linux book from your local bookstore. At last count, at least a dozen books were available on the installation, use and administration of Linux.

After a somewhat lengthy installation process, Linux allows your IBM-style personal computer to behave exactly like a high-priced 32-bit UNIX workstation, including full networking, X-Windows support, compilers, and debuggers. We have successfully run the Parallel Virtual Machine

(PVM) message-passing library described later in this book, under Linux. PCs connected with a LAN can even be used as a parallel cluster to solve larger problems. If you want to get started in parallel/distributed computing and are working within a strict budget, Linux may be a possible solution.

Another alternative is the WinMPI system. This is discussed in chapter 5, and an example of its use is given in chapter 9. Parallel code may be debugged on a PC running Windows and ported to a parallel computer afterward. WinMPI should be an excellent learning environment. Obviously, there is no point to running parallel code on a single processor except as a learning or development exercise.

Homogeneous versus Heterogeneous Clusters

A distinction must be drawn between parallel computing on homogeneous clusters (where all processors are the same) and heterogeneous clusters (where processors from different vendors may be combined to run a single problem). Parallel processes running in a homogeneous network are generally faster, because all processors speak the same language, and no conversion of data is necessary when passing messages. In contrast, heterogeneous clusters may be composed of vastly different types of computers, each using its own internal instructions and data formats. To operate in a heterogeneous environment, typically the same program is compiled on each different processor in the cluster. Data conversion is performed by the message-passing library to assure that a floating point number sent from one architecture is converted to the appropriate representation on the receiving machine.

Surprisingly, heterogeneous computing is not as difficult as it seems. Most message-passing systems designed for parallel workstation clusters perform the data translation transparently. The only difficulty for the programmer comes with installing the message-passing system on the cluster, and making sure that each node is running the same version of the application. Though there is a performance penalty for converting data during message passing, it often is worthwhile to run a program on a heterogeneous cluster to gain the power of faster nodes, as in the work of Becker and Dagnum (1991) discussed later in this chapter.

Large-scale heterogeneous computing is an interesting topic of ongoing research. While it's fun to assemble a local cluster of computers using as many vendors as possible to run your program, it likely won't increase performance dramatically over a comparable homogeneous network. However, if you consider the possibility of building a computing cluster out of a 300-node IBM SP-2, a (vector) Cray C-90, and a 500 node Intel Paragon, things begin to get interesting. Further, if you consider structuring your application to take into account of the strengths and weaknesses of each machine, the potential computing power is enormous. These type of problems are the subject of the annual "Heterogeneous Computing Challenge" held as part of the IEEE Supercomputing conference. Annually, the gurus of heterogeneous computing attempt to tie as many different computers and supercomputers together as possible to solve extremely large problems. Recent winners have assembled SP-2s, CM-5s, Paragons, Crays, T3Ds, workstations, and even one developer's laptop into superclusters to meet the heterogeneous challenge. The subject of the 1995 High Performance Computing Challenge was to be the first to assemble a teraflop application using computers throughout the world. An interesting heterogeneous network was created by Becker and Dagum (1991). They did a particle simulation of a three-dimensional flow, using a Thinking Machines CM-2 SIMD machine coupled to a Cray YMP via a HPPI connection. Up to two million particles were used. The work was assigned to the most appropriate machines. The Cray YMP was used for sorting the particles, which is necessary in order to determine neighbors and consequent collision pairs. The calculation of collision results, moving of particles, and computation of macroscopic flow quantities was done on the CM-2.

Alternatives to Parallel Development

Distributed Batch: NQS, LoadLeveler and its Kin as Alternatives

It is reasonable to ask yourself: do I really want to run this problem as a parallel code? For example, suppose you want to examine a large number of cases of a problem. Perhaps you want to examine parameter space for an optimization problem. This problem is probably best solved as a large number of individual runs, with a separate code to analyze the collected data. This is something that automated batch-processing systems, such as the Network Queuing System (NQS), Condor, or IBM's LoadLeveler, are ideal for.

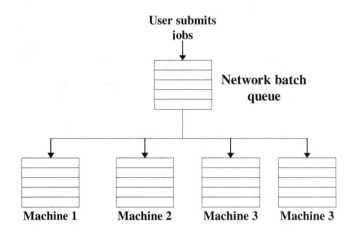

Figure 1.7: A Network Queuing System. Users submit jobs to a global network queue. They are then farmed out to machines on the network to maximize overall throughput.

These systems provide automatic scheduling for serial applications over a distributed network of computers. Though they do not generally run programs in parallel, they do provide extremely high usage of a computing cluster by scheduling jobs to underutilized computers. The efficiency will be better than any parallel implementation of an individual run, because each case is serial and completely independent of the others; the "parallel efficiency" is 100%.

LoadLeveler is a system for submitting a number of jobs to a network of computers, or to nodes of a parallel computer such as the SP-2; wowever, it is not merely a batch-processing system. It may be used to submit parallel jobs on the SP-2 at the Maui High Performance Computer Center, and is the recommended way of doing so. It is essentially a port of the Condor system (Tannenbaum & Litzkow 1995) to the AIX system of the

RS/6000 architecture. Condor supports check-pointing and migration of tasks between machines. It is available free via anonymous FTP from ftp.cs.wisc.edu/condor. NQS is probably the most widely used network queuing system worldwide. NQS is available as a public domain version from CERN on anonymous FTP. Search for NQS CERN from any Internet search engine or Archie server to find a site near you that has it.

Real-World Considerations

You Don't Own the Machine

Most users will find themselves sharing a large parallel machine with others. This sharing is typically done using two systems: batch and interactive systems. The SP-2 at the Maui High Performance Computer Center is a representative example. Of the 400 nodes, 200 are dedicated to running parallel batch processes; on each of these, there will be only one user process at any time. The other nodes are either reserved for system use or are in the pool of 127 interactive nodes. Users may log into these nodes, and an arbitrary number of users may be on any given node. If a user wants to multiprocess without using LoadLeveler, this is possible on the interactive nodes, but he cannot count on the exclusive use of any of these nodes. Performance will vary depending on the loading of other nodes due to other users. On such nodes, if the user's program is idle (for example waiting at a synchronization barrier for all of the user processes to catch up) it merely means that another user will be allotted the node. No waste of computer resources occurs. On many systems, such as the CM-5, users can generally expect to share nodes.

The practical implications of batch versus interactive systems on a busy parallel computer are essentially the same: it will take quite a while for your program to run. Under the batch system, you submit your job to a queue, where it waits its turn until enough nodes are available to run. The turnaround time, therefore, is highly dependent on the length of the queue and scheduling algorithm used. The longer the queue, the longer it will take your program to begin running. On an interactive node, your program will begin immediately, but must share available computer time and memory with other interactive users on each node. If your program does not have advanced techniques for migrating its workload from slower processors to faster ones, your program will (in general) be limited to the speed of the slowest processor. If other users have responsibly balanced their programs, and are not "hogging" the memory or CPU on a single processor, interactive processing can be fairly responsive. If, however, you have one or two irresponsible users, or too many users, individual nodes can run low on memory and begin swapping excessively, killing interactive performance.

A final practical limitation when using a large but distant shared parallel computer is how to handle the huge amounts of data generated by large parallel problems. Though most parallel computing centers have substantial computing capability, they are often woefully short of available disk space. Obtaining even a few hundred megabytes of disk space on one of these machines requires substantial negotiation with local administrators. A large parallel problem can generate gigabytes or even terabytes of data. One ill-fated parallel run of ours consumed an entire optical drive before dying for lack of disk space. Even if you can obtain enough disk space to complete a large problem, one is faced with the equally daunting task of post-processing the data. Most graphical post-processing is done on local workstations, meaning that you must spend hours or even days moving data from a remote parallel supercomputer to your local site. The only alternative is to fly yourself to the remote site, or to perform your parallel runs locally on workstation clusters or local parallel machines.

Parallelizing Compilers

It would be wonderful to have the computer parallelize your serial code. Just how realistic is this? At present, not particularly realistic. It is less plausible for MIMD architectures than for SIMD machines, which are a discredited architecture (see chapter 2 for definitions of MIMD and SIMD).

LINDA: A Shared Memory Paradigm

It would not be fair to leave this chapter without discussing the most popular alternative to message-passing systems, namely, Linda. This is a shared-memory "add-on" to existing programming languages, producing .C-Linda, Fortran-Linda, etc. Linda originated in the mid 1970s at Yale University with D. Gelernter and his colleagues. Data objects are called tuples; the shared memory is called "tuple space." Linda adds four basic operations to any language. Two, *in* and *rd*, effectively "get" data, the difference being that the former removes the data from the shared-memory or "tuple" space while the latter does not. These operations can associatively match against tuples in tuple space. They are synchronous, in that if a suitable tuple is not found, the process suspends until such a tuple appears. The other two operations, *out* and *eval*, move tuples into tuple space. The former is a sequential operation, and behaves somewhat like a procedure call. The latter creates parallelism. Each of these two operations evaluate the tuple fields supplied to create a new tuple. They invoke calculation as needed. The former invokes a single processor, the latter as many as appropriate, this being implementation-dependent. For more details, see, e. g., Cagan and Sherman 1993. This makes it easy to implement semaphores, the most basic of synchronization primitives. Simply execute out("semaphore") to signal that the critical section (resource) is free, and execute in("semaphore") to request the resource. The in will automatically block until a the corresponding out is executed if the resource is not free. Note that this shared-memory approach has a very similar flavor to that of a message-passing system, the difference being that messages are sent not between processors but to a manager of shared memory. Tannenbaum (1995) discusses the implementation of Linda.

Object-Oriented Parallel Processing

A number of systems, such as UC++ and ABC++, support an object-oriented approach to message passing based on C++. Both these languages support the concept of "active objects," which are processes.

ABC++ uses a "shared-object" paradigm. Thus, it is most appropriate for a shared-memory implementation. It may be implemented on a distributed-memory machine, with messages used to pass data as needed between machines, but this is hidden from and not directly controlled by the user; it is called "replication by need" in ABC++ literature. The

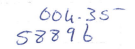

"active objects" or processes achieve "concurrency by inheritance," that is, the processes all share information through specifications that are syntactically the same as inheritance in C++. Processes are specified by pointers; dereferencing a pointer is forbidden to the user. Extensive use of templates and other C++ features is employed.

Modern Parallel Architectures

This section surveys the architectures currently available as well as some that have passed from the scene. Needless to say, development of new architectures may be expected. The U. S. Dept. of Energy has posted on the World Wide Web (www.dp.doe.gov/snew.html) documents describing the Accelerated Strategic Computing Initiative (ASCI), which may ultimately spend roughly one billion dollars to develop machines in the 1-100 Tflops range. Initially, two approaches will be supported: a massively parallel MIMD machine, and a shared-memory approach. Intel was awarded a $ 46 millon contract by Sandia to build the MIMD machine containing 9076 nodes based on the P6 Pentium Pro, running at 200 MHz, with a claimed 1.8-TFlop performance; the Livermore/Los Alamos cluster of shared-memory machines project was expected to issue a request for proposal (RFP) in Nov. 1995.

One lesson that apparently must be relearned periodically is that performance as measured in Mflops or some similar unit should be merely one figure of merit. A system with inadequate disk storage (because the available budget was all spent on processors) will quickly be found to be unusable. Software must also be included in the equation. The performance of the Paragon has been constrained by operating system memory requirements and speed, for example; Sandia National Laboratories has achieved substantial gains by using the SUNMOS operating system mentioned above. The efficiency and maturity of the associated software for message passing, etc. must not be discounted. Different message- passing schemes, such as PVM and MPI, have demonstrated differences of a factor of two on the SP-2, for example.

Network Architectures

A variety of network architectures are used in parallel computers. The architecture of the network controls the latency and bandwidth of message passing on a message passing machine, and the global memory access time on shared memory machines. Most modern parallel computers have very high bandwidth, low latency networks, with multiple paths between any two nodes. On most of these computers, the parallel programmer need not worry too much about the underlying network topology. However, a basic understanding can help the programmer avoid certain application pitfalls related to commonly used networks. For a full discussion of parallel network architectures see (Leighton 1992).

The performance of a parallel computing network is highly dependent on the applications running on it. An application performing an operation where each processor accesses only adjacent processors in the network will likely outperform one that accesses data in an all-to-all manner because adjacent processors can be accessed in a single communications step. Similarly, an application in which all processors send data to a single processor will necessarily create a bottleneck, because the destination can only accept one message at a time.

Three popular measures of parallel network performance are the *bisection width, diameter,* and the *degree* of a network. The *bisection width* of a network is simply the number of edges of the graph of the network that must be cut to sever the network into two disconnected halves. In essence it is a measure of the bandwidth of the network, because it tells us how many simultaneous messages may be sent from one half of the network to the other. In contrast the *diameter* of a network is the minimum distance between the two farthest nodes in the network, in terms of number of edges traversed. The diameter is a measure of the maximum number of steps it can take for any two processors to communicate. Finally, the *degree* of the network is the number of communications lines in and out of a single processor. This is a measure of the maximum number of simultaneous messages a single processor can create or accept at a time, and determines the maximum throughput of a single processor in, for example, an all-to-one communication pattern. The degree of a network also determines the difficulty of building and scaling the network, because building a network chip with larger degree is harder, and building a network with variable degree is even more difficult because the network chips must have more ports to accommodate more processors. Diameters and bisection widths are tabulated in Kumar et al. (1994) for a number of topologies.

Bus Networks

A bus network is perhaps the simplest network of all, though poorly suited for large-scale parallel computing. The most common example is the Ethernet, used widely for local area network computers. Ethernet LANs are used for most heterogeneous workstation clusters, the mainstay of parallel development, so the limitations of this network are important to parallel developers.

On a bus network, all processors are connected to a single shared bus. When a processor needs to communicate with another, it simply broadcasts its message on the bus. Each computer has collision detection software so it can determine if two computers tried to send messages at the same time. If this is the case, then each will try to resend its message after a random retry period. As long as the utilization of the network remains relatively low, this scheme works very well. As utilization increases beyond 50%, performance decays rapidly.

As a parallel network, bus networks are acceptable for small numbers of processors running small parallel jobs because (in general) all processors are not trying to send and receive data at precisely the same time. This makes them suitable for small multiprocessing computers and small workstation clusters. The bus network is not scaleable to more than a few parallel processors because its bisection width is only one, meaning only one message may be sent or received on the bus at a time. This is a serious limitation when one considers the need to support all-to-one and all-to-all communication patterns for large scale parallel applications.

Meshes

In a mesh network, all processors are essentially laid out on a two- or three-dimensional grid, where each processor has a communication link to its nearest neighbor. For the purpose of our discussion we will limit ourselves to the 2-D grid as shown in Figure 1.8, though a 3-D mesh has similar characteristics. The Intel Paragon is an example of a modern parallel computer based on a 2-D mesh network. A variation on the mesh is to connect the outer edges of the mesh together in a wrap-around manner. This configuration, most often called a toroidal mesh, reduces the diameter of the mesh by a factor of 2.

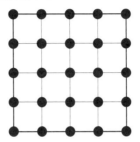

Figure 1.8: A 2-D mesh network. Lines show network connections, and circles show processors.

The bisection width of a 2-D mesh is $\sqrt{N}$ where N is the number of processors. The width is doubled for a toroidal mesh. The diameter of a 2-D mesh is $2(\sqrt{N}-1)$. The 2-D mesh has fixed degree of four. These are favorable characteristics, because many common communication patterns will take $O(\sqrt{N})$ (read "order of square root of N", meaning proportional to square root of N) communication steps to complete, and the mesh network hardware can be easily constructed and expanded to support more processors. Further, the mesh maps easily to many scientific calculations, including matrix and spatially decomposed problems. There are, however, some pathological communication patterns for a mesh, including the all-to-one (which takes *N/4* communications steps).

Hypercubes

The hypercube network, once the mainstay of parallel computing, has fallen out of favor in the most recent generation of parallel computers. A hypercube network is based on a multi-dimensional structure based on binary addresses. Hypercubes come in power of two sizes; $N = 2^D$ where D is the dimension of the hypercube and N the number of processors. It is easiest to understand a hypercube in terms of binary addresses. Because N is always a power of two, the address of any node can always be expressed as a binary number of length D. A 1-D hypercube has two nodes numbered 0 and 1. A 2-D hypercube has 4 nodes numbered 00, 01, 10, and 11. A 3-D hypercube has 8 nodes numbered 000, 001, 010, 011, 100, 101, 110, and 111. Each node is connected to its D closest binary neighbors, meaning that a hypercube network has degree D. This corresponds exactly to nodes whose binary address varies in one digit from its neighbors. For example the node 000 on a 3-D hypercube has three neighbors numbered 001, 010, and 100. Hypercubes of degree 1, 2, and 3 are shown in figure 1.9.

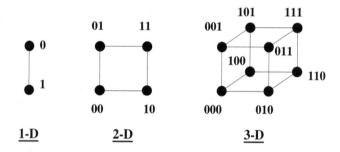

Figure 1.9: One, two, and three dimensional hypercubes with binary addresses shown on processing nodes.

Hypercubes have good network properties. The bisection width of a hypercube is $N/2$, and the diameter is $log_2 N = lg N$. Therefore communications are fairly fast across a hypercube, though again some common communications patterns can be pathological, depending on the routing algorithms used. The main disadvantage of a hypercube is that the degree of each node is a function of the size of the cube. As you increase the size of a hypercube, an additional communication line must be added to every node in the hypercube. This makes it difficult to build network chips for a scaleable system because every node in the network is altered by a machine expansion.

Trees and Fat Trees

The classical binary tree, with processing nodes at the leaves of the tree, would seem to be a good candidate for parallel computing. The diameter of a complete binary tree is $2\ lg\ (N+1)/2$, similar to the hypercube. The bisection width, however, is only one, meaning that messages traveling from one half of the tree to another will run into a significant bottleneck.

A solution to this is to create a tree whose bandwidth increases as you get higher in the tree, commonly called a *fat tree*. For a fat tree to be fully balanced, the network bandwidth must double at each level as one traverses from the leaves to the root of the tree. An example of a fat tree (with heavier lines indicating increased bandwidth) is shown in figure 1.10.

Figure 1.10: A simple fat tree network. Processors are located at the leaves, and network switches at parent nodes. The bandwidth of network connections doubles as we traverse up the tree (indicated by heavier lines).

A fully balanced fat tree network has a bisection width of N (weighting the "fatter" interconnects by their bandwidth) and a diameter of $O(2log\ N)$. The Thinking Machines CM-5 supercomputer used a modified version of a fat tree as its communications network. Its network was a four way fat tree where each parent network node actually had connections to four child nodes.

Supercomputers

Table 1-2 gives an overview of supercomputers (in their day). For historical perspective, examples of computers that were not massively parallel are listed, as well as modern supercomputers. This table should be taken with a very large grain of salt. The Internet cliché YMMV (your mileage may vary) is appropriate. The megaflop (Mflop) is a unit of computational speed: one million floating point operations per second. The megaflop rate is the peak rate; this is based upon the most wildly optimistic assumptions possible. On architectures with multiple floating-point units, it assumes that they are simultaneously kept busy.

On pipelined architectures, it is similarly assumed that there are no stalls. Under such assumptions, a machine on which a floating-point operation might require four cycles, i.e., would specify a latency of four cycles, might claim to pump out 2 answers per cycle due to pipelining and parallel units. Note also that floating-point divisions generally take a number of cycles, as typically about two quotient bits are generated per cycle on most architectures. This makes them very much slower than adds and multiplies. On modern architectures, floating point adds and multiplies are generally equally fast; there are usually separate hardware units for each. Division is therefore ignored in specifying Mflops. Thus, actual performance will fall short if division is frequently used.

Machine	Year	Cost (M$)	Num. Proc.	Clock ns	MFlops
Table 1.2: Past and present supercomputers, the number of processors and relative speeds in Mflops.					
Eniac	1946		1		(add) .05
IBM Stretch	1962		1		.1
CDC 7600	1967		1		300
Cray 1S	1976	5	1	12.5	800
Cray XMP	1983	15	4	9.5	840
Cray YMP	1989	20	8	6.25	2667
CM-5	1991	30	1024	30	128000
KSR-8	1991	.25	8	50	320
Cray C90	1990	31	16	15.	15360
Cray T3D	1993	9	256	3.3	77000
IBM SP-2	1994	20	400	15	106400
Intel Paragon	1992	60	2000	20	100000
NEC SX-R3	1992	16	4	2.5	6400
Hitachi S3800	1992		4	2	32000
Fujitsu VP2000	1992		2	3.3	8000
Fujitsu VPP500	1994	250	222	3.2	355000

IBM SP-2

The IBM SP-2 parallel computer is part of a new generation of parallel computers that make heavy use of existing high-end workstation technology. The SP-2 has high performance per node relative to other parallel computers. The SP-2 Power Parallel architecture is made up of a collection of high speed RS/6000 workstations based on IBM's POWER or POWER2 RISC microprocessors connected by a high speed network switch. Individual nodes are essentially off-the-shelf RS/6000 workstations running IBM's AIX operating system. The SP-2 may be configured with from 2-128 nodes, and up to 512 nodes by special request.

The largest two SP-2 sites at the time of this writing (late 1995) are located at Cornell Theory Center (512 nodes) and the Maui High Performance Computing Center (400 nodes).

Figure 1.11: One frame of the IBM SP-2 Supercomputer.

Nodes are available in two types, thin and wide, and are physically organized into 79-inch cabinets called frames. There are 2-16 processors per frame. Thin nodes are physically smaller with fewer bus slots, allowing up to 16 thin nodes per frame. Wide nodes have more slots for expansion and are larger, allowing only 8 wide nodes per frame cabinet. Thin nodes may have up to 512 MB of memory and 9GB of disk, as well as a variety of communication adapters. Wide nodes may have up to 2GB of memory per node and 18GB of disk space. Nodes are connected by IBM's high performance switch, and a control workstation, with parallel system administration software provides a single point of control for the system.

The high-speed switch is a synchronous multistage packet switch with wormhole routing. See Bernaschi and Richelli (1995) for a detailed description of the switch. The network topology is a complex 4-way communications switch, with characteristics similar to a fat tree. It supports better than 30 MB/s bidirectional bandwidth and less than 40 microsecond minimum latency. The point-to-point communication time of the switch is independent of relative location of the processors. The switch provides multiple paths between any two processors. Each switchboard contains eight crossbar switches. These are in two sets of input and output switches, with each switch in the first set connected to all switches in the second. The output switches connect to switches on all the other frames. Thus, any connection between nodes is routed through four switches. Crossbar switching provides simultaneous connection between any pairs of nodes, so long as the pairs are disjoint. Wormhole routing sends data in packets, with the first packet establishing the data path. This path is then maintained until the final data packet. This reduces the overhead for sending large amounts of data.

From a programmer's viewpoint, the IBM SP-2 appears very much as a collection of workstations. This makes transition from a workstation development environment to the SP-2 a fairly easy task. Users may log into any node and run interactively using PVM, MPI or IBM's Message Passing Library (MPL). Most sites also have batch queues running IBM's LoadLeveler, set up for larger parallel runs where dedicated computer time is needed. A discussion of the SP-1 hardware, which shares the same design principles but uses an earlier and less powerful version of the POWER architecture processors, may be found in Bernaschi and Richelli (1995). IBM was recently awarding a $7,000,000 contract by ARPA and Rome Laboratories to parallelize codes of interest to industry, such as the NASTRAN structural analysis code; one may take this as a vote of support for the SP-2.

Intel Paragon

The Intel Paragon is a MIMD distributed-memory machine with a 2-D mesh network. Processing nodes are built around the Intel si860 XP RISC processor. New multiprocessing nodes support up to three i860 processor per node, two of which are used for applications and the third as a communications processor. Processors have vectorized floating point pipelines and operate at 50MHz. The theoretical peak performance per processor is in the 75 Mflop range, according to current press releases. All processors on a node share a local high-speed memory of 64 to 128MB per node. The connecting network is a 2-D mesh, with a peak theoretical bandwidth of 175 MB/s and a 40 ns delay, making physical location of the nodes largely irrelevant when calculating network delays.

Figure 1.12: The Intel Paragon at Sandia National Laboratories, with 1904 nodes, currently the fastest computer in the United States.

There are two operating systems available for the Intel Paragon. The commercially available UNIX operating system (based on the Open Software Foundations OSF operating system) supports a full Posix compliant suite of software. Another popular Paragon operating system, called SUNMOS, was developed at Sandia National Labs and is widely used at Paragon sites. The chief advantage of the SUNMOS operating system is significantly lower memory usage than the OSF operating system. SUNMOS is popular on early Paragon systems like the Sandia Paragon, where memory is constrained to 32MB per node.

Figure 1.13: The Cray T3-D Supercomputer.

Cray T3D

The Cray T3D, is commercially available in 128- to 256-node configurations. Like the SP-2, the Cray T3D relies on commercial microprocessors; in this case, the 64-bit Dec Alpha. The Alpha is a powerful RISC microprocessor, running at 150 MHz and theoretically capable of up to 333 Mflops per node. The T3-D network is a 3-D torus mesh network (3-D mesh with edges wrapped around and connected) with peak network bisection bandwidth of 19.2 GB/s.

One significant aspect of the T3D is that there is a global message buffer. Thus, if there is a large number of sent messages awaiting consumption by the receivers, a computation can fail. This limits the ability to overlap computation and communication.

The T3D has a number of interesting features (Oed 1993). The hardware supports an atomic swap and a "Fetch-and-Increment" register. The former exchanges the contents of an arbitrary memory location and that of the "swaperand" register. The memory location and register can be located on different nodes. The operation is atomic, i.e., is not interruptible; as far as the universe can determine, the two locations change simultaneously. The "Fetch-and-Increment" register automatically increments when it is read, also atomically. Both these features are useful for protecting "critical sections" in programs that access shared data. This is used in software constructs such as locks and semaphores. See, e.g., Peterson and Silberschatz 1985 for examples of how to use these atomic instructions for mutual exclusion purposes.

There is a data cache and a pre-fetch queue (PFQ). The PFQ is a 16-entry first-in, first-out (FIFO) queue that can be used to request data before it is actually read. Support hardware implements a message queue (the "Messaging Facility") for guaranteed delivery of operating system messages. Hardware interrupts are generated upon receipt of the message. There is also hardware support for barrier synchronization. A barrier is a point in the code at which all processors must arrive before any one can proceed. Registers in each processor support maintaining a tree structure to facilitate passing the necessary messages. Synchronization at a barrier requires receiving arrival messages from all the other processors, i.e., "ANDing" the status of all other processors. The T3D also supports "ORing" the results, i.e., a form of messaging in which if any other processor has signaled, the process is notified. This Cray calls the "Eureka" mode, and suggests that it is useful for parallel search operations. Finally, nodes house a "Block Transfer Engine" for data transfers.

The T3D operating system is the standard UNICOS, a UNIX compatible Cray operating system. The standard message-passing library on the Cray is actually based on Oak Ridge National Lab's public domain PVM message passing interface, making it easy to port workstation-developed PVM applications to the T3D. A Cray-enhanced version of the popular Network Queuing System (NQS) provides batch job management and processor control.

Fujitsu VPP

The Fujitsu VPP500 is capable of holding up to 222 processors, with a peak performance of 355.2 Gflops in consequence (Johnson & Imai 1995). However, such a machine would cost roughly one-quarter of a billion dollars, if we estimate the cost by scaling up from the cost of 16-processor machines! Is it realistic to assume such a costly machine will be affordable? Perhaps, but only if some important problem needs such a rapid solution as to make such a machine cost-effective, and only if performance can be guaranteed. It might be difficult to prove performance to a sufficiently convincing degree to free up such large funding without building such a machine first and running the desired program on it. The

VPP500 uses a crossbar network, which should be expensive (due to its N^2 scaling). Japanese firms and government organizations are supporting a wide range of general- and special-purpose machines (Johnston & Imai 1994). An example of the latter is Hitachi's neurocomputer, which can be microprogrammed to emulate a variety of neural network functions. Just as the Cray T3D employs DEC Alpha chips, the JUMPP employs Supersparc-II processors, and the CP-PACS project uses Hewlett-Packard PA-RISC chips, while NKK is in a partnership with Convex computers to develop parallel systems based on their technology. The Numerical Wind Tunnel (NWT) project, involving Fujitsu, the National Aerospace Library, and the Foundation for Promotion of Material Science and Technology is also of interest. The machine consists of 140 vector processors in a crossbar network, each processor containing 256 MBytes and capable of 1.7 Gflops peak performance. A simulation was run at .12Tflops (Karp et al. 1995). (They were edged out by a group from Sandia National Laboratories running dense matrix solution problems at .14Tflops on an Intel Paragon with 1904 nodes.)

Others

Hitachi currently manufactures the machine with the fastest cycle time, namely 2.5 ns or 400 MHz. Superpipelining makes the concept of cycle time somewhat murky, because a faster cycle time is achieved by making each operation take more cycles. Consequently, when the pipeline stalls, the deleterious impact on performance is greater. This has been observed with the Intel P6 Pentium Pro, which is superpipelined.

Silicon Graphics is reported to have a new parallel computer based on its own RISC chipset, but details were unavailable at the time of this writing.

The Kendall Square Research machines were a MIMD architecture. A system called *ALLCACHE* provided a virtual address space of a terabyte (Rothnie 1991). Hardware processors called *search engines* moved data between the local caches; although they are called caches, they are in fact all the main memory of the machine, not small high-speed components. Memory is moved in 16KB pages rather than individual data items. The proprietary processors were arranged hierarchically, with "rings" of processors (called cells) arranged in a higher-order ring. It took two cycles to access data in the local cache, 150 for processors in the same ring, and 500 for processors in different rings. KSR had great difficulty in practice with multiple ring machines.

History records a number of bus-based multinode machines, such as the Sequent Balance, the Alliant FX series, the Flexible Flex/32, etc. Machines that used at most a few processors, such as the Convex C1 with a maximum of four, the Cray X-MP with up to four, and the Elxsi 6400 with a maximum of 16, use bus systems. Silicon Graphics has a family of shared-memory computers. The processors are in the MIPS family of RISC processors, and are connected to memory by a bus. The SGI Power Challenge with 16 processors costs about one million dollars, making for a system of less-than-supercomputer performance but with a very good price/performance ratio. Obviously, bus contention limits the scalability of such architectures

The BBN Butterfly uses a butterfly (also called a shuffle-exchange or omega) network to connect up to 256 processors to emulate a global shared memory. It is based on the Motorola 68020 processor with a custom coprocessor. With a maximum of 128 processors it would cost approximately three million dollars and give 2000 Mflops peak performance.

Distributed Heterogeneous Environments

An attractive use for parallel technology is the exploitation of unused computing power in networks. Networks are becoming ubiquitous, so exploiting the idle cycles of some machines comes almost free. Furthermore, the price-to-performance ratio of workstations makes the employment of small machines in a network, rather than large mainframes, attractive. Using such a distributed system requires the ability to provide for the exchange of both data and possibly requests for action between machines of different manufacture.

Large Networks of Workstations (NOW; Anderson et al., 1995) have been advocated and prototyped. They constructed a network of 100 nodes at U. C. Berkeley. Work has been done on adaptively scheduling parallel jobs on networks, using the most appropriate number of processors based on system loading; the Piranha system (Carriero et al. 1995) is an example. The term cluster is a popular alternative, with a book by Pfister (1995) devoted to the topic.

Distributed heterogeneous computing may be implemented in a number of fashions. The most convenient and popular approach is a client-server model. The client requests service, and the system determines an appropriate server to perform the requested action. This permits an adaptive response in which the loading of the various processors on the network are taken into account automatically. Message-passing models may be used, but this approach becomes awkward for the client-server model. Instead, the favored approach is that of remote procedure calls (RPC).

RPC, XDR (Open Look)

Remote procedure calls are a natural way to achieve parallelism. The structure of the serial program is not changed, so parallelism is achieved transparently. The only difference from the usual serial program is that the procedure called need not be on the same machine as the caller. This is generally achieved by the use of *stub* procedures (Singhal and Shivaratri 1995). Such server procedures emulate the behavior of the called procedure, and are indistinguishable from a local procedure insofar as the client (caller) is concerned. They "hide" the system interfacing necessary to call the server procedure on another machine.

RPCs have the apparent virtue that serial code can be parallelized virtually automatically, with little recoding effort for the actual computation. They also have the virtue, compared to messaging systems, that instead of the programming having to be concerned with both sides of communication (the "send" and "receive"). RPCs effect a blocking send (the procedure call). The server or receiver code is invoked dynamically as needed by the operating system, and is therefore less susceptible to errors in matching and synchronization of sends and receives. The associated shortcomings of RPCs compared to message passing are the overhead associated with all of the hidden work, and reduced flexibility. RPC calls are equivalent to the use of blocking sends, so the ability to use nonblocking (asynchronous) sends is lost. More significantly, the client-server model of RPCs constrains control flow to be one-directional. The client requests service as appropriate; the server cannot initiate a dialog or make requests of the client. In a master-slave model of parallelism, equating the client and the master works, but it becomes difficult to address multiple slaves as individuals, to control the topology of slave processes, to control data allocation and flow, etc. The overhead of starting up servers, as well as the additional costs of the stub procedures, makes the message-passing paradigm more efficient and flexible. RPC is a good choice for problems that fit well in the client-server model, and for use on a heterogeneous network, especially in a UNIX environment. RPC client-server is a model typically used for database query support, etc, rather than supercomputing. For other situations, which probably include most scientific and engineering applications, the message-passing model would be more appropriate. Finally, RPC is a relatively low-level method, so it is neither portable nor easy to implement. In practice, it will require substantial coding of the communications interface.

The Open Look alliance (Sun Microsystems, AT&T, etc.) have produced methods for distributed computing that have become de facto standards. The most important is probably XDR, eXternal Data Representation. This specifies a standard for encoding data so that it may be exchanged between any architectures. For example, all external data should be "big-endian," meaning that multibyte data (such as integers) have the most significant byte transmitted first. This is the ordering employed by the RS6000, HP RISC machines, and many others, while the Dec Alpha, Intel processors, and machines running Windows NT all use a little-endian ordering. Floating point numbers are in IEEE 754 format. This is the underlying protocol used by almost every heterogeneous message passing library to allow computers from different manufacturers to communicate. For details of the specification and how to use XDR, see the first section in the reference section of Bloomer 1992. This book is also a good reference for RPC in the OpenLook Open Network Computing (ONC) model. The importance of XDR goes beyond that of distributed parallel computing, to include data exchange in more general circumstances.

OSF DCE

The competitor to the Open Look alliance is the Open Software Foundation, which includes IBM and promotes the Motif standard windowing environment. The OSF standard for RPC is called the Distributed Computing Environment (DCE). See Shirley (1992) for examples of DCE client and server code.

Other approaches

There are other alternatives for interprocess communication that support communication between different machines on networks. Examples are named pipes and sockets. Both are firmly in the client-server camp. Sockets are similar to message-passing, with read() and write() calls used instead of sends and receives. See Stevens (1990) for more on this topic.

References

Anderson, T. E., Culler, D. E., Patterson, D. A., "A Case for NOW (Networks of Workstations)", *IEEE Micro*, pp.54-64, **15** (1) Feb. 1995.

Becker, J., and Dagum, L., "Distributed 3-D Particle Simulation using Cray Y-MP, CM-2," *UNAS News*, 6 (10), pp. 1-2, Nov. 1991.

Bell, G., "Utracomputers: A Teraflop Before its Time," *Comm. ACM* **35** (8), pp. 27-47, August 1992.

Bernaschi, M., Richelli, G., "Development and Results of PVMe on the IBM 9076 SP1," *J. Parallel and Distributed Computing*, **26**, pp. 75-83, 1995.

Bloomer, J*., Power Programming with RPC*, Sebastapol, CA: O'Reilly & Associates, 1992.

Brooks, E. D. III, "Massive Parallelism Overcomes Shared-Memory Limitations," Computers in Physics, 6 (2), pp.139-145, March/April 1992.

Cagan, L. D., Sherman, A. H., "Linda unites network systems," *IEEE Spectrum*, pp. 31-35, Dec. 1993.

Carriero, N., Freeman, E., Gelernter, D., Kaminsk, D., "Adaptive Parallelism and Piranha," *IEEE Computer*, pp. 40-49, Jan. 1995.

Cramblitt, B., "Rendering on a Network," *Computer Graphics World*, pp. 26-36, August 1994.

Cray Research, Inc, "The Cray T3D SC System", System Summary, 1993.

Denning, P. J., Tichy, W. F., "Highly Parallel Computation," *Science*, **250**, pp.1217-1222, 30 Nov. 1990.

Fet, Y. I., "Vertical Processing Systems: A Survey," *IEEE Micro*, pp. 65-75, Feb. 1995.

Flynn, M. J., "Very High-Speed Computing Systems," *Proc. IEEE* ,**54** (12), pp. 1901-1909, Dec. 1966.

_____, "Some Computer Organizations and Their Effectiveness," IEEE Trans. Computers, **C-21** (9), pp. 948-960, Sept. 1972.

Furht, B., "Parallel Computing: Glory and Collapse," *IEEE Computer*, **27** (11), pp.74-75, November 1994.

Gross, T., Hinrichs, S., O'Hallaron, D., Stricker, T., and Hasegawa, A., "Communication Styles for Parallel Systems," *IEEE Computer*, **27** (12), pp. 34-43, December 1994.

IBM Corporation, "RS/6000 SP System Component Summary", 1995.

Intel Corporation, "Intel Paragon™ Supercomputer Product Brochure", 1994.

Halsall, F., *Data Communications, Computer Networks and Open Systems*, Third Edition, Addison-Wesley Publishing, 1992.

Hillis, D., *The Connection Machine*, Cambridge, MA: MIT Press, 1985.

Hobbs, L.C., Theis, D. J., Trimble, J., Titus, H., Highberg, I., *Parallel Processor Systems, Technologies, and Applications*, NY: Spartan Books, 1970.

Johnston, S. C., and Imai, K.-I., "Parallel Processing in Japan: National and Corporate Trends," *IEEE Computational Sci. & Eng.*, pp. 32-41, Spring 1995.

Karp, A. H., Heath, M., Heller, D., Simon, H., "Judge's Summary: 1994 Gordon Bell Prize Winners," *Computer*, pp. 68-74, Jan. 1995.

Kumar, V., Grama, A., Gupta,A., Karypis, G., *Introduction to Parallel Computing*, , Redwood City, C. A: Benjamin/Cummings, 1994.

Leighton, F. Thompson, Introduction to Parallel Algorithms and Architectures: Arrays, Trees and Hypercubes, San Mateo, C.A.: Morgan Kaufmann Publishers, Inc., 1992.

Nordwall, B., "New Architectures to Spur Revolution in Computers," *Aviation Week and Space Technology*, pp.45-47, March 1, 1993.

Oed, W., "Cray T3D," Cray Research GmbH, Nov. 15, 1993.

Peterson, J. L., Silberschatz, A., *Operating System Concepts*, Reading, MA: Addison Wesley, 1985.

Pfister, G., *In Search of Clusters*, Englewood Cliffs, N. J.: Prentice Hall, 1995.

Rothnie, J., *KSR1 Memory System*, Kendall Square Research Corp., May 1, 1991.

Shirley, J., *Guide to Writing DCE Applications*, Sebastapol, CA: O'Reilly & Associates, 1992.

Singhal, M., and Shivaratri, N. G., *Advanced Concepts in Operating Systems*, N. Y.: McGraw-Hill, 1994.

Stevens, W. R., *UNIX Network Programming*, Englewood Cliffs, N. J.: Prentice Hall, 1990.

Tanenbaum, A. J., *Distributed Operating Systems*, Englewood Cliffs, N.J.: Prentice Hall, 1995.

Tannenbaum, T., and Litzkow, M., "The CONDOR Distributed Operating System," *Dr. Dobb's Journal*, **20** (2), pp. 40-48, Feb. 1995.

Wolfe, A., "U. S. plans teraflops push," *E E Times*, 1,136, June 19, 1995.

Zorpette, G., "Teraflops Galore," *IEEE Spectrum*, **26** (9),pp.26-38, Sept. 1992.

Chapter 2

Terminology of Parallel Computing

This chapter provides the background necessary to understand discussions of parallel processing issues. Much of what appears here is controversial. There are obvious incentives for making claims of success. Consequently, people tend to put the best possible face on their achievements, sometimes making results look better than they might appear to some critics. Practitioners in the field should be aware of these issues, both to defend their work and to understand the results of others.

Speedup, Efficiency, and Scalability

People doing parallel processing generally want to show that it's good for something. They want to demonstrate that doing the computation on an expensive machine or collection of machines is better than doing it on a workstation. Thus, they have to show performance achievements. The typical measure of achievement is the somewhat nebulous concept of "speedup." *Speedup* may be defined in a variety of ways, which leads to controversy. Generally, speedup is defined by a formula somewhat like $S(n) = T(1)/T(n)$, where $S(n)$ is the speedup achieved with n processors, and $T(n)$ is the timing achieved with n processors. The controversies arise as to how the timings should be measured, and what algorithms should be used (i.e., just exactly how the algorithm may change with n).

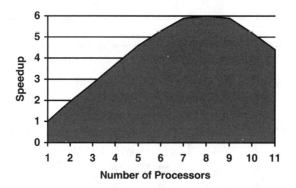

Figure 2.1: Sample speedup graph for a small problem. For
this problem, the optimal number of processors is eight.

A typical speedup curve for a fixed size problem is shown in figure 2.1.
As the number of processors increases, speedup also increases until a
saturation point is reached. Beyond this point, this particular problem
cannot be run any faster because losses to parallel communications and
synchronization are as large as the gains from adding additional
processors.

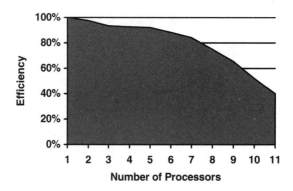

Figure 2.2: Sample efficiency for a fixed size problem. As
more processors are added, parallel efficiency generally
declines.

Parallel efficiency may then be defined as $E(n)=S(n)/n$. It measures how
much speedup is bought per additional processor. Cost may be defined as

C(n)= nT(n). Using the speedup example from Figure 2.1, we can calculate the parallel efficiency as shown in Figure 2.2. As might be expected, parallel efficiency generally declines as more processors are added to a fixed-size problem. This is due to the fact that additional processors add communications and synchronization overhead to the algorithm. This effect will be more fully explored in the next section.

A related buzzword is *scalability*. The adjective *scalable* can be applied to hardware or software, making it an especially useful term. A nebulous concept, scalability is widely taken to represent how well an algorithm or piece of hardware performs as more processors are added. The term is nebulous because performance always depends on the problem chosen, algorithm applied, hardware, current system load, and numerous other variables. Some state-of-the-art programs and hardware are said to be scalable to hundreds or even thousands of processors. Perfect scalability is the Holy Grail of parallel computing. Hardware makers especially make claims that their architecture is scalable to large numbers of processors.

Amdahl's Law and Speedup

Gene Amdahl (Amdahl 1967) presented a fairly simple result, actually little more than a mathematical identity. It has since become a cornerstone of parallel programming analysis, and even somewhat controversial. One reviewer of our manuscript insisted it be called Amdahl's "Law," and writes of it as such in his publications.

Imagine any algorithm for solving a problem. That algorithm has a fraction, *p*, that is parallelizable, perhaps with some considerable effort; the remainder, *s=1-p*, will not parallelize. The fraction of time devoted to the "serial" portion of the problem is assumed independent of the number of processors, while the time required for the "parallel" portion of the problem is assumed to be inversely proportional to the number of processors. Amdahl's law then gives the speedup as

S(n)= 1/(s+p/n) =1/(s+(1-s)/n)=1/((1-p)+p/n).

The crucial point to note about the "law" is that even with an infinite number of processors, *S(n)* cannot exceed *1/s*. Therefore if a serial problem takes time *T* to run, you cannot ever achieve better than *T/n* time on *n* processors. Moreover, this ideal run time can only be achieved when a parallel program has no serial component whatsoever. All nontrivial parallel programs have a serial component, so Amdahl's law is binding to them.

We illustrate Amdahl's law for *p=.8* in Figure 2.3.

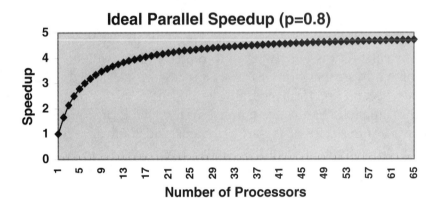

Figure 2.3: Amdahl's Law. Plot of Speedup vs. number of processors for p=0.8.

Another way to understand Amdahl's law is to look at it in the following way. Assume that a parallel algorithm exists that actually could run faster than *T/n* where *T* is the time for the best serial algorithm. If this is true, then we could simply simulate the parallel algorithm on a serial computer by multitasking and achieve the same theoretical performance. This algorithm would beat our best serial algorithm, which is a contradiction. Therefore, Amdahl's law applies and the best we can hope for is to achieve the equivalent of linear speedup where run time declines linearly as we add more processors.

Roger Hockney has an interesting way of rewriting Amdahl's law. First, note that the maximum speedup, such as would be achieved with an infinite number of processors, is $s_{max} = \dfrac{1}{1-p}$. The speedup can be written in terms of the maximum speedup $s = \dfrac{s_{\max}}{1 + \dfrac{n_{1/2}}{n}}$ where $n_{1/2} = \dfrac{p}{1-p}$ is

obviously the number of processors at which the speedup is one-half of the maximum possible. Empirically, this constant can be determined and used to characterize the behavior of the system, even if it does not exactly obey the idealized relation of Amdahl's law. The "constant" p might not behave as a constant, due to the effects of cache size, pipeline latency, synchronization delays, etc. The parameter p will, in fact, be a function of problem size; the parallel fraction of a computation involving modeling, say, one million particles will almost certainly be larger than for a simulation involving one thousand particles. Thus, $n_{1/2}$ will be a function of problem size, as might be expected.

If Amdahl's law were rigorously obeyed, the running time would decrease monotonically for a fixed problem as the number of processors is increased. In the real world, this does not happen. Rather, there is an optimal processor number. Adding processors beyond this increases overhead, resulting in an increase of running time! At least, this is generally true. It may happen that, for some problem parameters and ranges of processor count, "superlinear" speedup, or speedup values larger than the processor count, may occur. This can occur when the size of the problem on one processor is such that the cache hit rate improves (Nagashima et al., 1995).

Amdahl's law does not give a clue as to how to determine the serial and parallel portions of a problem. In fact, Karp and Faltt 1990 imply that its best use is to empirically determine the serial fraction s for given algorithms and problems; in other words, stand the law on its head. This may then be used as a metric to measure performance and efficiency.

Amdahl's law also neglects any additional overhead introduced by parallelizing a problem. For example, passing data between processors will generally require at least copying the data into buffers, and very possibly some data conversion if there is any heterogeneity in the processor network. Such costs invariably result in there being an optimal number of processors for any fixed problem, beyond which increasing the number of processors actually increases the duration of the computation. But Amdahl's law predicts a monotonic increase of $S(n)$ with n. It is therefore overly optimistic in this regard.

Load balancing is ignored. Implicitly, wall-clock time appears to be the time used in analyzing speedup and performance in Amdahl's law. It appears to be assumed that the load is static and may be balanced with perfect efficiency. If a processor is idle, waiting for others to catch up at a synchronization point, it contributes nothing useful to speedup. As long as we own the entire machine and are concerned only with wallclock time, this merely leads to a conservative benchmark.

How time is accounted for also enters into consideration. As noted, wall-clock time appears to be what is used. In heterogeneous systems or those with more than one user, this is not an effective choice as a figure-of-merit. Hence Amdahl's law is really only useful for homogeneous systems with a single user problem running at any time.

Clearly Amdahl's law must be seen as an inequality, limiting the best possible performance. And it is only useful insofar as the serial fraction may be accurately predicted or determined. In most situations, parallel performance does not nearly approach actual performance.

Table 2.1: Scaled Speedup			
Processors	Problem Size	Run Time (sec)	Scaled Speedup
1	1,000 cells	1,000	1.00
2	2,000 cells	1,050	1.90
4	4,000 cells	1,100	3.80
8	8,000 cells	1,200	7.20
16	16,000 cells	1,300	14.40
32	32,000 cells	1,400	28.80
64	64,000 cells	1,600	51.20

Scaled Speedup

A "loophole" in Amdahl's law was found by J. L. Gustafson and colleagues at Sandia National Laboratories (Gustafson 1988, Gustafson et al. 1988), who exploited this discovery to capture the first Gordon Bell prize. This result was hailed as a breakthrough (Denning 1988). Amdahl assumed the problem was fixed, i. e., independent of the number of processors n. The numbers s and p are therefore fixed constants. What if we changed the problem as we changed n? For example, suppose we were solving a partial differential equation by finite-difference methods. We would have to discretize the problem, that is, break it up into finite elements, gridpoints, etc. Suppose we increased the resolution, and hence the number of elements or gridpoints used, as we increased n. (Table 2.1) This would have the effect of changing the serial and parallel fractions of the problem. If we could make $s= q/n$, say, we could achieve arbitrarily large speedups. Gustafson showed that for some rather naturally parallel problems, this could indeed be approached.

Note that actual speedup, in the form of a shorter wait for the answer, is not achieved! The problem gets bigger at the same rate as the processor count, so with perfect parallel efficiency you will have to wait as long for the answer as for the result obtained via a single processor. However, you should get a better result, assuming the increased resolution is useful.

Scaled speedup is then the "speedup" achieved while scaling the problem, multiplied by the number of processors. Typically this is done by setting as constant the size of the problem per processor. For example, in a numerical application we might assign 10,000 elements to each processor. As we increase the size of the problem, we proportionally increase the number of processors to keep a constant 10,000 elements on each processor. The resulting speedup is measured relative to a single processor, also with 10,000 elements on it.

Some have called scaled speedup a swindle. It certainly has its limitations. For example, it clearly assumes you can scale up the problem, and wish to do so. It therefore indirectly assumes you have unlimited memory, computer time, patience, and disk storage (for the results from those huge numbers of gridpoints or whatever). It is certainly a swindle to present scaled speedup results and swallow the word "scaled" when doing so.

If the calculation you are interested in doing would require your waiting a prohibitive amount of time, scaled speedup is not a relevant figure of merit. If you genuinely need more resolution and are content to get such results but no faster than you get your low-resolution numbers, it is useful. Worley (1990) considers the effect of time constraints, that is, the need to get the answer faster, in just how relevant scaled speedup is vs. speedup. If the problem size is not allowed to grow in direct proportion to the number of processors, the relevant metric is somewhere in between, determined by just how long you are willing to wait for the result.

John Gustafson and others (Gustafson 1991) developed a benchmark specifically for scaled speedup performance, called SLALOM, which is based on solving the dense symmetric system of linear equations that arise from the radiosity method for computing the visual appearance of a region. The benchmark does not prescribe the method of solution. On some architectures, an iterative solver based on the preconditioned conjugate-gradient methods significantly outperforms a direct factorization method. This is a "scaled speedup" benchmark in that the problem size is allowed to be as large as desired; the achieved megaflop rate is the figure of merit.

Grama et al. (1993) argue for a figure of merit called *Isoefficiency*. Isoefficiency measures just how much the problem needs to be scaled up in order to maintain a constant parallel efficiency. If we define the problem size as W with the serial execution time proportional to W, say tW, the efficiency E may be taken as $tW/(tW+O)$, where O is the overhead and includes communication costs. These authors then invert this equation to solve for W, $W = E/(1-E)\ O/t$. For problems whose solution methods have known scaling properties, one can then decide how the problem size must scale for constant efficiency, or alternatively how efficiency degrades as more processors and elements are added. These authors do not make clear why it is desirable to maintain the efficiency at a particular value. Assuming you own the machine (i.e., you are the only user), you presumably want to maximize solution speed, i.e., minimize solution time, whatever the efficiency. If you feel you need greater resolution, you will add resolution until the wait for an answer strikes you as excessive. On the other hand, if you share the machine with others, efficiency is less important to you; time you do not use efficiently, such as having processors waiting for others to reach a synchronization point, will likely be used by others.

Amdahl's Law: Summary

Amdahl's law is nothing more than a mathematical identity relating speedup, processor count, and the serial fraction (or alternatively the parallel fraction, which is simply one minus the serial fraction). The controversy and confusion concerning Amdahl's law stems from the fact that the serial fraction is not generally a constant. It will depend on the number of processors, for example. The behavior of the serial fraction will depend on the assumptions of the analyst.

Speedup in Heterogeneous Networks: Superlinear Speedup

It is not obvious how to define speedup in a network of heterogeneous processors. Donaldson et al. (1994) define speedup as $\min(T(1))/T(n)$, where the serial time used for comparison is that of the fastest individual processor (for the problem at hand) in the network under consideration. This would appear to be a rather conservative definition of speedup. Nonetheless, it can lead to arbitrarily large speedups. These authors give an example of a problem that achieves a speedup of ten with two processors. How is that possible? The key factor is the inhomogeneity of the network. Consider a problem composed of some number of independent tasks running on a network of two machines, called A and B. Let the odd-numbered tasks be such that they run rapidly on A and slowly on B, and vice-versa for the even-numbered tasks. The problem running serially on either A or B will take a long time due to the half of the tasks that run slowly on each machine. In a parallel execution, we can see to it that only the odd-numbered tasks run on A and the others run on B. The example is contrived to exhibit a *superlinear* speedup, i. e., a speedup that exceeds the number of processors. Without heterogeneity, even in the absence of overhead due to parallelization, a homogeneous network would not show superlinear speedup.

Consider a homogeneous parallel computing system. Imagine that a problem (or sub-problem) can be split into a set of n tasks, each of which takes time t_i on any one of the processors. Then the serial execution time will be $\sum t_i$. The parallel execution time on n processors will be $max(\ t_i\ )+ O$ where O is the overhead (due to communication). The best possible speedup will be when all the t's are equal, in which case the speedup will be: $nt/(t+O)\ <\ n$. Thus, superlinear speedup should not be possible for any portion of a parallelizable portion of a problem, and therefore for any problem, given the assumptions inherent in this analysis. Note however that there may be loopholes: splitting the tasks may result in better cache utilitzation, for example, resulting in faster execution.

It should be realized that any parallel algorithm may be emulated and run on a single processor in serial fashion. Therefore, it is not possible for a parallel algorithm to be "better" than the best possible serial algorithm, where better means achieving gains in speed beyond those due to the division of labor among processors, because we can serialize any parallel algorithm.

Measuring parallel performance

The first inevitable question you will face after developing your first large scale parallel program will be "How well does it perform?" The correct answer is that "It depends." Indeed, parallel performance depends on a tremendous number of variables, many well outside the developer's control. These include the algorithm used, optimizations performed, the hardware you are using, characteristics of the problem you are running, and even what other users are doing on the machine at the time. We recommend an honest approach tat fully discloses the benchmarks being used and the limitations of parallel comparisons.

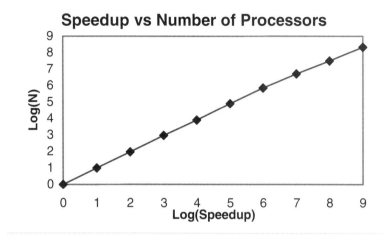

Figure 2.4: Beware the Log-Log plot! This speedup graph looks linear, but the final speedup is actually only 325 out of 512 processors, for 63% efficiency. Many parallel developers use "tricks" like this to inflate results.

Lies, Damn Lies, and Benchmarks

With the current emphasis on publications, the pressure on a research scientist to publish good parallel results is enormous. If an organization has just spent as much as $50 million on a parallel computer, or perhaps sells parallel computers, the pressure to report good results can be overwhelming. The combination of scientific exuberance, pending budget cuts, pressure from above, and a publish or perish mentality can combine to create some misleading results. In general, professional journals have tightened their standards over the last few years to reduce the number of questionable results reported. To a limited degree, makers of parallel computers have also improved their reporting by moving to popular standard parallel benchmarks such as the NAS parallel benchmarking suite. We feel it is important, however, for you to be aware of some of the questionable benchmarking techniques widely used to inflate parallel performance results. As a parallel developer, it is good to know when you are being snowed. An excellent review of this subject is available from Bailey (1992).

Some of the common questionable techniques include:

1. **Megaflops and Gigaflops:** Beware anyone who attempts to count flops (Floating Point Operations Per Second). Hardware manufacturers often quote peak (not sustained) flop rates for parallel processors doing no communications. Achievable application flop rates are seldom even half the stated rate. Similarly, parallel programmers often report the parallel flop rate by counting the number of flops used by all processors. This number is usually inflated over the serial flop rate, because some calculations are repeated on each processor. In fact, duplicating calculations increases the parallel flop rate.

2. **Comparing apples and oranges:** Many authors will attempt to compare their parallel version against a serial version of a program to show how much better the parallel version performs. Alternately they may compare their program against other parallel programs. The main problem here is that often one is comparing apples with oranges. For example, optimized parallel codes are often compared against unoptimized serial programs running on vectorized machines such as the Cray YMP or C-90.

3. **Choosing toy or optimal problems:** Authors will often choose *toy problems* rather than real world applications for their benchmarks. This is usually done to optimize parallel performance for a particular parallel hardware configuration and does not represent real world problem performance. An example would be choosing an easily partitioned square problem domain for a parallel benchmark when real problems might contain highly irregular domains, or choosing a problem with simple boundary conditions.

4. **Reporting only CPU time used:** Though this can be a useful measure, parallel performance numbers based solely on CPU time used can be misleading. The reason for this is that most operating systems will go into an idle state or switch to another process if a message is unavailable. On dedicated parallel machines, this means the CPU may be idle waiting for a message to arrive from another processor. Reporting CPU time used, however, excludes this idle time which may mask the fact that the program is poorly load balanced or has poor

communication patterns. The program may have nearly ideal CPU time speedup, while in reality it spends most of its time waiting for communications. Reporting average CPU time per processor can also be misleading, because one can trivially construct an ideal average CPU speedup curve by running the entire problem on one processor and leaving the others idle. The total CPU time used would be equal to the serial case, and the average CPU time per processor would match the ideal speedup curve, even though none of the problem was done in parallel. Including the standard deviation of run times along with the averages provides a more complete picture of parallel performance.

5. **Ignoring costs of I/O, initial data movement, etc**. (Self-explanatory).

Wall Clock - What Really Matters

The ultimate measure of performance for any computer program is simply the amount of time it takes a computer to get real problems done. We refer to this time as the wall-clock time. You can measure the wall clock time of any program using the UNIX command *time* as in *time myprogram*. For a parallel job running across several processors, the UNIX time() system call can be added at the beginning and end of the program to give a rough picture of the number of seconds elapsed since the program started. The maximum time taken by any processor is usually a good measure of the overall time to run your parallel program.

We do not recommend using CPU time as a measure for parallel performance unless you truly cannot get dedicated nodes to perform your performance benchmarks. CPU time usually excludes idle time spent waiting for messages to arrive from other processors, and as such may mask inefficiencies in your algorithm.

Parallel performance will vary widely depending on the problem being solved. Some problems can be quickly and evenly divided, while others may be difficult to divide or take a large number of communication steps to complete. Where possible, you should try to measure performance of different problems to identify which classes of problems are suitable and which might be better run on fewer processors or in serial (on a single processor).

When comparing a parallel algorithm against a serial algorithm, be careful to compare the best serial algorithm against your parallel algorithm. It is misleading to report a comparison of serial and parallel programs if the serial program has not been optimized.

When calculating scalability and speedup for a parallel program, we recommend you use the actual wall clock time of the single processor version as a basis. The speedup of a parallel version will then be the time it took for a single processor divided by the time it took in parallel. Parallel efficiency will simply be the speedup divided by the number of processors. It is often useful to run benchmarks using both speedup and scaled speedup, because the former helps determine the saturation performance of the program while the latter helps to determine how large a job may be exploited in parallel.

Bailey's (1992) article gives a very good example of the misleading nature of Megaflop rates. A convection-diffusion problem was solved by a number of methods, all iterative. The Jacobi algorithm achieved the highest rate, 1800 Megaflops. Because it had the poorest convergence, it required the largest number of floating-point operations, 3.82×10^{12}, and required the most CPU time, 2124 sec. The Multigrid method had the poorest Megaflop rate, 318. However, it required the least CPU time, 6.7 seconds, and the fewest floating-point operations, 2.13×10^{9}. In this case, the superior algorithm by any reasonable criterion is the Multigrid method. However, as it requires global rather than local communication of data, it achieves a lower Megaflop rate. The Jacobi iteration, in contrast, is simple, easy to implement, requires only local data, and consequently achieves high Megaflop rates. But it converges slowly, requiring many more iterations and consequently many more floating-point operations. The moral should be clear: the choice of algorithm should not be based on Megaflop rate alone.

In a similar vein, "speedup" should not be used as the figure of merit. Cvetanovic et al. (1990) present results comparing the behavior of the Successive Over Relaxation method (SOR) vs. the Alternating Direction

Implicit (ADI) for the solution of an elliptic partial differential equation. The results parallel those cited by Bailey (1992). The SOR method (which is quite similar to the Jacobi method) achieved far better speedup than the ADI method. On the other hand, the ADI was far superior in terms of elapsed time. ADI, like Multigrid, requires non-local data communication, which no doubt results in poorer apparent parallel performance when measured in terms of Megaflop rate or speedup. But the gains in convergence rate more than make up for such a drawback, as the total number of computations is greatly reduced.

Optimal Processor Number

As illustrated by Figure 2.1, there is an optimal number of processors for that problem. This is a general rule; at some point, adding processors adds overhead without any compensating benefit. This truism may be obscured by viewing plots of scaled speedup, because the problem changes with each datapoint: the more processors, the bigger the problem. But any fixed size, real-world problem will not get faster and faster no matter how large the machine is; a point of diminishing, and then negative, returns is reached.

Classifying Parallel Problems

Before attempting to develop a parallel program, it is critically important to understand how well particular problems are suited to parallel processing. An important result of the last 25 years of attempted parallel computing is that many problems are better-suited to parallel computing than others. Computer scientists have made an effort to formally and informally define classes of problems that are well-suited, so that major mishaps can be avoided. A basic understanding of these classes of problems may help to classify your particular problem before embarking on a major developmental effort.

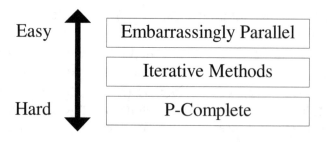

Figure 2.5: Some problem classes and difficulty in
parallelizing them. Most scientific calculations fall into the
middle class, and are moderately hard to run in parallel.
Problems in the P-Complete class are thought to have no
parallel solution.

Embarrassingly Parallel

Some problems can inherently be solved in parallel with great ease. This
class of problems is most commonly referred to as *embarrassingly
parallel*. Most of these problems have small degrees of data dependence,
meaning that rarely, if ever, does the outcome of one operation depend
upon another. A good example might be a brute-force chess program that
exhaustively searches for the best move by looking several moves ahead.
Because possible moves depend only on the current state of the chess
board, one could assign different initial moves to different processors and
allow them to search for alternatives until a criterion or time limit is
reached. All processors would then return their calculated best move
combinations back to a central point, where they could be evaluated and
the move made. Though clearly not an elegant approach, it could be
termed an embarrassingly parallel approach.

Another example of an embarrassingly parallel program would be one that
uses stochastic methods. Stochastic methods are based on making a large
number of almost identical simulations, where typically only the random
number seed is varied. Rather than a single outcome, the user is typically
interested in a range of outcomes and their corresponding probability.
These independent simulations can be done in parallel simultaneously on
many machines, with virtually no communications, placing them well
within the class of embarrassingly parallel problems.

If you are fortunate enough to be faced with an embarrassingly parallel problem, the most direct and simple solution is usually best. Break the problem up in the simplest way possible, and try to minimize the data passed between separate processes. This approach also works as a first step for problems that are more complex. In many cases, at least some small part of the problem is embarrassingly parallel, and can be solved simply before applying more advanced techniques.

Iterative Methods

Many problems, particularly involving linear algebra, require iteration (repetition of a sequence of operations). Generally, the iteration is terminated when some convergence criterion is satisfied, although occasionally a fixed number of iterations is specified. Linear systems are solved using methods such as the Jacobi, Gauss-Seidel, conjugate gradient, Quasi-Minimal Residual, etc. Often, the convergence can be markedly accelerated by "preconditioning," which is equivalent to multiplying the equation by a matrix chosen to be a crude inverse of the matrix in the problem, thereby reducing the spread in the eigenvalues. Eigenvalues, eigenvectors, and singular value decompositions must be found by iterative methods in general; eigenvalue determination is equivalent to determining the roots of a polynomial equation, and as that problem cannot be deterministically solved for polynomials of degree five or greater, eigenvalues cannot be found for similar-sized problems without an iteration. A variety of methods, due to Lanczos, Jacobi, etc. are popular, and are discussed in chapter 4.

Open Problems

A class of well defined problems exist that cannot easily be solved in parallel. The formal definition of this class requires knowledge of language theory and automata that are beyond the scope of this book. For a formal discussion see JaJa (1992, Section 10.5). We will therefore take an informal approach to these definitions. Before starting, we need to define the abstract concept of *order notation*. We informally define the order notation $O(n)$ to represent problems that can be solved in no more than cn computation steps, where c is some constant. Expanding this concept, we can say that problems which are $O(log\ n)$, where log denotes the base 2 logarithm (also often written as lg), can be solved in no more than a logarithmic number of time steps for inputs of size n.

We introduce the class of problems called NC, which represents all problems that can be solved on a PRAM (parallel shared memory) machine in $O(log^k\ n)$ steps for inputs of size n using a polynomial number of processors (JaJa, 1992) for some value of the constant k. These problems may be said to be easily parallelizable, because all can be solved in at most $O(log^k\ n)$ steps. We also introduce the class P, which consists of all problems that can be solved in a polynomial number of steps on any computer. It should be obvious that the class NC is a subset of the class P, because any problem that can be done in $O(log\ n)$ time on a parallel computer can be done in polynomial time on a serial computer (remember Amdahl's law?). It is an open problem in computer science, however, to determine whether all polynomial problems can be done in parallel that rapidly, i. e., whether P and NC are equivalent classes or not.

Though it remains to be proven, most theorists believe that the two classes above are not the same, meaning that many problems cannot be efficiently parallelized. These theorists define a third class, the class of *P-complete* problems, to be the set of problems that are solvable in polynomial time in serial, such that if they are also solvable in logarithmic time in parallel, any class P problem would be solvable in logarithmic time in parallel as well. P-complete problems are believed to be in the class P but not in the class NC. Two important results follow. First, because the P-complete class is well defined, problems that are P-complete cannot easily be solved in parallel. Second, it can be shown that all P-complete problems are equivalent, and therefore if someone can solve one P-complete problem in $O(log^k\ n)$ steps on a polynomial number of processors, then all P-complete problems can be solved the same way.

An example of a P-complete problem follows. The *Circuit Value Problem* is to determine the single output of a boolean circuit consisting of n binary AND, OR, and NOT gates and a given set of inputs. The circuit can be represented by the sequence $<g_1,\ g_2,\ ...\ g_n>$ where each gate g_i depends only on inputs or the gates g_j and g_k that came before it (i.e. $j,k<i$). This problem can easily be solved in $O(n)$ time on a serial computer by

evaluating the gate sequence $<g_i>$ in order for $i = 1$ to n. No one has yet demonstrated a way to solve this problem in $O(log\ n)$ time on a PRAM processor with a polynomial number of processors.

The Load Balancing Problem

A problem common to all parallel computations that evolve with time is the general problem of maintaining an equal processing load on all processors. In many real world problems, there is no easy way to determine an optimal way to partition pieces of the problem to different processors. The problem becomes even more complex if we consider that in addition to evenly balancing the computational load, we want to also select a partitioning that minimizes interprocessor communications. This problem is widely referred to as the general load balancing problem, as shown in Figure 2.6.

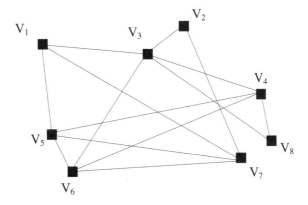

Figure 2.6: The general graph partitioning problem. Partition the weighted graph G into two parts of equal size such that the weights of the edges between the vertices are minimized. This is an NP-complete problem.

Using complexity theory again, it can be shown that the general load-balancing problem, which minimizes both communications and load imbalance, belongs to a class of problems called NP-complete. NP-complete problems are believed not solvable on a serial machine in a polynomial number of operations, so the load-balancing problem is considered difficult in that there is no known approach other than brute force testing of all possible alternatives; this typically requires a computational effort that depends exponentially on the size of the problem, and therefore becomes prohibitively expensive for sizable problems. In practice, various heuristics are used to approximate the optimal solution to the load-balancing problem. A few approaches are covered in chapter 4.

Beware Results Too Good to be True

If something is too good to be true, it probably isn't true. For example, parallel efficiencies greater than one make no sense. If some parallel algorithm achieved such an efficiency, it could be converted to run serially. Comparing the parallel algorithm to its serialized version, the parallel efficiency should then be at best unity. This might seem obvious. However, Miranker (1971), in an early and oft-cited review of parallel processing, refers to work of Shedler (1967) on finding the roots of equations, in which the parallel solution is more efficient that the serial solution. Reading Shedler's paper, we find that the serial and parallel algorithms are not the same; the parallel algorithms are "sectioned" by dividing the range of root searching. Depending upon the function whose root is being determined, this might (fortuitously) reduce the number of iterations, and hence function evaluations, required to determine a root. It might also decrease the efficiency in other cases. Clearly, the former was the case for Shedler's examples.

Parallel Portability

Portability refers to writing a program in such a way that it may be easily recompiled or *ported* to other machines. In the early days of parallel computing, there was no such thing as parallel portability. All early parallel programs were tailored to a single machine, because the operating system and parallel computing model were specific to the make and brand of the particular machine. Only in the last few years have makers of parallel computers started to focus on standards for the languages, operating systems, and parallel computing models required to make portable parallel computing a reality.

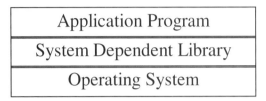

Figure 2.7: The most common way to achieve portability across a wide variety of systems is to isolate operating system specific calls in a separate library. This is called the "layered" approach to portability.

Why Portability is Important

Writing portable parallel applications is important for several reasons. These include a longer lifetime for your application, additional flexibility in being able to scale your application to different platforms, and an easier transition from development platforms to large supercomputers.

One of the top reasons to build portability into any parallel application is the rapid pace of change in parallel computing. The average parallel computer is obsolete in as little as two years, barring significant upgrades. This means a specialized application based on a particular vendor's library will also be obsolete in that time frame. Even worse, your vendor may be out of business shortly after you complete your development. Supercomputer makers are, quite frankly, dropping like flies. In the past two years alone, major computer makers like Kendall Square Research, Thinking Machines Corporation, and Cray Computer Corporation have all filed for bankruptcy. Considering that several man-years may go into a complex parallel scientific application, designing portable code is smart insurance in a rapidly changing computer market.

A second reason for incorporating portability into any new parallel application is the additional flexibility it provides. One of the fundamental concepts behind scaleable parallel computing is the idea that you can choose hardware that is suitable for the size of problem you are running. For example, many medium-size problems that are too large to run on a single scientific workstation can be run on a workstation network. Larger problems can be run on large parallel supercomputers, and small developmental test problems on a single workstation. In addition, if supercomputer A happens to be down for maintenance, as often happens, you can easily move to supercomputer B to get the job done. You clearly cannot achieve this kind of scalable flexibility by writing your program for a single vendor's computer or relying on special features available on only one vendor's computer. A portable application is required.

A final reason for writing portable parallel applications is the convenience of developing on a local computer and then porting applications to larger computers. It is generally easiest to develop on your local workstation or minicomputer, because you will be most familiar with the tools and development environment there. If you write your application in a portable way, you can then easily move to larger parallel computers with relatively little effort.

Portability and Languages

Choice of language is critically important to creating a portable program. It is important to note that you can write parallel programs in almost any language, and the one you are most familiar with is probably the best choice. FORTRAN '77 and ANSI C are currently the dominant languages for most scientific and engineering applications, and we advocate their use for parallel applications. FORTRAN tends to dominate older legacy applications, while C is the up-and-coming language for many new scientific applications. In terms of parallel portability, compilers for both languages are widely available, and are part of the standard distribution of every modern large-scale parallel computer the authors have ever worked on. Each has advantages and disadvantages for parallel portability, so we will discuss both in detail.

FORTRAN has been the dominant science and engineering language since its inception as FORTRAN IV in the 1950s. FORTRAN is fairly easy to learn, and has the largest suite of scientific and engineering libraries available for it. One of the main reasons for the dominance of FORTRAN in supercomputing has been raw performance. FORTRAN arrays, do loops, and other constructs are relatively simple for a compiler to recognize and optimize for vectorized and pipelined processors. Further, 30+ years of optimized FORTRAN compiler technology have made FORTRAN compilers hard to beat. Informal tests performed by the authors have determined that simple FORTRAN programs often outperform comparable C programs, largely due to better compiler technology and simpler language constructs. The primary disadvantage of FORTRAN versus C is the lack of modern dynamic data structure support and few direct interfaces to the operating system. It is a little harder to implement some operating-system specific operations in FORTRAN because FORTRAN lacks a C-like macro-preprocessor for changing out blocks of code, requiring separate modules to be written for different machines.

In contrast, C has full support for dynamic memory allocation, composite data structures, and full access to the Unix operating system. Because of these features, performing some operations in C may be easier than comparable FORTRAN code. The complexity of C comes with a price, however, since it sometimes hurts overall performance.

The C language actually comes in two versions. The more robust version is called ANSI C, based on the ANSI C specification. It supports strict type checking, which generally results in fewer runtime errors. ANSI C is the dominant compiler on most modern machines. The older version of C is commonly referred to as Kernigan and Richie (K&R) C, after two of the original developers of C and the UNIX operating system. It does not include strong type checking. K&R C is important only because it is still widely used on some older Sun workstations. ANSI C compilers can compile K&R C programs, but the older K&R compilers cannot compile some ANSI programs. A popular method to work around this portability problem is to include full ANSI prototypes for all functions and creatively #ifdef them in the header files, so they do not interfere with K&R compilers like the ones on older SUN computers.

Two new variations on C and FORTRAN are becoming more popular for scientific computing. These are C++ and FORTRAN 90. C++ supports all of the ANSI C constructs, plus adds complete object-oriented features to make C a full object-oriented language. Similarly, FORTRAN 90 adds dynamic memory allocation, composite data structures, and many new features to FORTRAN. Both of these languages can be used with existing C and FORTRAN libraries and code fragments, because both are backward compatible with their respective languages. In both cases, you will probably pay a slight performance penalty for using the new features, but the new features may also significantly speed development if used correctly. The strongest case for not using these new languages is, again, a loss of portability. Though most large supercomputing sites now have compilers for C++ and FORTRAN 90 available, many workstation clusters do not. Ultimately, you will have to examine what is available in your computing environment before developing in C++ or FORTRAN 90.

Two other languages are worth mentioning here. These are High Performance FORTRAN (HPF) and C* (C-Star). These two languages are based on the data-parallel model, and are used primarily on SIMD or simulated SIMD machines; in fact, C* is specific to the Thinking Machines family of Connection Machines. The main idea behind these languages is that a large array of data exists and needs to be manipulated by many processors. These languages allow arrays of data to be described as parallel data, called *shapes* in C*, allowing the compiler to automatically run operations on these arrays in parallel. For example, a statement to add a number to every item in the array would automatically be divided between the processors so that every processor added the number to part of the array. A few data-parallel operations for the C* language are shown in Figure 2.8. For applications where a lot of similar operations are to be done on large data sets, this type of language can be very easy to use. The drawback, of course, is in performance and portability. Though these languages perform very well when working on the parallel arrays, synchronization of data can be very expensive. Further, because the manner of passing data is determined by the compiler, one can unknowingly create algorithms with very poor performance. In terms of portability, these two languages are probably the most widely available special-purpose parallel compilers. Unfortunately, they are still not nearly as widely available as C or FORTRAN.

```
/* Simple C-Star example to define an array and
 * perform some data parallel operations on it */
shape [100] ShapeA;       /* Defines shape of array */

main(int argc, char **argv)
{
 int sum;
 /* Define a data parallel array called val,
   * consisting of 100 elements */
 int:ShapeA val;

/* Initialize the value of each "val" to be its
 * integer coordinate
 * In C this would appear as
 *    for(i=0; i<100; i++)
 *              val[i] = i;
 */
val = pcoord(0);

/* Compute the sum of all of the values using the
 * special operator += on the "val" shape. This
 * single statement performs an operation
 * equivalent to the following C code
 *        sum = 0;
 *    for(i=0; i<100; I++)
 *       sum = sum + val[i];
 */
sum = (+= val);

/* Add 10 to all values */
val = val+10;
}
```

Figure 2.8: A C* programming example showing some simple operations and their equivalents in C. The data parallel paradigm makes many operations more compact to write.

A great many special-purpose parallel languages exist and might be suitable for your particular parallel development, along with various parallelizing compilers. Some parallel languages are well suited to solving particular problems, and might make it possible to significantly speed your development. The main drawback to using any specialized language will be portability. While a FORTRAN or C message passing application can be run on any serial or parallel UNIX computer, the specialized languages, such as C*, often run on only a few. In addition, using a specialized language might mean starting from scratch versus being able to utilize an existing working serial code as a starting point. The decision ultimately depends on the situation and application, but we recommend that any loss of portability be carefully considered before starting a new development.

Portable Message Passing

A dominating concern in the development of any parallel program is the choice of communication paradigms and specific protocols. As mentioned in chapter 1, most early parallel computers only allowed a single proprietary protocol to be used. Parallel developers often had no choice but to use the paradigm and protocol given to them on whatever machine they happened to have access to. In the last 3-4 years, however, we have seen the development of a number of portable parallel communication systems. Most are based on the popular message passing paradigm, but some provide shared memory and data parallel services. We will concentrate on portable message passing systems in what follows, because they offers the largest degree of portability and flexibility for developing large, general-purpose parallel programs. Portable data parallel and shared memory paradigm tools do exist, and may be appropriate if you are developing special applications.

The first widely used, truly portable message-passing system was the Parallel Virtual Machine (PVM) project developed at Oak Ridge National Laboratory in 1989. It was first publicly released free of charge in March of 1991 as PVM version 2.0. The current PVM 3.x version was initially released in March of 1993, and has had a number of minor version upgrades since then. The concept behind PVM is to link separate hosts, possibly of varying type, to create a single so-called *virtual machine*. PVM allows you to take virtually any network of UNIX- based computers and treat them as a single parallel computer. In addition, PVM works on networks of heterogeneous computers by translating various data formats transparently during message passing. This allows you to assemble different types of computers to perform a single *parallel virtual machine*. PVM has a somewhat limited message-passing subset, providing basic send and receive operations and some simple collective communications, but not providing the rich set of features that more formal message passing systems, like the Message Passing Interface (MPI), provide. PVM does, however, provide a complete environment for parallel computing, including the PVM console, and includes features for dynamically adding and deleting machines from your own virtual-machine configuration. PVM's primary advantage is its portability. It can be copied and compiled on any UNIX computer or supercomputer in a matter of minutes, and its console interface remains unchanged, making it one of the best choices for highly portable parallel applications. PVM will be covered in additional detail in chapter 5.

Table 2.2: PVM Portability List				
Dec Alpha	BSD 386	CM-2	CM-5	Convex
Cray2	Cray YMP	Cray C-90	Free BSD	HP 300
HP PA	Intel 860	KSR-1	Linux	Maspar
MIPS	Net BSD	Next	Paragon	IBM RS/6K
IBM SP-2	SCO	SGI	Sun 4	Sun Solaris
Sun MP	Cray T3D	Vax		

Recently, a standard for message passing has really started to take hold in the parallel computing world. The Message Passing Interface (MPI) standard started at a workshop on message passing standards held in April of 1992 in Williamsburg, Virginia. A working group was established, and the first draft of the MPI standard, now called MPI-1, was published in October of 1993 and widely circulated at Supercomputing '93 in November of that year. The standard enjoyed the broad support of all of the major supercomputer makers from the very beginning. The MPI Forum was established in November of 1992, and opened to anyone interested in message passing. In June of 1995, an MPI 1.1 document was published to correct unimplementable features defined in MPI-1. The final specification draft of MPI-2 is not scheduled for completion until December of 1996. The MPI standard represents the work of over 175 universities, government organizations, and industrial partners from around the world. Most professionals agree that MPI represents the premier message passing system to be used in parallel computing for the foreseeable future.

MPI has a much larger feature set than PVM, which makes it both more powerful and more complex to use than PVM. The only major criticism of MPI that we have is that the specification only covers the programming interface. The MPI standard does not define how a program is started or a machine configured for use, leaving these details up to individual implementers. While this is not a large problem for people who work only on one machine, it can cause problems for people who want to work on a variety of platforms, because the user must learn and remember each different vendor's particular implementation to configure and start a parallel program. This can be alleviated in part by using a portable MPI implementation, such as MPICH (covered below), as a basis for development. Details of the MPI message passing standard and some simple examples are included in chapter 5.

With the MPI standard now in a stable state, portable implementations are beginning to appear for a variety of computers. One of the most popular public domain versions is MPICH, from Argonne National Laboratory. MPICH was started shortly after the MPI-1 draft was published, making it one of the first portable MPI efforts. MPICH is actually built over two earlier message passing systems called P4 and Chameleon. Currently, versions are available for most UNIX workstations and all of the major parallel computers, making it an excellent choice for developers who want a portable, international standard to use as a development base. MPICH also supports heterogeneous parallel computing, much as PVM does, by translating messages as needed between heterogeneous systems. The MPICH system is relatively easy to set up and use on any system, though it does not yet have an interactive shell like PVM does. A number of other popular portable MPI implementations exist, and are covered in chapter 5.

Another solution, which we recommend, is to develop an interface layer or library between your application and the underlying message-passing library. This actually has several advantages over direct use of even a portable message-passing library such as PVM or MPI. First, by creating an independent message passing layer, your application is truly isolated from the underlying protocol. This means that if you need to port your application to a machine which may not support your favored message-passing library, you now have the option to use another without major changes. Most likely, you will be driven to another message passing protocol primarily for performance reasons. Though very high-performance PVM implementations exist for some machines, such as the IBM SP-2 and Cray T3D, many machines perform better using their native-mode message-passing system.

Parallel Application
Interface Library Layer

PVM	MPI	Other

Figure 2.9: A layered approach to message passing. The
machine independent interface layer isolates the application
from the underlying message passing, allowing many
underlying protocols to be used with relative ease.

An example of a layered message passing library is shown in Figure 2.9.
The interface library layer isolates the application, letting us easily move
from PVM to MPI and potentially to vendor specific message passing
architectures. A simple example of this approach is included with source
code in chapter 7. In addition to providing significant flexibility and
potentially better performance on some machines, this approach also lets
you add detailed timing and debugging features to the interface layer, as
discussed at the end of chapter 8. This makes it much easier to debug and
optimize your application on a variety of machines, because you can
extract detailed message passing statistics from the interface layer.

References

Amdahl, G. M., "Validity of the single processor approach to achieving
large scale computer capabilities," in *Proc. AFIPS Spring Joint Computer
Conference*, p. 30, Atlantic City, N. J. 1967.

Bailey, D. H., "Misleading Performance Reporting in the Supercomputing
Field," *Scientific Programming*, **1**, pp. 141-151, 1992.

Cvetanovic, Z., Freedman, E. G., Nofsinger, C., "Efficient Decomposition
and Performance of Parallel PDE, FFT, Monte Carlo Simulations,
Simplex, and Sparse Solvers," Proc. Supercomputing 1990, 465-474, New
York: IEEE Press, 1990.

Denning, P. J., "Speeding Up Parallel Processing," *American Scientist*, **76**
(5), pp.347-349, July-August 1988.

Donaldson, V., Berman, F., Paturi, R., "Program Speedup in a Heterogeneous Computing Network," *J. Parallel Distributed Computing*, **21**, 316-322, 1994.

Grama, A. Y., Gupta, A. N., Kumar, V., "Isoefficiency: Measuring the Scalability of Parallel Algorithms and Architectures," *IEEE Parallel and Distributed Technology*, **1** (3), August 1993.

Gustafson, J. L., "Reevaluating Amdahl's Law," *Comm. ACM*, **31** (5), pp.532-533, May 1988.

_____, Montry, G. R., Benner,R. E., "Development of Parallel Methods for a 1024-Processor Hypercube," *SIAM J. Scientific Statistical Computing*, **9** (4), pp. 609-639, July 1988.

_____, Rover, D., Elber, S., Carter,M., "SLALOM: Surviving Adolescence," *Supercomputing Review*, pp. 54-56, December 1991.

JaJa, Joseph, *An Introduction to Parallel Algorithms*, Reading, M.A.: Addison Wesley Publishing, 1992.

Karp, A. H., Flatt, H. P., "Measuring Parallel Processor Performance," *Comm. ACM*, **33** (5), pp.539-543, May 1990

Miranker, W. L., "A Survey of Parallelism in Numerical Analysis*,"* SIAM Review*, **13** (4) 534-547, October 1971.

Nagashima, U., Hyugaji, S., Sekiguchi, S., Sato, M., Hosoya, H, "An Experience with super-linear speedup achieved by parallel computing on a workstation cluster: Parallel calculation of density of states of large scale cyclic polyacenes," *Parallel Computing*, **21**, pp. 1491-1504, 1995.

Shedler, G. S., "Parallel Numerical Methods for the Solution of Equations," *Comm. ACM*, **10** (5), 286-291, May 1967.

Worley, P. H., "The Effect of Time Constrains on Scaled Speedup," *SIAM J. Scientific Statistical Computing*, **11** (4), pp. 838-858, Sept. 1990.

Chapter 3

Starting a Parallel Effort

The preceding chapters have discussed whether a parallel programming effort is appropriate, or alternatives, such as a multiprocessor batch system, are more suitable. We will assume that you have decided that a parallel system is needed because of required performance and the inability to separate the problem into independent jobs or programs. This chapter will aid you in making some fundamental decisions about your application in order to start designing a parallel application.

One fundamental theme that will be echoed throughout this chapter, and indeed the remainder of the book, is the need to *maximize parallel processor utilization* while *minimizing communications*. This is the key to achieving high parallel efficiencies, scalability, and a fast application capable of solving large problems. The fact is that, for all modern systems, a single communications operation is thousands of times more expensive than a single processor operation, so any operation that can contribute to the overall solution without generating excessive communications will help to improve parallel performance.

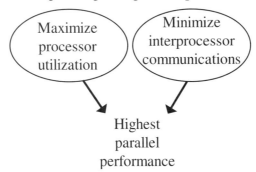

Figure 3.1: The formula for parallel success. Minimizing communications while maximizing processor utilization will result in the best overall parallel performance.

The problem to be solved may be either real-time or not. Real-time problems are those for which the utility or value of the answer is a function of the time delay in obtaining the solution. In so-called "hard deadline" problems, if the answer is not obtained within a certain delay, it is considered worthless. An example of a hard deadline system might be the flight control system for a flight vehicle. A point-of-sale data processing system, which automatically processes retail sales, updates inventory information, etc., would be an example of a "softer" real-time system; long delays would result in lost sales, angry customers, etc. Rogers (1995) discusses a continuous speech-recognition system. It is highly computationally intensive, requiring a number of DEC Alphas working in parallel to achieve a claimed 350 MFlops with acceptable speed and accuracy. The system used involves digital signal processors to initially process the sounds, and a multithreaded symmetrical multiprocessor (SMP) system with 2 GB of shared memory. An SMP system generally involves a common system bus, shared memory, and co-equal processor boards. Developing real-time parallel systems often requires parallel hardware capable of preempting tasks (such as threads) as well as specialized data collection hardware, which we will not cover in detail here. Rather, we will focus on the bulk of parallel computing applications, which do not require a real-time response.

Large scientific simulation is a very different problem for parallel processing. Most scientific calculations are never run at a speed remotely close to real-time. In fact, many run for several hours to complete only a few nanoseconds of simulated time. The requirement for parallel processing in these simulations arises for the sheer number of computations that must be performed, creating unacceptably long processing times using conventional serial computers. Large parallel problems would take weeks, or even months to complete on an average single workstation. Some problems are so large that they cannot even be run on the largest serial computers for lack of memory and processing power. It is these very large scientific problems that we intend to focus on. A typical scientific application run is shown in Figure 3.2.

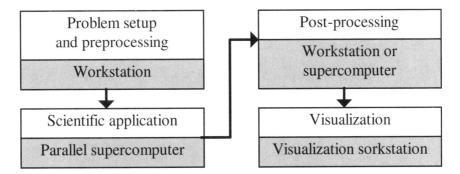

Figure 3.2: A typical scientific application run. Parallel supercomputers are usually used for only the most intensive scientific calculations. Workstations are typically used for preprocessing, postprocessing, and visualization.

A major consideration is whether the parallel code is to be a conversion of an existing serial code or is to be written from scratch. Another issue is how fine- or coarse-grained the parallelization process may be. We will explore both of these issues in the following sections.

Identifying Parallelism: Graininess

The *graininess* of a parallel application is a measure of how small a unit we can partition problems into. The smallest imaginable unit would be to store a single value on each processor, and have each processor perform calculations on that value. This would be called *fine-grained* parallelism. At the other extreme, we might approach a problem by breaking it up into the largest possible components. This would be called *coarse-grained* parallelism.

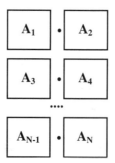

Figure 3.3: Sample problem. The matrix pairs (A_1,A_2) to (A_{N-1},A_N) must be multiplied together in parallel.

A simple example will illustrate our meaning. Suppose you had to multiply a number of pairs of moderately-sized matrices together. Coarse-grained parallel partitioning might assign the multiplication of a matrix-matrix pair (or sets of pairs, if you had more pairs than processors) to a processor. Fine-grained parallel partitioning would assign the computation of the elements of the product matrix to different processors, perhaps by partitioning the rows and columns of the multiplier and multiplicand matrices among different processors.

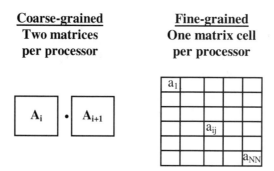

Figure 3.4: Coarse- vs. fine-grained approaches to the matrix multiplication problem. The coarse-grained approach distributes a complete matrix pair to each processor. The fine-grained approach distributes a single matrix value to each processor.

This example, while artificial, illustrates a number of principles. Note that fine- and coarse-grained parallelism are not necessarily mutually exclusive. If we had a large number of processors, we could allocate each matrix product determination to a set of processors, and use a fine-grained decomposition within each set for the product computation. In some cases, it is perfectly acceptable to mix fine and coarse grained partitioning in a single parallel application. For example, a problem might be coarsely partitioned at the top level, while still using a fine-grained partitioning for some time-consuming lower-level calculations, such as performing embarrassingly parallel operations (like ray tracing objects). The key in all parallel design decisions is to maximize processor utilization while minimizing communications between processors.

The extreme case of fine-grained processing is in dataflow or systolic hardware architectures. Such machines have relatively simple processors that wait until the necessary data is delivered, perform a specified operation on that data, and then forward the data to the next processing element. Dataflow architectures are generally proposed for special purposes (such as real-time signal processing), or for highly regular computations (such as matrix linear algebra). Their value for general-purpose computing is debatable.

Coarse-Grained Parallelism Provides the Best Performance

The example above also suggests why, if the number of processors were limited and you had to choose which approach to take, the coarse-grained approach would likely prove superior. The matrix-product computations are independent, and would require no communications overhead (except, of course, to allocate the matrices to processors and, if needed, send the resultant matrix products to a destination processor). The fine-grained approach would require considerably more effort to coordinate the computation and distribute matrix elements among processors. To compute a row of the product requires the row of the first (multiplier) matrix and a column of the multiplicand. Thus, to compute a row of the product requires the entire multiplicand matrix. Various strategies can be developed for assigning blocks of elements to processors and computing with these blocks, collecting the partial results and processing these (in our example, adding) to obtain the final results. There will generally be more communication and additional synchronization barriers required in such an approach.

Two different communications effects slow down fine-grained approaches. First is the actual overhead of the communications, including message startup latency and transit time. These delays can be substantial, with even short messages taking as much as hundreds of milliseconds overall on modern parallel systems. Internal calculations typically take place on the order of nanoseconds. The second effect that can significantly slow fine- grained parallelism is the fact that each communications step enforces an implied synchronization of the processors. Because each processor must wait for every communications step, no processor can get ahead of another and all are forced to wait. Therefore synchronizing often during a fine-grained algorithm causes substantial delays. You can think of it like putting a stop sign at every block in your program.

The distinction between coarse- and fine-grained is sometimes cast in terms of the use of "heavyweight" vs. "lightweight" processes (Howe and Moxon, 1987). This terminology is most often used in real-time transaction-processing systems. A lightweight process is a simple, single-task process. In AI circles it may be referred to as a daemon or an agent.

For any fixed problem size, there will be an optimal number of processors to use. The use of more than this number will actually result in the computation ending later. This is entirely due to the parallel overhead, which will be principally due to communications costs. The coarser-grained the computation is, the more likely that this optimal number will be larger, resulting in faster computation. Note, however, that many problems cannot be decomposed in a coarsely grained fashion, and will have to be done at a fine-grained level or else in serial on all processors.

Speculative (Optimistic) Parallelism

Speculative execution is an approach to gain the benefits of parallelism in some problems that are not obviously parallel. The most common application is that of discrete event simulation. Assume we have a complex system of "actors" or "agents." These could be nodes on a network, process locations, or workers in a factory, etc. They interact, sending others tasks to be processed. In general, such requests for task processing could be preemptive, i.e., require the receiver to stop what they are doing and take up the new task. The "pessimistic" approach would be to have each such actor proceed only so far as they could without the possibility of being interrupted. This would require considerable message traffic. There are a number of possible approaches to such pessimistic simulations, depending on whether agents broadcast the earliest time at which they might next send out tasks, or whether agents request such information from others. The connectivity, etc. of the problem determines which approach is better.

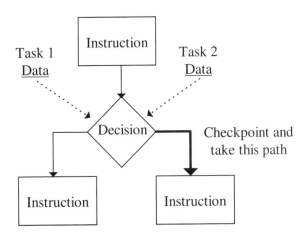

Figure 3.5: Speculative Execution. Rather than have tasks synchronize at a decision, each task will checkpoint at the decision, and continue with a given assumption. Tasks that are incorrect can later return to the checkpoint and continue with the correct answer.

An alternative, called "optimistic," is to compute away with each agent, periodically checkpointing or saving the state of the calculation. If a tasking request is received by an agent, and the simulation of that agent has passed the time at which the request would have been received, the simulator backs up to the last checkpoint before that time, recomputes up until the task request time, and then proceeds as it would given that the new request was received. Obviously, such an optimistic simulation approach requires careful tuning of parameters such as the frequency of checkpointing, the amount of storage allotted to preserving earlier states, discarding of earlier saved states as soon as possible (i.e., when all processors have advanced beyond that simulation time), etc. One does not want to use system checkpoint/restart, but needs the facility built into the simulation program itself for best efficiency. If earlier states can be saved in memory instead of using disk storage, considerable speed could be gained. This is an area of much active research due to the great practical significance. It need not be limited to discrete-event simulations. Adaptive optimization of tuning parameters is a good field for research. See Baker (1993) for an overview of these optimistic methods.

Common Scientific/Engineering Applications

Simulation of physical systems is of great importance in science and engineering. Hydrodynamic simulations are used in climate and weather modeling, astrophysical simulations, and engineering applications such as designing aircraft and jet engines. See, for example, Gardner and Fang (1994) for a discussion of the parallelization of a materials response code. The study of large, gravitating systems is now commonplace in astrophysics due to advances in computing power, particularly parallel applications. Structural mechanics models are used in designing flight vehicles, trusses, etc. Electromagnetic simulations are used in the design of microwave sources, "stealth" aircraft, and high-speed computer circuits. There are a great many "particle in cell" (PIC) codes to simulate the interactions of charged particles with fields. These are used to design microwave tubes (klystrons, backward wave oscillators, gyrotrons, etc.), particle accelerators, free electron lasers, etc. Taxing semiconductor simulations are also of increasing significance; see, for example, Shur et al. (1991) for a brief overview of this topic. A wide range of techniques are used, including finite difference, finite-element, and particle methods. Particle methods are the most immature and are therefore the object of the greatest research interest. Molecular dynamics simulations are of increasing interest, with a great many parallel codes developed for that purpose.

Closely related to particle methods are Monte-Carlo methods. These use random numbers to solve physical problems, particularly transport problems (especially neutron and radiation transport). There has been theoretical interest in the question of parallel random number generation (to insure that the "random" numbers are not correlated between processors, as would be the case if each processor used the same algorithm with the same initial seeds). Monte Carlo methods have even been applied to linear algebra problems (Kamgnia 1991)!

The connectionist or massively-parallel approach, along with ideas from the "Game of Life" spawned a computational approach based on lattices. Cellular automata were investigated as mathematical models for many physical systems. One is the lattice gas. Here a regular array of "sites" admits of collisions between mass particles. With appropriate rules, such systems can model fluid flow (Krafczyk and Rank 1995; Orszag and Yakhot 1986; Frisch, Hasslacher, Pomeau 1986). Lattices have been used for modeling quantum chromodynamics (QCD). A four-dimensional lattice in space-time is used. The simplification of assuming that particles can be located only at lattice points is a valuable reduction in the complexity of the model. Special parallel architectures have been developed for such simulations.

Spectral and modal methods expand the unknown solutions in series of functions chosen for various properties (orthogonality or orthonormality, satisfaction of boundary conditions, etc., depending upon the technique in use). Multi-resolution methods, especially involving wavelets, are of great interest. These approaches often require quadrature for the determination of expansion coefficients. These approaches are most often applied to linear problems, such as elasticity or quantum mechanics, where because of linearity the expansion results in independent problems. Multi-grid methods have been shown to be related to multi-resolution methods, at least in theory; they will be discussed in Chapter 4.

Particle methods are often used in physical simulations. In addition to the PIC codes discussed above, astrophysical simulations of gravitating systems such as stars and galaxies are of great interest. Gravity is a long-range force that causes all particles to interact with one another. If N particles are being simulated, there are order N^2 pairwise interactions; this rapidly becomes computationally infeasible. A variety of methods, such as the fast multipole method (FMM), have been developed to reduce computational costs. The basic idea behind FMM is that the gravitational effect at any point is not sensitive to the detailed distribution of particles far away. It is therefore possible to approximate the distant mass distribution in terms of a few of the lower order moments. This may be done economically in a number of ways, such as through interpolation onto a grid. See, for example, van de Velde (1994) for an overview of particle methods and Salmon and Warren (1994) for a critical discussion of the topic.

Particle and vortex methods are used in hydrodynamics. A variety of methods, such as Smooth Particle Hydrodynamics (SPH; Monaghan, 1991), Reproducing Kernel Particle Methods (RKPM; Liu, Jun, Zhang, 1995), Element Free Galerkin (EFG; Lu, Belytschko, Gu, 1994), etc., have arisen to solve a variety of hydrodynamic and structural mechanics problems. Molecular Dynamics (MD; e.g., Nanano, Kalia, Vashishta, 1994) models have been used for a wide variety of problems; a relatively new application being quantum simulations of small-scale semiconductor devices (Nanano, Vashishta, Kalia, 1994). Vortex methods, which rely on discrete vortices to model fluid flows, are of increasing interest. The vortex methods often use methods similar to FMM to compute the velocity fields at points of interest, due to the vortex distribution (e.g., Almgren, Buttke, Colella, 1994). The MD and other models mentioned have finite-range force interactions. Consequently, it is necessary to determine the "neighbors" of each particle. This may be with a variety of methods, such as octrees or hashing to an underlying grid.

Kaufmann and Smarr (1993) give a good overview of scientific problems requiring a large dose of computer resources. This book is in the Scientific American Library series, and therefore does not contain full technical discussions or complete bibliographical references to the technical literature. It is also not specifically concerned with parallel computing issues. Nonetheless, it is a valuable resource to see how others have approached simulation of major scientific problems.

Domain Decomposition

Many physical problems are naturally partitioned spatially. This has come to be called domain decomposition. It is sufficiently important to deserve its own chapter. See chapter 4 for details. Domain decomposition is probably the most often-used parallelization method for physical problems.

In particle simulations, one may divide the problem domain into regions and assign to a processor the particles within a region. It is also possible to assign particles to processors without redistributing them as a consequence of their motion. Generally, the former appears to be the best approach in terms of minimizing the communications overhead, but this may not be the case with all problems.

Choosing a Programming Model

There are a number of approaches to parallel programming.

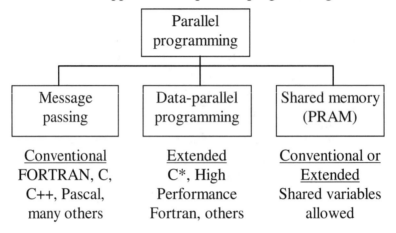

Figure 3.6: Parallel programming paradigms and languages.
Most message passing programming is done in conventional
languages, while data parallel and shared memory
programming is usually done in specialized or extended
languages.

The programming approaches tend to mirror the machine architectures.

Table 3.1: Programming model paired with hardware architecture		
Software paradigm	Hardware architecture	Exemplar language
Shared-memory	Shared-memory	ABC++
Data Parallel	SIMD	HPF
Message-passing	"Loosely Coupled" (MIMD)	MPI
Data flow	Systolic	Lucid, VAL

It is possible to use a MIMD machine to run other programming models, such as ABC++ programs (shared-memory model) or data-flow algorithms, for example. The table merely gives the most "natural" programming model for an architecture, not the required programming model.

Parallel vs. Conventional Languages

Most parallel programming languages are extensions to existing languages. For many-message passing systems (PVM, MPI, P4, etc.), there is no change to the language, merely calls to procedures that implement the messaging. Linda is a shared memory system that adds four subroutine calls to existing languages. There is a Linda-C, Linda-FORTRAN, etc. High performance FORTRAN (HPF) adds directives in the form of special comments (beginning with !HPF$) to direct the distribution of data, to give "hints" as to the parallelization of do-loops, etc. Many systems based on C++ provide class hierarchies to support parallelization, particularly via the data-parallel model discussed below. As noted in the first chapter, there is a plethora of such languages. The tower of Babel will undoubtedly shake out, but how and when?

There are a number of reasons for avoiding the approaches based on C++ for the moment. Aside from their uncertain futures, C++ support is not uniformly good, nor is the language truly standardized or portable. In addition, there is generally a performance penalty in using C++ due to the creation and use of temporary variables. As C++ standardizes and matures, these problems will undoubtedly decrease.

Data-Parallel vs. Message Passing

The data parallel model for parallel programming achieves parallelism by automatically partitioning data between nodes. This approach is most suitable for highly parallel problems on architectures such as shared-memory machines. The Linda shared-memory paradigm, discussed in chapter 1, can be added to FORTRAN or C code relatively easily. If shared-memory is your favored approach, this might be the way to go.

However, Linda is by no means transparent. In general, we have found shared-memory to be a good approach for problems that are "embarrassingly parallel" or nearly so. In such cases, contention for memory and the details of how the physical memory is actually distributed are less important. Where flexibility is required, message-passing should be used. The data-parallel model is awkward, at best, if dynamic load balancing (i.e., load rebalancing) is needed.

The data-parallel model is most appropriate for SIMD machines, which naturally implement only data-parallel problems (Johnsson 1993; Boghosian, 1990). Every node does the same thing on different (possibly "null") data. With the full flexibility of MIMD machines, the limitations of the data-parallel model are evident.

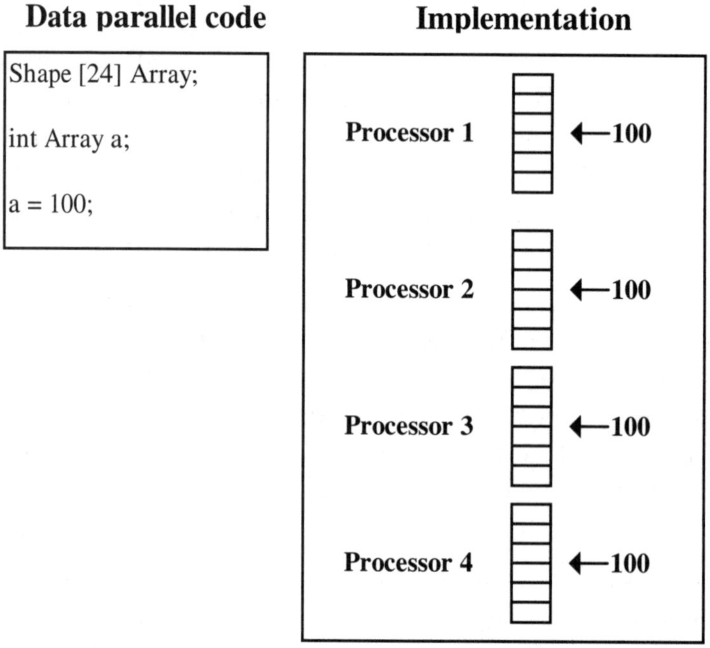

Data parallel code	**Implementation**

```
Shape [24] Array;

int Array a;

a = 100;
```

Processor 1 ←100

Processor 2 ←100

Processor 3 ←100

Processor 4 ←100

Figure 3.7: Data parallel operation to initialize a data parallel array of 26 integers to 100. The code on the left is implemented as shown on four processors. Each processor operates on its portion of the array. Allocation of variables to processors is done by the compiler.

It is appropriate at this point to note here other models. The "object-oriented" model is exemplified by µC++ and ABC++. Here, one partitions "objects." In practice, this approach is similar to data parallelism, hidden within C++ classes. Another approach is the "functional" programming model, typified by the Sisal language. Here, the details are hidden under the abstraction of function calls and the user is at the mercy of the implementor. Functional programming can be succinct and powerful (as in the APL language of old), but obscure. For example, to take the inner (dot) product of two vectors, a typical functional program code fragment might look like (/+@(AA*)@TR)<a,b> where a and b are the two vectors, TR means "transpose the associated vector," (AA *) means "apply to all elements a (pairwise) multiplication, and /+ means "add all the terms" (Douglas 1983).

Portable Message Passing

We advocated at the end of chapter 2 a layered approach to achieve portability, using PVM and MPI. The latter is as portable as parallel programming gets, because it is a standard. The former should permit parallel program development on serial machines, as well as allow development and production on networks of homogenous or heterogeneous machines. This layering has been done with no degradation of efficiency when running MPI, and minor overhead increases in running under PVM. Experience on the SP-2 shows that this is appropriate, as the MPI implementation there has lower latency and higher transfer rates than the PVM implementation; therefore, where speed is the issue, the MPI version should be used.

Converting an Existing Program

The first question to ask is: Is the serial program suitable for parallelization? This will be a function of the language, algorithm, and other practical considerations. In some cases it may be better to start from scratch than try to convert an old legacy code to run in parallel.

FORTRAN Considerations

If the serial program is written in FORTRAN 77, serious consideration should be given to converting the program to FORTRAN 90. This new standard has many virtues for parallel programming. One is the ability to dynamically allocate and free memory. The ability of the programmer to dynamically manage memory is often crucial for efficient memory usage. Another is the ability to deal with array sections. This enables the treatment of "slices" or "stripes" of arrays as objects with relative ease, greatly easing splitting problems for allocation among processors. Pointers are supported, which also facilitate working with arrays. Vector subscripts are another interesting feature. All in all, working with arrays in FORTRAN 90 has become easier than in C. Finally, intrinsic operations such as MATMUL for matrix multiplication and DOT_PRODUCT for the dot product of vectors hold out the hope that they will be efficiently implemented, with parallelism support built in on parallel machines.

Morton et al. (1995) provides a case study of porting and parallelization issues involving a FORTRAN code. Their code was originally developed on an RS/6000 using PVM, and was therefore developed for parallel use from the outset. It was a linear system solver. They found that by using the Basic Linear Algebra Subroutines (BLAS), good performance gains could be achieved on the T3D. Presumably the BLAS library on the T3D was carefully optimized for that machine. They also found that using T3D-specific options, which use the shared-memory features of the machine (see chapter 1) via low-level routines, produced some performance gains by speeding up communication. These machine-specific optimizations were encapsulated so as to make porting changes relatively minor. As we discussed in chapter 2, there is a tradeoff in optimizing the scalar performance of an individual processor vs. communications overhead. An algorithm that is more effective in the scalar sense might require more communications effort.

We would recommend C as the language of choice in a parallel programming effort begun from scratch. This is because of C's ability to interface with the operating system more seamlessly. In a parallel program, this is often necessary or desirable, as illustrated by the work of

Morton et al. (1995). C is also more flexible in its use of pointers and various forms of indirect addressing.

FORTRAN code is often better optimized, particularly for vector processors, than C code. This is due to a number of factors, including greater experience with vectorizing FORTRAN compilers, and the ability of the FORTRAN compiler to make assumptions about the independence of arrays; C treats arrays as pointers and cannot conclude so easily that two different pointers do not reference overlapping, and consequently dependent, data. On some machines, it is desirable to write some subroutines in FORTRAN to be called from a predominantly C-coded program. This situation should change for two reasons. First, compilers are maturing and their writers are concerned with such issues. Secondly, the hardware trend is for pipelined (or micro-pipelined) machines that support in hardware out-of-order execution, register renaming, and various other "tricks" to get the most out of the pipeline. Formerly, the approach was to depend on the compiler to order operations so as to reduce the incidence of pipeline stalls. It was realized that at compilation time it was not possible to recognize all such opportunities. With these hardware improvements, less burden will be placed upon the compiler to detect and exploit all possibilities for "vectorization."

Identifying Parallelism in an Existing Program

A key question in converting an existing code is: Should the algorithmic structure of the serial code be preserved? Identifying parallelism in an existing algorithm is usually done by examining the existing code in detail and determining which parts can be easily modified to run in parallel. For parts of the algorithm that cannot be run in parallel, new algorithms must be examined. Strategies for partitioning parallel algorithms will be presented in detail in chapter 4.

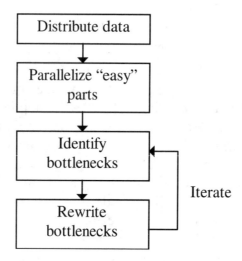

Figure 3.8: One method for converting an existing application. Distribute and parallelize the easy portions of the algorithm; then try running it in parallel before attacking some of the "hard to parallelize" parts.

For example, in solving a sparse linear system, it may be more suitable to use a direct solver on a serial processor; but use an iterative solver, such as the preconditioned conjugate gradient method, in a distributed environment. Or, if a dense linear system needs to be solved, while an LU solver employing partial pivoting almost certainly is the method of choice on a serial machine, in a parallel environment a QR solver might be the best choice. The QR solver, while more costly in terms of total number of floating-point operations, is stable without pivoting. Consequently, if the matrix at hand is poorly conditioned, communications overhead due to pivoting could render the QR approach superior.

Obviously, the decision will be dictated by the relative amounts of communications overhead. It might also, in these examples at least, be determined by the libraries available. In such a case, the decision will be relatively easy as changing algorithms would require relatively little user effort. However, solving linear systems is a particularly common problem and is used here as an example. The user will often find that searching methods, etc., are not as well-supported in system libraries and may need to be changed to take best advantage of hardware. It is therefore well to modularize such code so that it may be changed without undue grief.

Rapid Prototyping

One successful strategy for developing parallel applications us to use *rapid prototyping*. In rapid prototyping, one attempts to quickly develop the important parts of a parallel application quickly to identify potential bottlenecks and problems before completing the larger effort. In some cases, prototypes are used as a basis for the complete application, in other cases, prototypes are discarded after use.

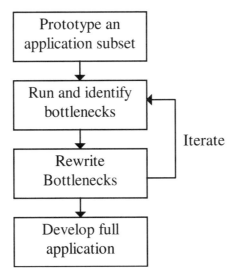

Figure 3.9: Rapid prototyping is a risk reducing development method. The idea is to quickly implement a subset of the application's features to identify problems quickly.

The key feature of any prototype is *limited scope*. It is important to fully define the purpose and scope of a prototype before starting, to avoid wasting time on unnecessary features. For example, if the purpose is to demonstrate that something is feasible in parallel, it may be appropriate to select a simple problem, choose an appropriate algorithm, and simply hard code the problem into your simulation to show it can be done. If, on the other hand, you intend to use the prototype as a basis for your final application, you may want to spend time laying out appropriate data structures, diagramming communication patterns, and considering how to structure your prototype so it can easily be expanded to the final prototype.

Another key feature of rapid prototyping is being able to develop your simulation rapidly. Ideally, you want to be able to implement *quick and dirty* algorithms and data structures for the prototype, and be able to easily replace these components with more elegant solutions later on. For example, you might initially hard-wire your test problems or some simple boundary conditions into the code, with the intention of replacing these with options read from a file later on. In another case, you might implement an underlying data structure as a sequential array initially, with the intention of replacing it with a faster data structure such as a hash table.

We strongly recommend the use of *object-oriented* concepts for the implementation of all prototype software. The central idea is to encapsulate your data and operations into a single entity called an object. An object is typically a data structure or service, along with all of the operations to operate on it. An object has a well defined interface, in that the object can only be modified by calling one of its operations. This well-defined interface allows us to create "stubs" internal to the object, which we will later replace with working code. You do not necessarily need an object- oriented language to create objects, or use the object-oriented paradigm. While object-oriented languages have a number of powerful features that make some operations easier, their use in prototypes is not always desirable. In rapid prototyping, we use objects to isolate certain portions of our code, so that later we can replace the underlying internals of our objects without changing the prototype. This allows you to fast prototype sections of your application, and then fill in the details and optimize the results later.

Data dictionary Object	Add(Item)
	Delete(Key)
	Find(Key)

Figure 3.10: Object oriented concepts can be used to reduce risk when prototyping. For example, this Data Dictionary Object could be implemented using a simple array initially, and could later be replaced by a faster hash table implementation

A simple example (Figure 3.10) will help to clarify the object oriented concept, and how it might be applied to fast-prototype an application. Suppose that for your final application, you wish to have a complicated fast data dictionary for storing data. The dictionary would implement *Add, Delete,* and *Find* operations based on a *key* for each data item. The user might choose, for a rapid prototype, to implement this dictionary as a simple array. Later, as performance becomes more important, the dictionary object internals could be replaced with a faster hash table implementation.

Another approach to creating extendible prototypes is to use *layering*. Similar in concept but less stringent than object oriented programming, the goal of layering is to isolate critical functions (but not necessarily data). In many languages that are function- and module-oriented, such as Fortran and C, layering is a more appropriate choice for isolating modules to be expanded later. Layering is also widely used to increase parallel portability by isolating the application from details of the message-passing system or operating system. We saw an example of the layered approach in chapter 2, where an intermediate message passing layer is used to isolate the application from the underlying message-passing system. By creating a well defined interface to a generic message-passing paradigm, we greatly increased the portability of our application. Layering can also be used to create stubs for features in a prototype that we will want to improve or expand upon later. The key in layering is to create a well-defined set of functions whose details can be expanded to meet the needs of the final application.

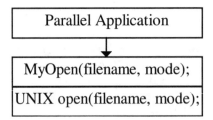

Figure 3.11: A layered approach to file I/O. The MyOpen()
call is layered over the UNIX open() call. This allows us to
later place a parallel file system call in place of the UNIX
system call without changing the parallel application.

An example (Figure 3.11) of a functional layered approach might be to isolate all of the input and output calls for your program for future expansion. For example, you might create your own *MyOpen(), MyRead(), MyWrite()* and *MyClose()* calls for manipulating files. In the prototype, these calls, might directly call the underlying UNIX system calls (i.e. *open(), read(), write(),* and *close())*. However, when we move to the final application, these simple calls might be replaced by calls to a parallel input/output system so that large amounts of data could be better handled. Note the difference between this layering example and the object-oriented example above. In the object-oriented approach, both data and operations to be performed on the data are encapsulated. In the layered approach, only the operations are isolated.

Some of the key areas to isolate when building a parallel prototype are the internal data structures, message passing, parallel input and output, problem input and configuration, and overall program control. In each case, use of the object-oriented or layered approach may be appropriate, depending on your particular prototyping strategy. Often it is appropriate to isolate external interfaces, such as the operating system or input/output system using a layered approach, and use an object-oriented approach for internal data structures and constructs. Use of these paradigms will significantly speed development, and will make the transition from prototype to final application an easy one.

I/O for Parallel Computations

Parallel input and output (I/O) is one of the great open problems of modern parallel computing. Parallel programs and modern parallel processors have the ability to create unimaginably large volumes of data, yet most have infantile methods for handling it. In addition, there is no standardization of parallel I/O systems between machines, so a portable parallel application must be structured to deal with a variety of parallel I/O systems. Postprocessing the data is equally daunting, because parallel post-processing is required for the largest problems, and few parallel commercial visualization tools are available.

The I/O Bottleneck

A simple example will illustrate the input/output problems caused by massively parallel computing. Consider a large parallel numerical simulation that the authors wish to use as a basis for a movie. They want to create a 60-second movie at 20/frames per second. This will require 1200 frames overall. They are running the problem on 100 processors, each with 50,000 double-precision values to output, for a total of a moderate 400K per node. Multiplying by the number of processors, we get approximately 40MB per dump file, or 48 GB overall. While this may not seem like a lot of data, consider the alternatives for outputting and post-processing this data. The two basic approaches are to output the data from a single node, or output the data on all nodes to separate devices. In the former case, it will take a very long time to gather the data on a single node and write all 48GB to disk. The single output node becomes an intolerable chokepoint, and might even fail for lack of memory or network bandwidth to handle the data. The latter approach solves the chokepoint problem while the program is running, but now we must contend with gathering and postprocessing data from 100 different processing nodes.

The problem above represents a very moderately size problem, with only 5 million data values to be written. A large parallel problem might have several million computed cells each, with 50 or more double-precision values. For example, a moderate 5-million-cell problem with 50 values per cell corresponds to over 2GB of data. Split over 100 processors, we have a moderate memory requirement of only 20MB per processor. However, if we have a long-running problem, we may want to checkpoint the program periodically for restarts in case the program or machines fail during computations. These restart files can combine with the normal output files to create very large output requirements, in the hundreds of gigabytes and even terabyte (trillion byte) range. Generating these large amounts of data is only half the problem. Postprocessing the data is equally challenging.

Approaches for Parallel I/O

There are several approaches commonly used to solve the parallel I/O bottleneck. We've found it is best to use a combination of approaches depending on the type of access and the particular system you are running on. We will introduce several paradigms for parallel I/O.

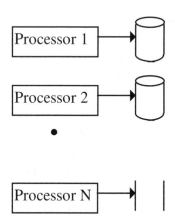

Figure 3.12: The local file approach to parallel I/O. Each processor writes to its local disk, and the user is responsible for gathering data from all local disks for postprocessing.

One paradigm for parallel input/output is the *local file* system. Here each processor has a local file system where all of its output is read or written.

Typically the input files are pre-staged to the local disk of each processor, and output files are later gathered from each processor for post-processing. For output, each processor only writes to its own file space so there is no output bottleneck. This results in relatively fast parallel output, since the processors do not even need to synchronize their output, and can each dump their local portion of the problem in parallel. The major limitation is that typically the data needs to be gathered for postprocessing, because most postprocessing problems are still run on serial computers. On input, the input must be pre-staged to the local file space of each processor before the program is run. The local file system paradigm is very easy to implement because standard serial UNIX open, read, and write calls can be used directly. This paradigm is appropriate for running large problems on clusters of workstations or parallel computers that do not have a dedicated parallel I/O file system. If output files are structured properly so that they don't depend on the ordering of the data, it is possible to simply append the output files from each processor together to generate a single file for postprocessing. The local file system is very portable, because it can be used on any parallel computer that has separate disks for each process. The only portability problem we have run into is the difficulty of pre-positioning and gathering data from parallel computers where the operating system, rather than the user, determines where a job runs. These systems present a problem because the user does not know in advance where to position data or gather it when the job is completed.

A related paradigm for parallel output is the *shared directory* system. Here, all processors are assumed to have a single disk or directory that is shared. On input, all processors can read their input data from the shared directory, and on output each can write either its own file, or processors can take turns writing to a single file. The shared directory paradigm has the advantage of providing a single input and output point for the user, which makes pre-processing and post-processing easier. The disadvantage of this system is that, for large problems, the single directory will become a bottleneck. The controller for the shared directory file system can generally only process I/O serially, so even if each processor writes to its own file in the directory, we will still have a significant serial bottleneck in our parallel program. We've found it is best to have the option of reading and writing from a single shared directory for small problems, because it is much simpler to deal with a single input and output location. We reserve the local file paradigm for larger problems, when performance is more important. The shared-directory paradigm is fairly easy to implement using standard UNIX calls. It is also fairly portable because most large parallel systems, as well as many workstation networks, have shared network directories available.

A variation of the shared-directory paradigm is the *single I/O node* input/output paradigm. Here we use message passing, rather than a shared file system to direct all I/O to a particular processor. The net result is similar to the shared-file system paradigm, in that all input and output can be directed to a single directory on a designated processor. The chief advantage of this system over the shared-directory paradigm is that this system will work even if no shared network directories exist. It suffers the same disadvantage in that the I/O processor becomes a bottleneck for large applications. This paradigm would be useful on a heterogeneous collection of workstations, or a supercluster of supercomputers where cross mounted file systems do not exist. This paradigm is somewhat more difficult to implement than the previous systems, because each read or write must be translated into a message to the I/O processor where data can be read or written out. Care must be taken to control the flow of data as well, because 100 processors could easily overload the ability of a single processor to handle simultaneous I/O requests. Assuming some provisions are made for controlling the flow of data, this is a highly portable form of parallel I/O. It makes no assumptions about the hardware, other than the existence of a disk on at least one of the processors. Again, we recommend that this paradigm be available as an option, because it is useful for running small to medium size problems on some architectures.

Log Files

Log files represent a special example of parallel I/O, and can be used to demonstrate some of the paradigms described above. In a serial simulation, a log file is often used to record the progress of the simulation, as well as to record problems and aid in debugging. A serial program typically opens a log file when it starts, and writes short entries as initialization, time steps, errors, and other significant events occur, so the user can monitor progress of the program. In parallel, we will look at implementation of a log file using the paradigms described above.

If we start by implementing our log file using the *local file* paradigm, we have the advantage of fast execution and easy implementation. In fact, if we are converting an existing serial program that has a log file, we need only change the *open()* system call to open a local file on each machine. The result of this strategy will be a separate log file on each processor, each log file containing only the log statements from its execution. To look at the log files, the user must gather them from each of the local file systems. Though this is acceptable when running on a few processors, it can be very cumbersome to determine what went wrong when a large run fails.

An alternative is to move to the *shared directory* paradigm. Here, each processor would still have its own log file, but all log files would be opened in the same directory, making it a little easier on the user. Again, the underlying code would use standard UNIX I/O calls, and this time each processor would open its own log file in the shared directory. For example, processor one might open "log.1", processor two would open "log.2" and so on. (*Aside*: It might have occurred to the reader that a better strategy would be to simply have all processors open a shared log file with the *append* operator, so that data written from each processor will be appended to a single file. Unfortunately this does not work on most networked file systems, because each processor keeps its own pointer to the end of the file, meaning they will overwrite each other after only a few log statements are written.) For the shared-directory paradigm, there might be a slight degradation of performance, but in general because the log statements are short, this paradigm would perform almost as well as the local file system. The only problem with this system is that the user again may have to wade through 100 log files (if the model is running on 100 processors) to figure out if anything went wrong.

Finally, we can try out the *single I/O node* paradigm on our log file. Rather than have each node directly access the file system, we will instead use the message passing system to forward log statements from processors to a single I/O node where the log file will be maintained. When a processor encounters a write to the log, it will instead *send()* a message to the designated I/O processor, which is usually node zero in the network. Similarly, node zero will periodically *probe()* for log file messages and then *receive()* and *write()* them to a single log when they are found. This avoids the requirement for a shared file system and creates a single log file with messages from all of the processors. The only drawback is the complexity of having to send messages to the I/O processor, and having the I/O processor periodically poll for log messages. The fact that the I/O node must poll for messages can also lead to some un-logged messages if the program fails before all messages are received and logged. Overall, this is the only portable I/O paradigm that works in all possible network configurations, yet still creates a single file much like a serial application.

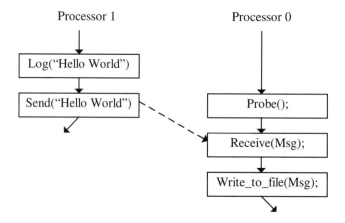

Figure 3.13: Single I/O node logging. Log statement on processor 1 sends the log message to processor zero where it is actually written to a file.

Proprietary Parallel I/O Systems

We will examine some of the common features of proprietary parallel I/O systems available on some of the largest parallel supercomputers. These systems typically involve a great deal of dedicated hardware to make fast parallel I/O available to applications. The major limitation of dedicated parallel I/O systems is the fact that there is, as yet, no standardization between various vendors. This means that code written for these systems will only run on a single parallel computer. The new Message Passing Interface I/O standard, described below, is an attempt to standardize parallel I/O, but has not been widely adopted to date.

Dedicated parallel I/O systems take advantage of message passing systems as well as special input/output hardware to reduce the parallel I/O bottleneck. A good example of a parallel I/O system is the one developed for the for the Intel Paragon. The Paragon has dedicated I/O nodes configured for every few nodes. These are hooked directly to RAID disk servers, and directly support a parallel I/O mode as well as standard UNIX I/O access. The operating system directly supports a number of parallel I/O modes, and files can be opened in any mode. These include local and shared I/O modes, similar in concept to the local and shared paradigms described above. The Intel system also supports a shared UNIX file mode where each processor has its own file index into a shared file, and can read and write to different sections of the file independently. A log file mode allows processors to write independently to a shared file, with the output placed in sequential order on a first-come, first-serve basis. Similarly, a global and synchronous mode allow all processors to share a single file pointer. In the synchronous mode, all I/O is processed sequentially by processor number, while the global mode requires that all processors perform the same operations in the same order on a single file. Perhaps most useful, the Paragon also has a record-oriented mode, where file operations are performed in a first-come, first-serve basis on a shared file, but fixed-length records written are stored in order by processor number. Applications can use different file modes to access different files as needed.

The MPI-IO Standard

As part of the Message Passing Interface (MPI) standardization effort to be covered in chapter 5, people from throughout the country are currently assembling a standard interface for parallel I/O systems called MPI-I/O. Though currently still in draft form, the standard advances a concepts that may someday be widely available for parallel applications developers. The MPI-IO standard is based on the idea that parallel I/O is similar to message passing. Writing to a file is similar to sending a message, and reading from a file is similar to receiving a message. MPI-IO extends the message- passing constructs developed in the MPI standard to use in parallel I/O.

Unlike most other parallel file systems, MPI-IO data is not defined by reads and writes of binary data. Instead, the contents of the file is defined in terms of MPI *derived data types*. Derived data types, to be covered in chapter 5, are simple complex data structures made up of primitive components. This is conceptually similar to a record in Pascal or a structure in C. A derived data type describes a collection of elementary data. Derived data types are, in turn, used to construct a *filetype* data type. Filetypes define the layout of the each processor's data used for parallel I/O. The filetype represents a data pattern tjat may be repeated several times in the final file. Different processors can access these different repeated filetype patterns. Because the filetype is defined when the file is opened, different processors may read separate filetypes. Finally, the defined filetype for a given parallel file can be *tiled* with filetypes from other processors to define a complete parallel I/O file. This tiling of data allows different processors to access different portions of the file without overlapping.

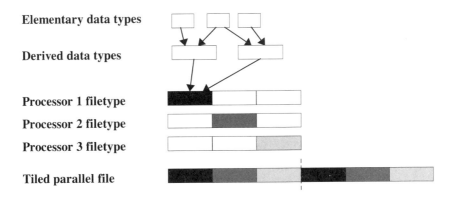

Figure 3.14: The MPI-IO file structure. Elementary data
types are grouped to form derived data types. These, in
turn, define filetypes for different processors. Finally,
filetypes are tiled to form the overall parallel file. This type
of structure makes for very fast parallel access, because I/O
is very well structured.

An example of the MPI-IO hierarchy is shown above. Primitive data
types are used to define filtypes, and filetypes from each processor are
then tiled to form the overall parallel file. The chief advantages of this
system over more traditional UNIX file-system approaches is a high
degree of portability and better performance. Because all data types are
well defined, all filetypes in a file are identical, and processor access
patterns are well defined, it is possible to efficiently read and write data
from all processors simultaneously. Dedicated parallel file system
hardware can be implemented to handle this type of file very efficiently.
The major drawback of this approach is some loss in flexibility, because
all data types, sizes, and formats must be well defined in advance. NASA
Ames is currently working on an implementation of the draft MPI-IO for
workstation clusters, and IBM is working on another implementation for
its SP-2 Parallel I/O File System (PIOFS), with full versions to be
available in 1996.

References

Almgren, A. S., Buttke, T., Colella, P., "A Fast Adaptive Vortex Method in Three Dimensions," *J. Comp. Physics*, **112**, 177-200, 1994.

Baker, L., *VHDL Programming*, N. Y.: John Wiley, 1993.

Boghosian, B. M., "Data Parallel Computaton and Connection Machine*," 1989 Lectures in Complex Systems, SFI Studies in the Sciences of Complexity*, Lect. Vol. II, ed. E. Jen, 325-370, Reading, MA: Addison-Wesley, 1990.

Corbett, Dror, Fineberg, Hsu, Nitzberg, Prost, Snir, Traversat, Wong, "Overview of the MPI-IO Parallel I/O Interface," The Workshop on I/O in Parallel and Distributed Systems, IPPS '95, Santa Barbara, CA, April 25, 1995.

Douglas, J. H., "New Computer Architectures Tackle Bottleneck," *High Technology*, 71-78, June 1983.

Frisch, U., Hassslacher, B., Pomeau, Y., "Lattice-Gas Automata for the Navier-Stokes Equation," *Phys. Rev. Letters*, **56**(14), 7 April 1986.

Gardner, D. R., Fang, H. E., "Three-Dimensioanl Shock Wave Physics Simulations with PCTH on the Paragon Parallel Computer," High Performace Computing 1994, La Jolla CA, April 111-13, 1994. Also available as report SAND93-2040C.

Howe, C. D., Moxon, B., "How to program parallel computers," *IEEE Spectrum*, 36-41, Sept. 1987.

Johnsson, S. L., "Massively Parallel Computing: Data distribution and communications," Parallel Architectures and their Efficiency, 1st Heinz Nixdorf Symposium, ed M. Heide and M. Rosenberg, Berlin: Springer, 1993.;

Kamgnia, E., "The von Neumann-Ulam Monte Carlo Method for Solving Systems of Linear Algebraic Equations on a Parallel Computer," *High Performance Computing II*, (ed. M. Durand and F. El Dabaghi), Amsterdam: Elsevier Science Publishers B. V., pp. 233-44, 1991.

Kauffman, W.. J. III, and Smarr, L. J., *Supercomputing and the Tranformation of Science*, New York: W. H. Freeman, 1993.

Krafczyk, M. and Rank, E., "A Parallelized Latice-Gas Solver for Transient Navier-Stokes Flolw: Implementation and Simulation Results," *Int. J. Num. Methods in Eng.,* **38**. pp. 1243-1258, 1995

Liu, W. K., Jun, S., Zhang, Y. F., "Reproducing Kernel Particle Methods*," Int. J. for Num. Methods. in Fluids*, **20**,1081-1106, 1995.

Lu, Y. Y., Belytschko, T., Gu, L., "A new implementation of the element free Galerkin method," *Comput. Methods Appl. Mech. Engrg.,* **113**, 397-414, 1994.

Monaghan, J. J., "Smoothed Particle Hydrodynamics," *Annual Review of Astronomy and Astrophysics*, **30**, pp. 543-574, 1992.

Morton, D., Wang, K., Obge, D. O., "Lessons Learned in Porting Fortran/PVM Code to the Cray T3D," *IEEE Parallel and Distributed Technology*, pp. 4-11, Spring 1995.

Nakano, A., Kalia, R. K., Vashishta, P., "Multiresolution molecular dynamics algorithm for realistic materials modeling on parallel computers," *Computer Physics Communications*, **83**, 199-214, 1994.

_____, Vashishta, P., Kalia, R. K., "Massively parallel algorithms for computational nanoelectronics based on quantum molecular dynamics," *Computer Physics Communications*, **83**, 181-196, 1994.

Orszag, S., Yakhot, V., "Reynolds Number Scaling of Cellular-Automaton Hydrodynamics," *Phys. Rev. Letters*, **56**(16), 21 April 1986.

Paragon User's Manual, "Parallel I/O Modes," pp 5-13 to 5-17, Intel Corporation

Rogers, R., "Voice Recognition Calls for Symmetry," *EE Times*, p. 43, July 3, 1995.

Salmon, J. K., Warren, M. S., "Skeletons from the Treecode Closet," *J. Comp. Physics*, **111**, 136-155, 1994.

Shur, M., Fjeldy, T. A., Jensen, G. U., "Supercomputer Simulation of Submicron Semiconductor Devices," *Supercomputing Review*, 29-33, June 1991.

van de Velde, E. F., *Concurrent Scientific Computing*, Berlin: Springer, 1994.

Chapter 4

Partitioning Your Problem

One of the most critical design decisions in any parallel program is how to partition your problem. A poor or rigid partitioning choice might result in disastrous parallel performance. A flexible partitioning choice, designed to optimize real world problems will result in much better parallel performance. We now examine some common classes of problems, and methods for partitioning them.

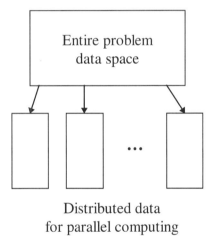

Figure 4.1: A fundamental issue in all parallel developments
is how to distribute data so it can be processed in parallel.

Embarrassingly Parallel Problems

Many problems of interest are relatively easy to parallelize. These problem can be partitioned such that no communication is required between sub-domains. These are the "embarrassingly parallel" problems. Others require communication at the interfaces between regions. Still others have "long-range" interactions that lead to the possibility that any portion of the problem domain can influence any other. There are a number of special problems that are naturally parallel, such as tracking multiple targets (Gottschalk 1988).

Visualization and Other Graphics and Geometrical Algorithms

Many algorithms concerned with geometry parallelize naturally if different regions are independent or nearly so. Visualization and graphics often involve such geometrical problems as sub-problems. For example, consider the problem of plotting contours of a field defined over a two-dimensional region, where the values are known at an irregular distribution of points. This sort of problem often occurs in cartography, for example. It is first necessary to tessellate the space, and this is usually done by Delaunay triangularization (O'Rourke 1994). Delaunay triangularization produces a mesh of triangles with the given points as the vertices. The construction of the Delaunay triangularization in one region is independent of the triangularization of a distant region, so this problem parallelizes well (Cignoni et al. 1995).

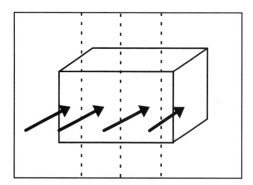

Figure 4.2: Many graphics algorithms, such as 3-D rendering, are embarrassingly parallel. Here a simple ray-tracing algorithm on a cube is shown on four processors.

Given the Delaunay triangularization of a point set, the Voronoi diagram may then readily be constructed as the geometrical dual. It is only necessary to construct the perpendicular bisectors of each line in the Delaunay triangularization, extending these only until they meet another bisector. This produces a set of polygons, defining the volumes closest to any point. Voronoi diagrams are of interest in crystallography and other fields, including the optimal location of facilities. Delaunay triangularizations are of interest in defining computational meshes (Rees and Morton 1991). The Delaunay triangularization maximizes the minimum vertex angle of any of the triangles. It is strictly defined only for convex regions, but Rees and Morton discuss the Locally Delaunay triangularization as a generalization for arbitrary regions.

Ray tracing, ray casting, and radiosity methods are computationally intensive and much of this work parallelizes well. Radiosity requires the solution of a sparse linear system, so is not strictly "embarrassingly parallel," but much of the work involves computing the view factors or elements of the matrix. Rays may be cast or traced independently. Cramblitt (1994) discusses rendering on a network. The Maui SP-2 has been used as a "rendering farm" (Wolfe 1995) in experiments to perform motion-picture-quality animation. The magnitude of the computations required can perhaps be guaged from the movie "Toy Story," said to be the first computer-generated feature-length film; it has 114,000 frames consisting of 34 Terabytes of data; each frame is 5 MB of data, produced from 300MB of initial data.

Stochastic Problems

Monte Carlo Methods are computationally intensive and therefore good candidates for parallelization. In its most general usage, Monte Carlo methods employ random numbers to solve problems. Almost always, "pseudorandom" numbers generated by an algorithm are employed, rather than truly random numbers. Monte Carlo methods are most often used to solve transport problems. The substance transported, such as radiation or neutrons, is modeled as a collection of particles. These interact with the underlying medium by probabilistic rules. For example, neutrons emitted in a region of a reactor are modeled by a single macro-particle, which moves in a randomly selected direction. It then will do a random walk out of the reactor. If its path crosses other material, the probability that it will interact (absorption or scattering) is computed, and a random number is used to determine what happens to the macro-particle. Obviously, the flight of each macro-particle may be computed independently of the others, at least over a time step. As the absorption changes the properties of a material region, and thereby alters the probabilities of absorption or scattering in given directions, the computation of the behavior of a macro-particle from birth to death is not completely independent of the behavior of the others. Therefore, there must be periodic synchronization to update the properties of the underlying media, amounting to a time step. An example of a parallel Monte Carlo code, for radiative transfer calculations for stars, is in Colombet et al. (1993). They used a network of workstations running PVM. The parallelization of percolation cluster simulations is discussed in Babalievski (1992); this work is of interest in fractal research.

Many statistical problems are highly parallel. Quantum statistical problem require the averaging over a large number of possible system configurations, called a statistical "ensemble." Obviously, each configuration's values may be computed independently of the others; they are all independent, possible "universes." A parallel implementation of hierarchical clustering may be found in a paper by Olson (1995).

Optimization and Combinatorial Problems

Note that the ensemble averaging approach, and many similar statistical or optimization problems in which a large number of configurations have to be examined, are naturally treated by the "LoadLeveller" type of batch processing approach. These independent problems are embarrassing parallel. All that is needed after the independent runs are completed is a post-processor that either determines the appropriate average for statistical problems, or finds the optimal configuration given all the output, in the case of the combinatorial optimization problems.

Other methods, such as the Simplex method for linear programming, may be parallelized as other matrix methods. See Anderson and Setubal (1995) for an example of a parallel method for the Maximum-Flow Problem.

AI Applications

There are numerous approaches to "artificial intelligence." These include the "connectionist" approach, which involves massively parallel hardware (or the simulation thereof) along the lines of neural networks, often modeled on biological systems. This is perhaps best exemplified by the work of Carver Mead and his associates to produce a silicon cortex, silicon retina, and silicon white matter. This is a project in massively parallel, special purpose hardware.

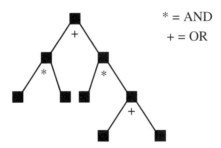

* = AND

+ = OR

Figure 4.3: AI applications such as this AND-OR tree can be done in parallel by distributing different parts (branches) of the tree to different processors.

The major forms of parallelism in AI expert systems relate to so-called "And" and "Or" parallelism. Expert systems rely on rules of the general form "if {antecedent conditions}, then {consequent conditions or actions}." Large numbers of these rules are used together to draw inferences by various "chaining" methods, typically forward- or backward-chaining. Generally, the antecedents are a conjunction of logical clauses (clauses "anded" together); such rules are called Horn clauses (see, for example, Baker 1989) and have desirable properties. Often, these clauses may be evaluated independently, in parallel, to determine if the consequent should be activated (assigned the logical value True if a logical proposition, or, if an action to be taken, acted upon). Similarly, if we have two or more antecedent clauses "ored" together, if any one is true the consequent will be True. Therefore, the clauses may be evaluated in parallel if independent, and, if any one is true, the consequent may be assigned and the other, parallel, evaluations of clauses, terminated ("short-circuited").

Signal Processing

Signal processing, particularly for sonar and radar systems, was an early motivation for parallel systems. Systolic arrays may be used to advantage. Typical applications involve Fourier transforms (particularly fast Fourier transforms or FFTs), convolutions and correlations, and filtering. Inputs from arrays of sensors are naturally processed via arrays of processor elements, and matrix operations can naturally implement FFT. Matrix multiplications can then be used for convolutions or filtering operations. See, for example, Miklosko et al. (1989) for a discussion of signal processing arrays (as well as coverage of many other topics of interest related to specialized hardware). Mastin, Plimpton, and Ghiglia (1993) discuss massively-parallel processing of synthetic aperture radar data.

Domain Decomposition

Domain decomposition refers to spatially partitioning the computational domain. This is not necessarily a tessellation: the domains may or may not overlap. The Schwarz method described immediately following is an example of an overlapping decomposition. On the other hand, Lai (1993), for example, describes a non-overlapped decomposition used to solve semiconductor device simulations. Multigrid methods, described later, can be implemented with or without overlap of the domains, although there appear to be good reasons for using some overlap. Overlap can contribute to minimizing communications overhead if used carefully.

Fundamental Tradeoffs in Domain Decomposition

Certain very fundamental parallel principles are at work when we decompose a problem spatially. The effectiveness of all spatial decomposition methods can be explained in terms of *volume* and *surface area*. When we consider partitioning any regular problem, such as a numerical grid, spatially, the volume enclosed by a particular partition will correspond roughly to the number of cells. Similarly the surface area of the section will correspond roughly to the communications needed for that partition to communicate with its neighbors.

Volume and Surface Area vs Number of Processors

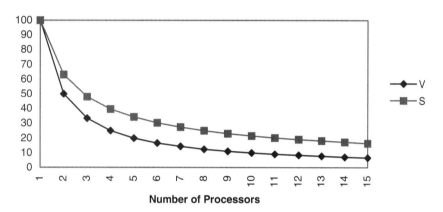

Figure 4.4: Volume(V) and surface area(S) of a partitioned unit cube, expressed as a percentage of the original volume or surface area. Surface area declines more slowly than volume, limiting the theoretical speedup that can be achieved using spatial decomposition.

Consider partitioning the simplest possible problem, a regular cube with a certain number of cells along each edge, into smaller cubes. As we increase the number of processors, we need to slice the overall cube into smaller and smaller pieces. If we look at the volume of each piece, it is decreasing in direct proportion to the number of processors. At any stage, then, an even partitioning of the volume of the cube V between N processors will result in V/N volume for each processor. This corresponds to the amount of work done computing cells by each processor. Similarly, it can easily be shown that the surface area of the processors is declining at a rate of only $6 \cdot A \cdot N^{-2/3}$ where A is the original area of the cube.

Therefore, the volume allocated to each processor is declining much faster than the surface area of each processor for large numbers of processors. This means that the work is declining faster than the communications as we add more processors. This creates a fundamental limit for spatially partitioning this kind of problem. For any nontrivial problem, the communications time will eventually overwhelm any advantage gained by applying more processors to the problem. In essence this is another expression of Amdahl's law, as covered in chapter 2. In this case, however, we can see clearly how adding more processors will eventually result in a diminishing return because communications overhead does not decline linearly as more processors are added. This result applies only to the evenly spaced, evenly partitioned cubic grid we used to create it. Clearly, highly irregular spatial problems may have highly advantageous partitioning directions or configurations that could perform much better than this result. However, most spatially partitioned problems have a regular grid similar to this one, so it is important to understand the tradeoffs. It is also worth mentioning that 2-D problems suffer somewhat less from this effect, because the communications overhead declines with the function $4 \cdot L \cdot N^{-1/2}$ where L is the length of the original square. In either case, this effect can be mitigated somewhat by increasing the problem size as we increase the number of processors, which corresponds to using the measure of scaled speedup described in chapter 2.

Simple 1-D, 2-D, or 3-D partitioning

One of the easiest-to-implement spatial decomposition methods is dimensional partitioning. Using this method, we simply carve the problem space up into pieces along the main coordinate directions. We will start with a description of the one-dimensional method, which can easily be extended to two or three dimensions. Dimensional partitioning can either be done in a *weighted* or *unweighted* mode. We will describe both methods.

In the unweighted 1-D partitioning, we simply choose a direction along which to partition. It is usually best to choose the longest direction spatially, because this will result in less communication. For example, suppose we want to partition a 30x20 grid to run on three processors.

Here we would choose the X direction to partition along, because there are 30 cells in the X direction vs only 20 in the Y. The next step is to simply divide the domain into three equal pieces along the X direction. In this example we would get three partitions, each 10x20 cells, with processor borders between processor pairs (0,1) and (1,2).

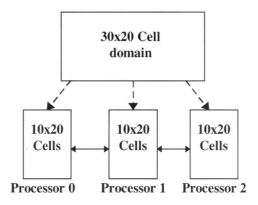

Figure 4.5: Example of 1-D domain decomposition. A 30x20 cell problem is partitioned into three 10x20 cell domains by direct unweighted partitioning along the X axis.

Expanding our example into unweighted 2-D partitioning, we could divide the problem along both the X and Y axis if we have more than four processors available. Applying 2-D partitioning with four processors to the problem above would result in four processor domains, each a 15x10 grid, corresponding to dividing the domain into quarters. Similarly, for a 3-D problem we can easily partition our problem space along all three axes as long as we have eight or more processors (for a cubic array). Using the principles described in the section on fundamental tradeoffs discussed previously, it is possible to show that for a regular cubic grid, 2-D partitioning is best for 2-D problems and 3-D partitioning is best for 3-D problems. This result follows simply from the argument that applying 1-D partitioning to a 2-D cube creates partitions with a larger surface area than applying the 2-D method to the 2-D cube. The result for 3-D partitioning follows from a similar argument. Therefore, it is appropriate to apply N-D partitioning to an N-D regular grid problem where N is the number of dimensions. The only exception to this is elongated or irregular grids, where more advanced methods will create much better results.

Processor weight	Percent of cells
200	20%
100	10%
500	50%
200	20%

Table 4.1: A simple four-processor weighted allocation. Processors are allocated problem cells based on their weight. Weighted load balancing can be used to dynamically balance the computing load during a run.

A variation of the dimensional partition method is the *weighted* domain partitioning method. This is an attempt to apply simple 1-D, 2-D or 3-D partitioning to problems that may have irregular or uneven grids. To use this method, we assign a weight to each computed node and then attempt to balance the sum of the weights to minimize the difference between nodes. One simple way to do this is to apply the Orthogonal Recursive Bisection method described in this chapter. Other methods, based on characterizing weights in various dimensions, or making initial guesses and then improving on them locally, have been developed, but the basic concept is to spatially partition based on weights. Weighted methods, including Orthogonal Recursive Bisection, will be covered later in this chapter.

Schwarz Methods

Consider the situation where we have to solve the Poisson equation, $\nabla^2 \phi = \rho$, in some simple domain, in parallel. Suppose for simplicity the one-dimensional domain $0 < x < 1$, with Direchlet boundary conditions (i.e., the specification of the function values) at the endpoints of the domain, x=0 and x=1. Suppose we partition the problem between two processors, allocating the right half of the problem to one and the left half to the other. We need to match the solutions of the two processors at the interface, that is, x= .5. The Schwarz method is probably the oldest and simplest approach to doing so. It is an iterative method. We allow the solution domains of the two processors to overlap slightly. The entire domain is initialized. We then calculate in one processor, say the "right" processor, solving a Direchlet problem, with the value of the leftmost points of that region taken as boundary conditions. The values at those points will not change. Now, solve in the "left" processor's region analogously. The rightmost points in solving that subdomain problem would have been altered from the initial values by the solution in the "right" processor. Iterate until convergence. Note that it will not generally be worthwhile to solve each subdomain problem exactly, as the boundary condition on one side (from the overlap region) will not be exact. Note also that each subdomain solution must be synchronized with the other, in order to have the proper values for the overlap region. The virtues of the Schwarz method are that only data from small "strips" of adjacent regions need be communicated between processors, and only data between adjacent regions need be communicated. The convergence rate, the efficiency of the calculation, etc. are dependent on the choice of overlap region size, sequencing of the calculations, etc. As suggested by our example, the Schwarz approach, often called the alternating Schwarz method due to the sequence of subregion solutions, is typically used for solving elliptic partial differential equations such as the Poisson equation. It is probably one of the oldest parallel methods (Schwarz 1890).

Multigrid Methods

Multigrid methods are iterative methods for solving systems of elliptic partial differential equations. Such systems have global influence, i.e., a change at any location affects the solution at any other point, however distant. Convergence of many methods is slowed by the need for a change at some gridpoint to propagate to another. In some of the simplest iteration schemes, if the value at some point changes, it may require N iterations for this to influence the value at another point N cells away. Multigrid methods take note of this and try to speed up the process by using a set of grids instead of one. The simplest case would be a system with a regular array of gridpoints, with 2^N in any direction. This would be our finest gridding. Then, in each direction, we would have a grid of every other point, thus containing half as many points, then a grid of every other one of these points, etc. There are a variety of ways to sequence through solving on each of these grids, and using the results of solving on one grid to "update" the values on the others. Multigrid approaches to nonlinear problems have been developed. Brandt and Diskin (1994) discuss parallel multigrid solvers for nonlinear elliptic problems. High computational efficiency is claimed if the number of gridpoints per processor is large, even on the coarsest grid. Among the tricks used to minimize communications cost is to overlap domains. See, for example, Baker (1991) for a gentle introduction to multigrid with code for 1-D and 2-D Poisson solvers; a standard reference for multigrid methods is Wesseling (1992). One difficulty of multigrid methods for parallel environments is that, on the coarsest grids, the relatively small amount of computation results in a large (relative) communications overhead.

Orthogonal and Unsymmetric Recursive Bisection

Recursive bisection refers to partitioning the problem by recursively dividing the problem in one direction, then another, etc. When this partitioning is done by dividing the problem among sets of processors by assigning regions in orthogonal directions, it is called orthogonal recursive bisection or ORB. Unsymmetric recursive bisection is a generalization of the basic ORB method (Freitag et al. 1995). ORB is often called Recursive Coordinate Bisection (RCB). These recursive methods are sometimes referred to as multilevel methods, because each level of recursion partitions a subdomain.

These methods are easiest to describe (and implement) when the available number of processors is a power of two. Suppose, for example, we have a three-dimensional problem of some sort. Assume the problem is mapped or embedded within a unit cube, extending from 0 to 1 in the three coordinate directions x, y, and z. Consider first the basic ORB method. We first divide the problem into two "halves" by choosing a direction, say x, and determining a plane, say x= .65. The choice is may be estimating the computational effort required within any subvolume and choosing the division point to equalize it between halves. The half of the problem for x<.65 is assigned to half the processors, and the other half of the problem volume to the other set of processors. Each of these sets now recursively applies the same division algorithm starting with another direction, say the y direction (the best direction to use may be determined by some algorithm rather than rigidly following some prescribed sequence).

Unsymmetrical recursive bisection attempts to put the dividing line near the center of the volume to be partitioned. Suppose, for example, eight processors were available. ORB would divide the problem work approximately in half, assigning each half to four processors in the first step. Then each set of four would split the problem in half, assigning each half to two processors, etc. URB might, in the first step, split the problem up so that two processors were assigned one of the "halves" and six were assigned the remainder, if this more evenly assigned the load or if another criterion for more evenly dividing the problem volume were satisfied. URB strives to do this volume division to reduce the frequency of rezoning.

Spectral Recursive Bisection

Spectral recursive bisection is an improved approach to determining when the divisions are by consideration of the required communications overhead between regions, along with attempting to equalize the work required within one region. the method has also been called Recursive Spectral Bisection (RSB) and Eigenvector Recursive Bisection (ERB). Typically, RSB is somewhat slower than ORB to compute the partition, but results in somewhat faster execution of the partitioned problem.

Recursive Spectral Bisection (Pothen et al. 1990, Simon 1991) is used to partition a graph recursively along the lines discussed above. Suppose we assign the value +1 to each vertex assigned to the "right" half and -1 to each vertex assigned to the "left" half. The communications cost may then be modeled as proportional to

$$\frac{\sum\left(x_i - x_j\right)^2}{4}$$

which is the count of links in the "cut set" connecting vertices of the two sets, where the sum is taken over all pairs of vertices that are adjacent and therefore require communication. Minimizing this sum is a difficult problem. But if we use not the adjacency matrix A but the related Laplacian of the graph, defined as a matrix of elements l_{ij} which are 0 if the vertices are not adjacent, and -1 if they are, and along the diagonal the elements are equal to the degree of the vertex (the number of adjacent vertices). Note that this matrix $L=D-A$ differs from the adjacency matrix, apart from the sign, by the diagonal terms. The Laplacian matrix has a zero eigenvalue, its smallest, associated with the eigenvector of all ones. The next smallest eigenvalue is positive as the matrix is positive semi-definite. RSB now employs the approximation that to minimize the sum, we use the sum associated with Laplacian matrix instead of the adjacency matrix, and we allow the elements to treated as continuous variables instead of integers. The smallest eigenvalue gives us an eigenvector that would ideally consist of elements with values +1 or -1. This of course, will not happen in practice, but the values can be used to separate the points into two sets (Walshaw and Berzins, 1995, and the references cited therein).

Spectral methods require the computation of an eigenvector, which is relatively expensive. It does not do well if the initial graph is not connected (this should be tested for initially and corrected if discovered). It also does not do well near the edges, in part due to the approximate nature of the heuristics. Therefore, it is best to use a hybrid approach (to be discussed shortly) in which the result of RSB is post-processed by a greedy method. The result will most likely be a very good partition, but one that has cost a significant amount of computation to determine.

Divide and Conquer

Methods such as ORB are examples of a general technique for parallelization known as "divide and conquer." The problem at hand is recursively apportioned to subsets of processors. In the forgoing examples, the problem was first split in two. Each new half of the original problem becomes the responsibility of half of the processors, with one processor of each group becoming in effect the "master" and the remainder the "slaves." The recursion can continue, with each subset fissioning itself, until the point of diminishing returns is reached. In many problems, division by two is not the best choice. For example, division of spatial regions is typically done by means of quadtrees and octrees, in two and three dimensions, respectively. This is similar to ORB, except that ORB splits any region into halves, i. e., one dimension. Quadtrees split two-dimensional, rectangular regions into four rectangles, while octrees split a three-dimensional rectangular parallelepiped into eight smaller ones. Often, squares and cubes are used, respectively, rather than the more general structures. We will discuss in chapter 5 an example of the use of divide and conquer for performing broadcast communications.

Divide and conquer figures in many computational methods. When it can be used recursively, as in ORB, the result is an algorithm that scales as the logarithm of the problem size in time. One example is in the solution of recurrence relations (Stone 1987). A recurrence of the form $x_i = a_i x_{i-1} + b_i$ may be solved for e x_i $i=1,...,n$ given x_0 as a starting value by a simple serial method using n additions and multiplications. It may be solved in logarithmic time using n processors, assuming n is a power of two, as follows. Assign to ith processor the ith-subscripted coefficients. As the first stage, the ith processor computes the coefficients of the corresponding recurrence expressing its dependence upon x_{i-2} : $x_i = a_i (a_{i-1} x_{i-2} + b_{i-1}) + b_i$. It is crucial to the process that this recurrence may be put in the same form as the original recurrence, i. e. $x_i = a'_i x_{i-2} + b'_i$. The first processor has meanwhile computed x_1. In the second stage, these primed coefficients are used in a precisely similar manner to obtain the recurrence relating the ith and $(i-4)$th variables, while x_2 and x_3 are computed on the second and third processors using the values of x_0 and x_1, the value of x_1 being passed from the first processor between stages. In the next stage, the next four variables in the recurrence may be computed using the four determined values and the recurrenced coefficients determined in the second stage. This approach is called "recursive doubling," as the distance between indices doubles at each step. It contrasts to the recursive halving used in ORB, but the effect is the same. The computation time for the recurrence scales logarithmically in n. Note however that in the serial algorithm, there is one addition and one multiplication per step, while two multiplications and one addition is needed to compute the recurrence coefficients. Thus, the speedup (neglecting communications costs) is $F n/lg\ n$, where $F= 2/3$ assuming that the costs of floating-point additions and multiplications are approximately the same; $F=1/2$ if we neglect the cost of additions compared to multiplications, which is more appropriate to software floating-point. Note also that additional storage is required compared to the serial algorithm. Finally, note that the communication pattern is favorable, in that at each stage the first $2i$ processors each communicate with the processor whose index is greater by $2i$, so that it should be possible to overlap all data transfer.

This method may be applied to recurrences such as

$$x_i = \frac{a_i x_{i-1} + b_i}{c_i x_{i-1} + d_i}$$

because a recurrence relating x_i to x_{i-2} has the same form. The evaluation of continued fractions may be put in this form. The serial iteration requires two additions, two multiplications, and two divisions per stage, whereas the recurrence requires six additions, ten multiplications, and 1 division. Assuming equal cost for multiplication and addition, the value for the coefficient F in the speedup formula will be *(4+d)/(16+d) where d=(cost of division/cost of multiply or add)*. Recursion will therefore be more attractive for this formula than for the linear recurrence, due to the high cost of division. More complicated recurrences, such as linear recurrences involving more than just the preceding variable, may be treated in a similar manner; these include the recurrences for Fibonacci and Lucas numbers. As these are defined by the recurrence

$$\begin{pmatrix} x_{n+1} \\ x_n \end{pmatrix} = \begin{pmatrix} 1 & 1 \\ 0 & 1 \end{pmatrix} \begin{pmatrix} x_n \\ x_{n-1} \end{pmatrix}$$

they may be computed by computing the powers of the matrix shown and multiplying the initial vector by the resultant matrix. The repeated matrix product may be computed by recursive doubling, because matrix multiplication is associative and the product of two similar matrices is a similar matrix.

In general, the matrix representation may be used to parallelize such problems by converting them into a series of matrix products. Because the cost of multiplying two $m \times m$ matrices is order m^3, the speedup will be of order $N/(m^2 \log N)$, making the parallel approach less attractive for more complicated recurrences. However, this approach does not take advantage of the special structure of the matrices. Just as the special structure of the matrix representing a Fast Fourier Transform may be used to factor the matrix and achieve a more economical computation, so may the special structure of a recurrence be used to better this pessimistic result; see, for example, Chung et al. (1991).

A similar application of divide and conquer is cyclic reduction. Consider a tridiagonal system of linear equations, each equation of the form: $a_i x_{i-1} + b_i x_i + c_i x_{i+1} = d_i$. This may similarly be reduced to two systems of equations which involve only odd or even subscripts. As these resulting systems are each tridiagonal, the process may be used recursively. Care must be used, however, as the process can be numerically unstable; see Stoer and Bulirsch (1993) for a discussion of the method of Buneman to stabilize the process. That work also gives references to generalizations of the method to other elliptic problems.

A related application of divide and conquer that does not permit recursion, and therefore will not give a logarithmic scaling, is applicable to red-black ordering, which will be discussed in chapter 9 when we consider a parallel Poisson equation solver. For simplicity, consider solving Poisson's equation using the standard finite-difference stencil, in one dimension. This again gives rise to a tridiagonal system. If we attempt to apply the SOR method (see chapter 9) to solve this system, we find that we must wait for results for all lower values of i before we can determine the value of x_i at any iteration stage. Instead, split the points in the problem grid into two sets, arranged as the red and black squares of a checkerboard in general (hence the name red-black ordering). In one dimension, red-black ordering splits the points into odd and even points. We do not recurse or further subdivide these sets. If we re-order the equations with the odd points in the first half of the solution vector and the even points in the second half, we find that we can perform a stage of SOR iteration on the even points, and then on the odd points. Notice we have done no additional computation whatsoever; we have merely changed the sequence of calculations. Again, it should be noted that reordering the calculations can change the convergence properties, although in this case, the reordering is not detrimental.

Clustering Methods

Clustering methods use (primarily) local information. A simple example of such a method is called Recursive Graph Bisection or RCB. Assume that the graph to be partitioned is connected. Define the distance between two vertices as the number of vertices on the shortest path between them. First, the two most distant vertices of the graph are determined. This choice may not be unique. Starting from one of them, we find the half of the vertices that are closest to that vertex, and that cluster is one of the two halves.

Greedy (Local) Methods

The clustering approach can be employed in a purely local manner by choosing a number of initial vertices and growing clusters starting from these sites. If the number of sites equals the number of processors, no recursion is needed. Obviously, the key is to choose the initial sites wisely. A number of alternative choices may be made, and the best result chosen.

Neighboring processors can compare workloads and adjust the boundaries of their computational domain. One potential problem with such an approach is that the inter-processor boundaries tend to become crenellated, convoluted shapes. This increase in the surface to volume ratio implies an increase in communications overhead. Such schemes should therefore have some penalty function for communications, which will act as a "surface tension" term in the formation of new interface surface area.

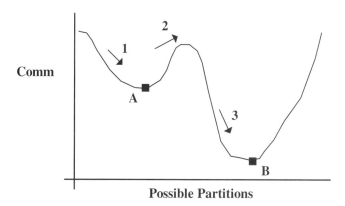

Figure 4.6: Simulated annealing is a communications minimization method. The algorithm generally tries to go "downhill" along the gradient (1 and 3), but occasionally proceeds against the gradient (as in step 2) to reach the global minima at B.

Simulated Annealing

Partitioning is an optimization problem, namely, to distribute the load to minimize the computational cost of a given computation by distributing the elements (cells, gridpoints, etc. depending on the method) among processors. Simulated annealing (SA) has become a rather standard approach to such optimizations. A good discussion of the method is in Press et al. (1992). The approach is to start with an initial guess and attempt to minimize with a typical gradient-driven technique. SA attempts to evade local minima in the hunt for a global minimum by occasionally proceeding against the gradient. This is done randomly, based on a "temperature" parameter; as the calculation proceeds, it "cools" and it becomes less likely that such a step will be taken.

Typically, the cost function to be minimized at optimum will have two terms, one due to load imbalance between processors and one due to communications overhead. Williams (1991) found that the cost of the SA partitioning was substantial, but so was the savings in execution time compared to other methods.

Hybrid Methods

Hu and Blake (1994), discuss a number of hybrid methods. The MINCUT method uses heuristics to improve the results of a bisection. For each vertex, it computes a table of the changes in connectivity when that vertex is moved to the other half of the bisection set. The vertex that will reduce the number of "cut edges" (those between the two sets) the most is moved to the other set and "locked" into that set. The procedure is iterated until all vertices are locked or no gains are registered. The initial bisection may be generated randomly, but the results are not insensitive to the initial configuration. Hu and Blake propose a method called MINGRAPH, which uses RGB for the initial selection and refines the bisection via MINCUT.

Time-Dependent Problems: Dynamic Load Balancing

In many problem formulation, the relative load changes. In particle codes, particles may migrate between regions assigned to different processors. This makes rebalancing desirable. On networks of workstations, it is possible that changes in loading due to other users sharing the resources would make it desirable to periodically monitor the load balance to shift computation to the more lightly loaded machines. One important trade-off is the frequency with which this is done. That depends on the cost of the load-balance calculation as well as the cost to transfer the requisite data to effect the rebalance. Local greedy methods should almost certainly be used due to the costs of a global rebalance and the data transport that would be required.

Walshaw and Berzins (1995), suggest a method for reducing the cost of RSB and making its cost acceptable for dynamic load balancing. The idea is to cluster vertices far from interfaces between processors, collapsing each cluster into a single vertex. This will of course greatly reduce the size of the matrix and hence the cost of the eigenvector determination. Heuristics must be used to determine how large such clusters should be, and how far from boundaries they need to be. The trade-off is, again, the cost of the approximate RSB vs. the effectiveness of the partition achieved in reducing communications costs.

Willebeek-LeMair and Reees (1993) classified dynamic load-balancing strategies in five categories:

1) Sender Initiated Diffusion (SID)

2) Receiver Initiated Diffusion (RID)

3) Hierarchical Balancing Method (HBM)

4) Gradient Model (GM)

5) Dimension Exchange Method (DEM)

The Dimension Exchange Method (DEM) model is closest in philosophy to ORB, etc., the recursive bisection methods we have discussed previously. In the Sender Initiated Diffusion (SID) method, processors that decide they are overloaded attempt to send their surplus load to neighbors. The method is therefore local and asynchronous. The similar Receiver Initiated Diffusion (RID) method has underloaded processors requesting more work from their neighbors.

The Gradient Model (GM) is somewhat similar to RID, with underloaded processors requesting load from their overloaded brethren. However, instead of the relatively simple approach of RID, in which pairwise transactions between adjacent processors occur, GM uses a relaxation method that makes tasks "gravitate towards underloaded points" which might be separated by moderately loaded processors whose total loads do not change. Two levels of load are defined: the Low Water Mark (LWM), and the High Water Mark (HWM). Nodes are considered lightly loaded if the load is below the LWM and heavily loaded if above the HWM. Otherwise, the load is considered "moderate" and is not altered. The nodes carry a variable called "proximity," which represents the shortest distance to the nearest lightly loaded node. All nodes have their proximity initialized to the diameter of the system, the maximum possible value. If the node is lightly loaded, its proximity is zero. All other nodes compute their proximity as one more than the minimum proximity of their neighbors. This is similar to Dijkstra's shortest-path algorithm. Nodes notify neighbors if their proximity changes, resulting in recomputation of proximities. This process is triggered when loads fall below the LWM. When there is at least one heavily-loaded and one lightly-loaded processor, the load is propagated against the gradient. Note that this scheme is general, and does not presume a spatial domain decomposition. If we are using spatial domain decomposition and intend to use GM, boundary motion would have to occur on all intermediate processors along the path. It is likely GM would not be the approach of choice in such a case.

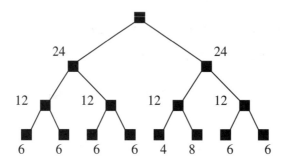

Figure 4.7: A Hierarchical Balancing Method (HBM) with eight processors at the leaves of the tree. A value at each node in the tree tracks the load of the subtree. Here the load imbalance between processors 4 and 5 can be handled by moving two units of work from processor 5 to 4. Larger imbalances would be handled at a higher level in the tree.

The Hierarchical Balancing Method (HBM) is a global method in which the demand for rebalancing propagates up a tree. At the lowest levels this can proceed asynchronously, without any global synchronization barriers. The rebalancing is as local as it can be, or global as it needs to be.

Willebeek-LeMair and Reeves (1993) evaluate the approaches and find RID as perhaps the most attractive. An artificial problem (set of tasks) was used for testing as well as analytic results. The authors have used global rebalancing methods with some success on small heterogeneous clusters, but global methods typically become excessively expensive for problems with a large number of processors.

Linear Algebra

Linear algebra is probably the most important single class of numerical techniques in scientific and engineering problems. The most common problem is the solution of linear systems. Even the solution of nonlinear problems usually relies on linearization and the solution of the associated linear problems, as in the Newton-Raphson and related methods. Discretization of physical problems via finite-difference or finite-elements result in linear systems, generally with special structures that can be exploited. Eigenvalue and eigenvector problems and linear programming problems are also of substantial interest. Numerical linear algebra problems fall into two categories: dense and sparse. Sparse systems have relatively few nonzero elements compared to those elements which are zero. The solution of the linear systems provide solutions to the problem, while the eigenvalues and eigenvectors may be of interest in determining vibration frequencies and modal structure.

Solution methods for linear systems fall into two categories: direct and iterative. For dense systems, on serial processors, the direct method of LU decomposition with partial pivoting is universally preferred and used. Gallivan et al. (1990) discuss the state of the art of parallel, non-iterative methods. On parallel systems, the difficulties associated with pivoting make QR decomposition attractive for poorly-conditioned systems, due to the ability to omit pivoting while retaining stability. Similar considerations apply to symmetric systems, which generally employ a Cholesky decomposition with pivoting usually unnecessary. An interesting compromise between LU and QR methods is the "linear rotation" method discussed by Jou (1989) and Chirico et al. (1995); this uses Gaussian Elimination (LU decomposition) without pivoting, but with a rotation designed to stabilize the system.

For sparse systems, preconditioned conjugate gradient methods are probably the most frequent choice for sparse symmetric systems, serial or parallel. For general linear systems, variants on the conjugate gradient method such as GMRES or BiCSTAB are used, with preconditioning. Special cases, such as special sparsity patterns, e .g., tri-diagonal matrices, are exceptions and may make a direct method the preferred approach. See

Alaghband (1995) and Geshiere and Wishoff (1995) for direct sparse solvers, and Sun (1995) for the "parallel diagonal dominant" algorithm for solving tridiagonal systems.

Eigenvalue and eigenvector problems are typically solved using Lanczos methods if only a single eigenvalue is needed (as for RSB partitioning). The Lanczos method is related closely to the conjugate gradient method. When all eigenvalues are needed, the Jacobi method is preferred. See Gotze (1994) for a discussion of parallel implementations of the Jacobi algorithm, as well as the Kogbetliantz algorithm for performing the singular value decomposition.

As a general rule, it appears that parallel algorithms for well-conditioned systems have been intensively studied and are quite advanced. The situation for poorly conditioned systems, however, is not so satisfactory. Special pivoting strategies for parallel processing have been considered (Davis and Yew 1990). Stable factorizations using the QR method have also been studied (Sameh and Kuck 1978; Bojanczyk, Brent, and Kung 1984; Pothen and Raghavan 1989). See Heller (1978) for a good, if somewhat dated, overview of parallel linear algebra., and Demmel et al. (1993) for a more recent review. Ortega (1988) covers the solution of linear systems on parallel and vector machines. Golub and Ortega (1993) is a text that focuses primarily on setting up and solving linear systems for scientific problems. It discusses both direct and iterative solvers, and covers a broad range of topics such as multigrid methods, etc., and should serve as a good introduction to parallel scientific computing. The Center for Research on Parallel Computation has a program on linear algebra methods for distributed-memory machines, focused on LAPACK-DM, a distributed-memory version of the LAPACK linear algebra package (which includes the BLAS), ARPACK, for eigenanalysis, and an object-oriented interface via templates to LAPACK (Choi, Dongarra, Pozo, Sorensen, Walker 1994).

Because of the significance of linear algebra, it is rarely desirable or necessary for the user to write his own software. Intel, for example, provides "Turbo" software to solve dense linear systems on Intel Paragons.

Dense Systems

Linear algebra problems are probably most effectively treated using the BLAS Level 3 libraries, which should be available on most parallel machines. These use a partitioning of matrices into sub-matrices. This is generally referred to as "block partitioning." "Striping" (assigning sets of adjacent rows or columns) is a special case of block partitioning. Block methods can substantially reduce memory traffic and improve the utilization (hit rate) of cache (hierarchical) memory systems (see Golub and Ortega, 1993). Once blocks are determined, there are various schemes for assigning blocks to processors, such as the "torus-wrap" mapping (Hendrickson 1993, Hendrickson and Womble 1994). See Jalby and Philippe (1991) for an example of an algorithm being "blocked," in this case the Gram-Schmidt procedure to form a set of orthonormal vectors from an set of independent vectors. It is found in this case that simply blocking the method, which amounts to treating sets of columns simultaneously with matrix operations, reduces the numerical stability. In the case of the Gram-Schmidt algorithm, an additional iteration of the orthogonalization, while increasing the cost somewhat, suffices to repair the numerical damage. The potential for increased numerical difficulties with blocked algorithms should be considered, however.

Matrix multiplication requires $O(N^3)$ operation for matrices of N rows and columns, using the conventional or straightforward algorithm. In 1969 Strassen published an algorithm with an exponent of 2.807 instead of 3, and Winograd and Coppersmith later developed a version with an exponent of 2.376. For approximately two decades, Strassen's result was considered of relatively little practical import, as it had a higher coefficient multiplying the power of N and it also had considerable "bookkeeping" costs due to its complexity. It was felt that the "crossover" point at which Strassen's method become more economical than the conventional method was at such large a value of N as to be of little interest. Bailey et al. (1990) showed that on Crays the crossover system size was on the order of 128; this implied that for matrices of size 2048 x 2048, the use of Strassen's method would cut the computation time in half. These authors wrote a procedure called SGEMMS to perform matrix multiplication and replace the BLAS 3 matrix multiplication routine. Later Douglas et al.

(1994) wrote GEMMW, based upon the Winograd variant, in Linda-C. These authors also discuss using complex arithmetic and parallel implementations. Optimized Level 3 BLAS and LAPACK routines are also discussed in Ling (1993).

Matrix multiplication and the solution of linear systems via LU factorization are closely related; Strassen's original paper on faster matrix multiplication is titled "Gaussian elimination is not optimal." Consequently, a faster GEMM procedure should lead to faster linear system solvers. This is discussed in Bailey et al. (1990). The LAPACK solver for dense linear systems is SGETRF, which performs LU factorization. It repeatedly calls SGETF2 on a diagonal submatrix with a block size specified by the parameter NB, which calls the BLAS 3 routines STRSM which solves triangular systems of matrices, and SGEMM which does the matrix multiplications. Matrix multiplications are performed on matrices of dimension $J \times NB$ multiplying matrices of size $NB \times (N - J)$ where (due to the blocking) $J = NB, 2NB, ..., N$. Discussions of blocked algorithms for solving linear systems may be found in the LAPACK manual (Anderson 1992), which uses the Cholesky factorization of a symmetric matrix as its example, and Dongarra et al. (1991). Poorly conditioned systems to be solved on parallel machines probably should not use LU decomposition at all, however.

Schneider et al. (1993) discuss the solution of a sparse linear system (derived from circuit simulation, and therefore not of banded structure) on a cluster of workstations, using LU decomposition. Special cases such as tridiagonal (Stone 1973), banded systems (Wright 1991), triangular systems (Same and Brent 1977), etc. have received attention. See also Choi et al. (1995) for parallel matrix transposition

Sparse Systems

Sparse systems are of great importance in scientific and engineering calculations. Some methods are so common and natural that it is easy to lose sight of the fact that a sparse linear system is in fact being solved. The use of simple finite-difference stencils will generally result in simple banded linear systems, in which the matrices have diagonal stripes or bands of nonzero elements. Unstructured meshes, such as finite-element systems generally employ, tend to yield linear systems with the nonzero elements concentrated in blocks. Great effort has been focused on reordering variables and equations to achieve the arrangements of sparsity patterns to minimize fill-in.

Most linear algebra operations, such as the "elementary row operations" applied to sparse matrices, change some of the zero entries into nonzero entries. This reduction of sparsity is call "fill-in." As an extreme example, inversion of a sparse matrix will result in a full matrix in general. This problem results in the preference for iterative methods for sparse matrices, as fill-in does not occur. In general, for iterative methods to be computationally competitive, preconditioning methods must be used to improve the convergence of the iterations. Iterative methods can be formulated in terms of matrix operations which can be efficiently implemented, as in the discussion of dense matrix problems, assuming account of sparsity it taken. Parallel implementations of conjugate gradient methods are discussed in many papers, e. g., Meurant (1989). That paper discusses preconditioners specifically chosen for their parallel efficiency. Again, there is the tradeoff between the cost of the preconditioner, both in computation and communication, against the effectiveness of the preconditioning and the consequent reduction in the number of iterations. There is a vast literature on parallel preconditioned conjugate gradient methods, and related methods for non-positive-definite systems. See, for example, Greenbaum, Li, and Chao (1989), van der Vorst (1989), and Natarajan and Pattnaik (1992). The Quasi-Minimum Residual (QMR) method is related to the BiCSTAB and is discussed in van de Velde (1994; see chapter 3 for reference), Chan et al. (1994), Freund and Nachtigal (1994) with attractive convergence properties.

Block algorithms were discussed above for dense systems. They are not irrelevant for sparse system, however. Rothberg and Gupta (1994) discuss blocking applied to sparse Cholesky factorization, for example.

The standard reference on the solution of sparse, positive-definite systems is the book of George and Liu (1981). Pissanetzky (1984) and Duff, Erisman, and Reid (1981) discuss sparse-matrix algorithms. These monographs do not address the issue of parallel computation, but should provide useful background material to those working with sparse matrices in any computing environment.

Data Distribution

Laying Out Irregular Shapes

As noted above, there are two possible approaches. One is to simply embed the problem domain within a regular structure and apply techniques such as ORB to that simple region. Alternatively, the shape may be mapped, approximately or exactly, to such a region, by a coordinate transformation (such as conformal mapping). ORB or the other methods discussed previously may be used. A major disadvantage of this approach is that the problem must typically be generated on one node, then partitioned and distributed to the other nodes. Even if done during preprocessing, this problem generation and distribution will take a lot of time and memory to accomplish.

A simple alternative that the authors have used is to not actually generate the problem when determining partitioning, but have partitioning proceed from a trial setup of the problem domain. Using this method requires that the problem can be generated on the fly from an input file, or requires two passes through an input data file, one to partition and one to distribute. The initialization would proceed like this: First, we call the section of code that would generate all of the cells in the problem domain. Internal to this function, we call another function with the position and weight of each cell generated. This internal function records the weight and location appropriately for our partitioning algorithm, allowing us to complete one stage of the partitioning.

For example, assume we are using the Unsymmetric Orthogonal Recursive Bisection algorithm on a large problem, and wish to make our original partition without actually generating all of the cells on a single node. Let us assume that the original problem can be defined by a small file describing the shapes in the problem. From this list of shapes, we can easily generate the positions of all cells in the problem. To implement our ORB quickly, we might generate the positions of all cells in the domains based on our list of shapes, and accumulate these positions in a series of counters along the partitioning direction. From these counters, we can determine the approximate mean value along which to split the domain. Repeating this process on other processors, we can complete the ORB partitioning algorithm and arrive at our final processor partition before generating any cells at all. We can then complete a fully parallel initialization of the problem, as we will describe in the next section. This completely avoids having to generate or partition any part of the problem serially, and lets us run much larger problems than would be possible using a traditional initial partitioning strategy.

Parallel vs Serial Initialization

True scalability requires that the partitioning and initialization of the problem be done in parallel. Otherwise, large problems would fail almost instantly, as they would exceed the capacity of a single node to perform the initial partitioning. In fact, it is easy to imagine a problem that can be run in parallel, but would require a Cray supercomputer to perform the initial problem setup because of the memory required. For example, a 10-million-cell problem with 100 data points per cell requires 100 MWord or 1.6 gigabytes of main storage just for the data in double precision. Only the worlds largest serial computers can be used to set up such a problem. Initializing the problem in parallel, however, lets us significantly reduce the per node memory requirement. Dividing this problem between only 32 processors results in a memory requirement of only 3.125 MWord per node or 50 MB, which many parallel processors have. Wherever possible, it is best to initialize a problem in parallel to allow for the possibility of very large problems being run. Further, if we use parallel initialization in conjunction with a parallel I/O system, it is possible to perform initial setup and even restarts quickly, increasing overall performance.

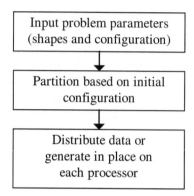

Figure 4.8: One method for parallel initialization. An initial
partitioning is done based on the problem configuration
before actually generating data on all processors.

Parallel initialization is done in two stages. First, an initial partitioning of
the problem needs to be determined. If the partitioning is static, this can
be done easily by reading the partitioning from a file. If partitioning is
dynamic, you can use a method like the one in the previous section, which
allows you to partition a problem without actually generating it. The
second stage is to actually generate the data. This can be done in a
number of ways.

The most effective is to use a descriptive format for the problem setup,
such as a list of shapes and boundary conditions. This allows the
relatively small problem description file to be passed between processors,
and actual data to be generated in parallel from the descriptions. This
works particularly well for spatially partitioned problems, because you can
use processor boundaries as boundaries for shape generation, significantly
speeding initialization. Another method is to generate data points on a
single processor and distribute them via message passing to the other
processors as they are generated. This provides the simplicity of writing a
serial initialization routine without overloading a single processor's
memory capacity. This method is much slower than the fully parallel
model, because it is done serially. A final method is to use a preprocessor
to generate an input file of all of the data. Though serial preprocessors are
widely used in existing codes, we discourage their use in parallel codes

because of the memory limitation on the preprocessor itself, and the high degree of overhead associated with reading the file in. Unless special parallel I/O software is used, or partitioning is known in advance, it is very costly to read the entire problem in from a file. See the sections in chapter 3 on parallel I/O for a full discussion of this problem.

References

Alaghband, G., "Parallel Sparse Matrix Solution and Performance," *Parallel Computing*, **21**, 1407-1430, 1995.

Anderson, E., Bai, Z., Bischof, C., Demmel, J., Dongarra, J., Du Croz, J., Greenbaum, A., Hammarling, S.,McKeney, A., Ostrouchov, S., Sorensen, D., *LAPACK User's Guide*, Philadelphia, P. A.: SIAM, 1992.

Anderson, R., Setubal, J. C., "A Parallel Implementation of the Push-Relabel Algorithm for the Maximum Flow Problem," *J. Parallel and Distributed Computing*, **29**, 17-26, 1995.

Babalievski, F. V., "On the parallelization of percolation cluster simulations*," Computer Physics Communications*, **67**, 453-455, 1992.

Bailey, D. H., Lee, K., Simon, H. D., "Using Strassen's Algorithm to Accelerate the Solution of Linear Systems," *J. Supercomputing*, **4**, 357-372 (1990).

Baker, L., *Artificial Intelligence in Ada*, N. Y.: McGraw-Hill, 1989.

Baker, L. *More C Tools for Scientists and Engineers*, N. Y.: McGraw-Hill, 1991.

Bojanczyk, A., Brent, R. P., Kung, H. T., "Numerically Stable Solution of Dense Systems of Linear Equations Using Mesh-Connected Processors," *SIAM J. Sci. Comput.*, **5**(1), 95-104, March 1984.

Brandt, A., and Diskin, B., "Multigrid Solverson Decomposed Domains," *Contemporary Mathematics*, **187**, 135-153, 1994.

Chan, T. F., Gallopoulos, E., Simoncini, V., Szeto, T., Tong, C. H., "A Quasi-Minimimal Residual Variant of the BiCGSTAB Algorithm for Nonsymmetric Systems," *SIAM J. Sci. Comput.*, **15**(2), 338-347, March 1994.

Chirico, M., Di Zitti, E., Bisio, G. M., "A Linear Rotation Based Solution of Large Systems on a Transputer Array," *Microprocessors and Microsystems*, **19** (6), 321-26, August 1995.

Choi, J., Dongarra, J. J., Pozo, R., Sorensen, D. C., Walker, D. W., "CRPC Research into Linear Algebra Software for High Performance Computers," *Int. J. Supercomputer Appl.*, **8** (2), 99-118, Summer 1994.

Choi, J., Dongarra, J. J., Walker, D. W., "Parallel Matrix Transposition Algorithms on Distributed Memory Concurrent Computers," *Parallel Computing*, **21**, 1387-1405, 1995.

Chung, K.-L., Lin, F.-C., Yeh, Y.-N., "A Three-Phase Parallel Algorithm for Solving Linear Recurrences," *Computers Math. Applic.*, **21**(2-3), 187-195, 1991.

Cignoni, P., Laforenza, D., Perego, R., Scipigno, R., Montani, C., " Evaluation of Parallelization Strategies for an Incremental Delaunay Triangulator in E3," *Concurrency: Practice and Experience*, **7**(1), 61-80, Feb. 1995.

Colombet, L., Desbat, L., Menard, F., "Star Modeling on IBM RS6000 Networks using PVM," *2nd Int. Symposium on High Performance Distributed Computing*, Spokane, WA, IEEE Press, pp. 121-128, July 20-23, 1993.

Cramblitt, B., "Rendering on a Network," *Computer Graphics World*, 26-36, Aug. 1994.

Davis, T. A., Yew, P.-C., "A Nondeterministic Parallel Algorithm for General Unsymmetric Sparse LU Factorization," *SIAM J. Matrix Anal. Appl.*, **11**(3), 383-402, July 1990.

Demmel, J. W., Heath, M. T., van der Vorst, H., "Parallel numerical linear algebra," *Acta Numerica*, 111-197, Cambridge: University Press, 1993.

Dongarra, J. J., Duff, I. S., Sorensen, D. C., van der Vorst, H. A., *Solving Linear Systems on Vector and Shared Memory Computers*, Philadelphia, P. A.: SIAM, 1991.

Douglas, C. C., Heroux, M., Slishman, G., Smith, R. M., "GEMMW: A Portable Level 3 BLAS Winograd Variant of Strassen's Matrix-Matrix Multiply Algorithm," *J Computational Phys.*, **110**, 1-10 (1994).

Duff, I. S., Erisman, A. M., Reid, J. K., *Direct Methods for Sparse Matrices*, Oxford: Clarendon Press, 1986.

Freund, R. W., Nachtigal, N. M., "An Implementation of the QMR Method Based on Coupled Two-Term Recurrences," *SIAM J. Sci. Comput.*, **15**(2), 313-337, March 1994.

Frietag, L., Jones, M., Plassmann, P., "Parallel Algorithms for Unstructured Mesh Computation," Proc. Third U. S. National Congress on Computational Mechanics, ed. J. N. Reddy, p. 248, June 12-14, 1995, Dallas, TX.

Gallivan, K. A., Heath, M. T., Ng, E., Ortega, J. M., Peyton, B. W., Plemmons, R. J., Romine, C. H., Sameh, A. H., Voigt, R. G., *Parallel Algorithms for Matrix Computations*, Philadelphia, PA: SIAM, 1990.

George, A., Liu, J. W.-H., *Computer Solution of Large Sparse Positive Definite Systems,* Englewood Cliffs, N. J.: Prentice Hall, 1981.

Geschiere, J. P., Wijshoff, H. A. G., "Exploiting Large Grain Parallelism in a Sparse Direct Linear System Solver," *Parallel Computing,* **21**, 1339-1364, 1995.

Goetze, J., "On the Parallel Implementation of Jacobi and Kogbetliantz Algorithms*," SIAM J. Sci. Comput.*, **15**(6), 1331-1348, Nov. 1994.

Golub, G., Ortega, J. M., *Scientific Computing: An Introduction with Parallel Computing*, San Diego, C. A.: Academic Press, 1993.

Gottschalk, T. D., "Concurrent Multiple Target Tracking," *Third Conference on Hypercube Concurrent Computers and Applications*, Pasadena CA, Jan 19-20, 1988, Vol. II, ed. G. Fox, 1988.

Greenbaum, A., Li, C., Chao, H. Z., "Parallelizing Preconditined Conjugate Gradient Algorithms," *Computer Physics Communications*, **53**, 295-309, 1989.

Heller, D., "A Survey of Parallel Algorithms in Numerical Linear Algebra," *SIAM Review*, **26** (4), 740-777, 1978.

Hendrickson, B., "Parallel factorization using the torus-wrap mapping," *Parallel Computing*, **19**, 1259-1271, 1993.

Hendrickson, B., Womble, D. E., "The torus-wrap mapping for dense matrix calculations on massively parallel computers," *SIAM J. Sci. Comput.*, **15**(5), 1201-1226, 1994.

Hu, Y. F., and Blake, R. J., "Numerical Experiences with Partitioning of Unstructured Meshes," *Parallel Computing*, **20**, 815-829, 1994.

Hoffman, K.-H., Zou, J., "Parallel Efficiency of Domain Decomposition methods," *Parallel Computing*, **19**, 1375-1391, 1993.

Jalby, W., Philippe, B., "Stability Analysis and Improvement of the Block Gram-Schmidt Algorithm," *SIAM J. Sci. Stat. Comput.*, **12** (5), 1058-1073, 1991.

Jou, I. C., "Linear Rotation Based Algorithm and Systolic Architecture for Solving Linear System Equations," *Parallel Computing*, **11**, 367-379, 1989.

Kauffman, W. J. III, and Smarr, L. J., *Supercomputing and the Tranformation of Science*, New York: W. H. Freeman, 1993.

Lai, C.-H., "Domain Decompositon Methods for Semiconductor Device Problems on a Cray S-MP, *Int. J. Supercomputing Applications*, **7**(4), 337-348, Winter 1993.

Ling., P., "A Set of High-Performance Level 3 BLAS Structured and Tuned for the IBM 3090 VF and Implemented in Fortran 77," *J. Supercomputing*, **7**, 323-355 (1993).

Mastin, G. A., Plimpton, S. J., Ghiglia, D. C., "A Massively Parallel Digital Processor for Spotlight Synthetic Aperture Radar," *Int. J. Supercomputer Appl.*, **7** (2) 97-112, Summer 1993.

Meurant, G., "Practical Use of the Conjugate Gradient Method on Parallel Supercomputers," *Computer Physics Communications*, **53**, 467-477, 1989.

Miklosko, J., Vajtersic, M., Vrto I., Kletter, R*., Fast Algorithms and their Implementation on Specialized Parallel Computers*, Amsterdam: North-Holland, 1989.

Natarajan, R., Pattnaik, P., "Performance of the Conjugate Gradient Method on VICTOR," *J. Comp. Phys.*, **100**, 396-401, 1992.

Olson, C. F., "Parallel Algorithm for Hierarchical Clustering," *Parallel Computing*, **21**, 1313-1325, 1995.

O'Rourke, J., *Computational Geometry in C*, Cambridge: University Press, 1994.

Ortega, J. M, *Introduction to Parallel and Vector Solution of Linear Systems*, N. Y.: Plenum, 1988.

Pissanetzky, S., *Sparse Matrix Technology*, N. Y.: Academic Press, 1984.

Pothen, A., Raghavan, P., "distributed Orthogonal Factorization: Givens and Householder Algorithms," *SIAM J. Sci. Stat. Comput.*, **10**(6), 1113-1134, Nov. 1989.

Pothen, A., Simon, H., Lou, K.-P., "Partitioning Sparse Matrices with Eigenvectors of Graphs," *SIAM J. Matrix Anal. Appl.*, **11**(3), 430-452, July 1990.

Press, W. H., Teukolsky, S. A., Vetterling, W. T., Flannery, B. P., *Numerical Recipes*, Cambridge: University Press, 1992.

Rees, M., Morton, K. W., "Moving Point, Particle, and Free-Lagrange Methods for Convection-Diffusion Equations," *SIAM J. Sci. Stat. Comput.*, **12**(3), 547-572, May 1991.

Rothberg, G., Gupta, A., "An Efficient Block-Oriented Approach to Parallel Sparse Cholesky Factorization," *SIAM J. Sci. Comput.*, **15**(6), 1413-1439, Nov. 1994.

Sameh, A. H., Brent, R. P., "Solving Triangular Systems on a Parallel Computer," *SIAM J. Num. Anal.* , **14**(6), 1101-1113, Dec. 1977.

Sameh, A. H., Kuck, D. J., "On Stable Parallel Liner System Solvers," *J. ACM*, **25** (1), 81-91, Jan. 1978.

Schwarz, H., A., *Gesammelete Mathematische Abhandlungen*, Vol. II, Berlin: Springer, pp. 133-143, 1890.

Simon, H. D., "Partitioning of unstructured problems for parallel processing," *Comput. Syst. Eng.*, **2**, 135-148, 1991.

Schneider, M., Wever, U., Zheng, Q., "Solving Large and Sparse Linear Equations in Analog Circuit Simulation in a Cluster of Workstations," *The Computer Journal*, **36**(8), 685-689, 1993.

Stoer, J. & Bulirsch, R., *Introduction to Numerical Analysis*, 2nd ed., Berlin: Springer, 1993.

Stone, H. S., "An Efficient Parallel Algorithm for the Solution of a Tridiagonal Linear System of Equations," *J ACM*, **20** (1), 27-38, Jan. 1978.

Stone, H. S., *High-Performance Computer Architecture*, Reading, M. A.: Addison-Wesley, 1987.

Sun, X.-H., "Application and Accuracy of the Parallel Diagonal Dominant Algorithm," *Parallel Computing,* **21**, 1241-1267, 1995.

van der Vorst, H., "ICCG and Related Methods for 3D Problems on Vector Computers," *Computer Physics Communications*, **53**, 223-235, 1989.

Walshaw, C., Berzins, M., "Dynamic Load-Balancing for PDE Solvers on Adaptive Unstructured Meshes," *Concurrency: Practice and Experience*, **7**(1), 17-28, Feb. 1995.

Wesseling, P., *An Introduction to Multigrid Methods*, N. Y.: J. Wiley, 1992.

Willebeek-LeMair, M. H., Reeves, A. P., "Strategies for Dynamic Load Balancing on Highly Parallel Computers," *IEEE Trans. on Parallel Distr. Systems*, **4**(9) 979-993 (1993).

Wolfe, A., "Three look to star in Hollywood role," *Electronic Engineering Times*, p. 1, 114, issue 861, August 14, 1995.

Wright, S. J., "Parallel Algorithms for Banded Linear Systems," *SIAM J. Sci. Stat. Comput.*, **12**(4), 824-842, July1991.

Chapter 5

Parallel Development and Debugging

Development Strategy

How should you best develop a parallel code and get it working? The approach we advocate is to first get the code working as a serial program, and then parallelize it. That, of course, does not mean that no consideration of the ultimate, parallel fate of the code should be given when the serial code is being written. Obviously the code should be structured with an eye to migrating to a parallel environment.

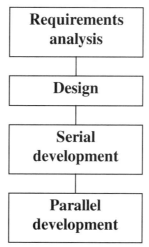

Figure 8.1: Recommended serial development process. It is best to develop a working serial code before extending to a full parallel development.

We will use the basic development process shown in Figure 8.1 to create our application.

Design Decisions

The first step in parallel development is to get a good grasp of the requirements. A complete list of requirements can be used to prioritize development and form a basis for data structures and design. It is important to identify as many requirements as early in the development as possible. While the main algorithm of a scientific program will lead to the primary design, it is important to consider the auxiliary features, as these can significantly affect the design. For example, what output is required? What diagnostics will be necessary to debug and use the program? How will run-time options be handled? Unless you have already spent several years working with an existing serial program in your field, it is unlikely you will know which features and algorithms are most important. Some research will be required. For many complex numerical codes, you may need to consult an expert in the field or obtain an existing serial code to determine exactly what is required. The time you spend researching your application up-front will pay large dividends later.

Creating a Serial Code Suitable for Parallelization

It is assumed that you either have written or are about to write a computer program which will ultimately be run in parallel. The first consideration is the appropriateness of the overall algorithm for parallelization. Where possible, encapsulation into modules should be used to make the program as flexible as possible with regard to ease of replacing or modifying the algorithms used. As discussed in chapter 2, it is often not possible a priori to determine the most effective algorithm; the more "local" methods may parallelize more easily, with less message traffic, but be otherwise so inefficient (e.g., require more iterations for convergence, and consequently more computation) that another method with more "global" communication would be preferable.

All the usual strictures concerning good programming practice apply. Modular code will be much easier to parallelize. The modules must be as independent as possible, without variables shared between modules, or subtle bugs will likely creep in. Computation should be concentrated into as few functions as possible, consistent with the desire for modularization. Subroutine calls inhibit optimization and add overhead, resulting in slower execution.

We believe C is the language of choice for parallel processing. Some "embarrassingly parallel" problems may be more easily coded with the parallel FORTRAN 90 extensions, but where flexibility and portability count, C is the clear winner. Object-oriented C++ approaches, are gaining in popularity but are by no means universally available. The resulting code is also rather opaque. Treating processes as objects with pointers syntactically identical to data may be "neat" but it is hardly intuitive. Such languages are most suitable for shared-memory approaches to solving "embarrassingly parallel" problems, but for a message-passing approach with maximum flexibility, they fall short. Another danger with ABC++, UC++, μC++, etc., is that their future is uncertain. Even the locations that currently support these systems may not do so in the future. The user will then be on their own in updating the system to take into account system changes.

Applying Parallelization

The modular, debugged, serial code should then be parallelized one module at a time. For example, suppose you have a complicated simulation code that performs a number of computational steps, including initialization. An example might be an electromagnetic PIC (particle in cell) code, as discussed in chapter 4. This code has two main computations: determining the electric and magnetic fields given the particle motions, and computing the updated particle positions and velocities given the fields and the consequent forces on the particles. The first version of the parallel code should parallelize only the "particle push" stage of the computation. You will of course have to modify the initialization to assign different portions of the problem to different processors. Make the first version of the parallel initialization as simple as possible. Leave the field computation and the initialization to the master (root or rank 0) processor. Then, parallelize the field computation. Only after the rest of the code is working should you parallelize the initialization. There may be reasons for altering this sequence, but the basic approach should be followed. While you are parallelizing the "push," you can then be reasonably assured that the initialization and the field computation are correct. And when anomalies in the results show up while parallelizing the field computation, you may reasonably assume that the particle push is not the source of the difficulties, as it has already been debugged.

Try to use the higher-level "structured" parallel operations where possible. That is, use broadcasts, multicasts, scatter/gathers, reductions, parallel prefix scans, etc., where possible. Our layered code attempts to use multicasts where possible. These "structured" operations are less likely to cause deadlocks or other problems than user code to implement the same operation using lower-level sends and receives. They are also likely to have been optimized in performance. It's always better to take advantage of the work and experience of a number of system's programmers than to do the job yourself. (On the other hand, you might try to make sure that the library is well-optimized, particularly if your program's performance seems unsatisfactory.)

Developing on Workstations, PCs, or Networks

It is possible to debug parallel applications on networks of workstations, or even on single machines. For a number of very practical reasons, this is much more convenient than debugging at a supercomputer center. Information does not need to be shipped between sites. The wait for machine access will probably be shorter at a local site (particularly if you use your own machine) than if you have to contend with users for a national resource. Finally, it is more efficient not to use massive resources on small, short debugging runs. You will likely not win friends or impress people at the site if you tie up individual nodes with debugging runs. It is far better to begin using the supercomputer center only when your code is ready.

One advantage of developing and debugging on a single machine is that there will be only a single clock. If there are tracing reports on when a given process reached a certain point, the user can be sure that the time ordering is not distorted by differences in the internal clocks of a number of different machines.

We have mentioned the WinMPI system in chapter 5, and used it to develop the code of chapter 8. It is based upon the mpich system layered over p4. This system enables the user to run parallel programs conforming to the MPI standard on personal computers running Windows 3.1. The major change needed to make your program compatible with WinMPI is to rename your main() to int MPI_main(int argc, LPPSTR argv). The WinMPI system was compiled with Microsoft's Visual C++ compiler, so use this compiler if possible to avoid compatibility problems. The source code implementing WinMPI calls functions such as malloc() and memcpy(), so it is likely that most C programs written for UNIX environments will not require substantial rewriting for compatibility.

The pvm system may be brought up on personal computers running Linux, and mpich most likely can be implemented under Linux as well. Consequently, there are numerous ways to run parallel programs on personal computers, if the machine is sufficiently powerful.

Any of these systems could presumably be used for preliminary debugging of parallel programs. Of course, full-size runs are probably precluded given the resources of a typical Windows environment. But if it is possible to perform even preliminary verification of the parallel code on your own desktop, the opportunity should not be passed up. You would then be independent of other users and would not have to compete with them for resources on shared machines while debugging. They would not impact you, and you would not risk impacting them with an unreliable program. Debug in the comfort of your home, office, airplane, etc.

Once the code is working in serial and initial debugging is completed, if possible use a local area network (LAN) of workstations to run more realistic problems before transitioning to a massively-parallel computer. The turn-around should be superior for debugging runs. pvm is ideal for this environment.

Debugging Parallel Programs

Parallel Debugging is Nondeterministic

A serial code with a bug will generally fail the same way each time it is run. There error message might be missing, uninformative, or even misleading, but at leas there will be some basic consistency. In debugging parallel code, you will find that the error will generally not be completely reproducible. Messages will not be received in the same order every run, due to variations in the loading, etc., of each processor. Consequently, the code may or may not fail at a certain point, depending upon the sequence of message arrival. Or the code may fail at the same point, but due to differences in the data received at that point, report a different situation at that point. Be prepared for this phenomenon. Do not be disconcerted by it, but rather ensure that your debugging statements print out enough information. If you generally get beyond a point of difficulty, you should still debug it before tackling the subsequent bug, as its fix may remove the cause of the subsequent problem.

Using Serial Debuggers

It is extremely important to have the code thoroughly debugged in serial mode before proceeding to debug the code in parallel. If something "funny" happens during parallel testing, you want to be sure it is because the job is being run in parallel.

Run the Same Test Case Serial and Parallel

Obviously, you want to then run the same problems in parallel and compare results. You will probably note that some small differences creep in. There will be a great temptation to write these differences off as "roundoff" due to differences in the order of computation. It would be an error to obstinately pursue a phantom error. If the problem is not ill-conditioned, small roundoff errors should not substantially alter the desired, significant result. If small differences are noted between the serial and parallel results, the first appearance of any difference should be localized, and it should be determined if it is roundoff due to altered sequence of computation.

Tracing

Tracing is a standard debugging technique for serial or parallel code. The complications of tracing for parallel execution are obvious. Unless all machine clocks are synchronized, the times reported for a given event by each processor may be inconsistent and misleading.

As discussed in chapter 6, the PICL system is the only major message-passing system to support tracing, and it may be considered obsolete. Even its authors have gone on to something else. Tracing and logging facilities are promised for later versions of popular systems, but they are not yet implemented, and may be unreliable in their first release. Therefore, the user will probably have to do his own tracing. We have included working code to do this in chapter 6.

Synchronization Points (Barriers)

A barrier is a point in the code at which all processors must arrive before any of them may proceed. Barriers or synchronization points can be a useful debugging tool. Barriers are, in effect, a "foolproof" trace for SPMD code. Assuming the message-passing system code correctly implements barriers, one can put a barrier, followed by a print statement in the master or rank 0 process, and be reasonably assured that if the statement is not printed (and the code "hangs"), the problem is in your user code before the barrier. (Be sure to flush the print buffer so that all messages are printed out. On UNIX systems, for example, be sure to follow the printf(...), fprintf(...), or similar statement with an immediate fflush(fhandle) for the appropriate file handle. Otherwise, you will be unsure as to whether the output was not seen because the printf() was never executed, or that the output is merely being held in a buffer for printing.)

Barriers can typically be effected by a single statement in SPMD code. These can then be removed when the problem is located and fixed. It is therefore much more convenient than the tracing facility. A barrier can be erected at a single point, and the user can then reliably locate a problem. Tracing may produce a flood of irrelevant information telling you all about the sends and receives that you already know work.

Don't Trip Over Your Debugging Code

Code introduced for debugging purposes can introduce problems. If it sends messages to a log file to be created and managed by the master process, it is possible for the messages to cause a deadlock or race condition with the other messages in the system if the debugging sends or receives don't match up. If some receive is incorrect, either in the debugging code or elsewhere, it may gobble up the debugging information message that was not meant for it. That would result in curious behavior. The basic moral is: Be particularly careful with debugging code.

Parallel Debuggers

Some systems come with support tools for debugging. An example is the PADE environment for pvm, discussed briefly in chapter 5. These may be useful, particularly if the user is experienced and comfortable with such systems. Often, however, such systems are not worth the trouble to learn and use.

Test on a number of processors and processors counts

There are allegedly aborigines whose counting system is: one, two, many. There is a temptation in parallel processing to use the same counting system. If the code works on one, two, and perhaps up to four processors, we would like to consider our work complete and fully tested. Sadly, some problems can show up at large processor counts. One cannot conclude that a job that works for four processors will work on 128. An error that only occurs for a larger processor count will likely be more subtle, and probably more difficult to trace.

One problem that may show up only with large problems is memory leakage. On large production runs lasting a long time, small memory leakage builds up over time. This can be a particular problem if the realloc() function is used. It tends to be wasteful of storage if the reallocated pointer is to a region larger than the original. This is not strictly speaking a coding error, i. e., a failure to properly free memory allocated with a malloc, but is rather an inefficiency that needs to be considered. At the very least, one has to plan for periodic checkpointing and restarting of the job if the problem cannot be adequately circumvented by better memory management.

It is also useful to test code on a variety of hosts. After debugging on a network of RS/6000s, add a DEC Alpha and/or Sun Sparcstation to the mix if possible. (The use of the XDR protocol under PVM should facilitate this). At the very least, code that is not portable should show itself. We have detected a number of bugs in code in this manner. Often, compiler peculiarities show up.

Write SPMD Code

Current technology provides much better support for SPMD code than for MPMD programming. Implementations of MPI do not support MPMD at present. Debugging SPMD code is also somewhat easier than MPMD code. The if(master){} else /*slave*/{} structure of SPMD code makes it easier to see both sides of the passing of message, with the sending and receiving code in approximate proximity, making it easier to spot problems.

Chapter 6

Practical Message Passing

In previous chapters, we have argued for the message-passing paradigm as the most flexible approach to parallelism. We have also argued that the MPI standard provides the best long-term approach to a portable standard, while PVM provides the best development environment at present and the best option for parallel processing on heterogeneous networks. In this chapter, we discuss both PVM and MPI. In the remaining chapters, we will show how to implement parallel programs that can exploit both.

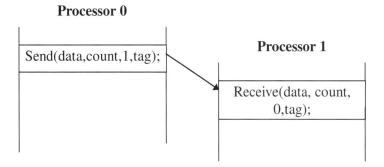

Figure 6.1: In the message passing paradigm, all interprocessor communications are done explicitly, most often using send and receive calls to exchange data.

MPI

MPI stands for Message Passing Interface. Many MPI documents, including the standard specification, may be found on the Internet (see chapter 10, Suppliers). The latest revision to the MPI standard (as of Dec. 1995) is June 12, 1995, version 1.1. The revision was not completely backward-compatible with the previous version, so if you encounter MPI code that fails with a segmentation violation or other curious problem, it may be because the code is from an earlier version. (For example, the level of indirection of some variables in MPI_Init, for example, changed, which would produce such errors early in the execution of a program.) Gropp et al. (1994) provides an excellent introduction to MPI. It may be purchased from MIT Press as well as obtained online. A variety of overviews, such as by Still (1994) and Walker (1994), are in popular publications. MPI is well on its way to becoming an accepted international standard. More than 15 implementations of MPI exist, though none permit distributed operation between implementations. MPICH is emerging as the most popular implementation. Many manufactures of parallel machines support MPI with optimized libraries for the MPI functions.

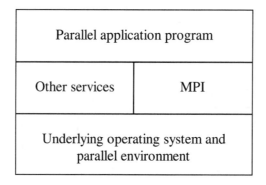

Figure 6.2: MPI is a library that provides message passing services. MPI does not provide a complete parallel environment, debugging tools or parallel I/O services.

The most crucial observation to note about MPI is that it "is a message passing interface, not a complete parallel computing programming environment" (Walker, 1994) This is not a problem if you work on only one machine, but it can be a problem if you hope to work on many systems. This is one of the reasons layering over PVM or another system, which provides such an environment, is highly desirable. There are at least four popular implementations of MPI: CHIMP, MPICH, LAM, and UNIFY. All of these differ in the practical details: how one specifies the count of nodes to be used, etc. There is no standard environment for debugging, etc. Usually, environmental variables are used to specify such details. Each implementation of MPI will require different specifications of the environment, different procedures for submitting and running jobs, etc.

MPI is intended for primarily for MIMD, distributed memory systems (Walker, 1994). (A SIMD machine would probably be programmed in a data-parallel paradigm rather than a message-passing approach. Shared-memory machines would read and write to memory rather than pass messages.) MPI does not specify configuration on heterogeneous networks; rather, it has features for specifying the topology of sets of processors, for example, which would be of use on parallel distributed-memory systems. MPI does not currently allow you to add and delete tasks as your job runs. MPI implementations such as MPICH can and do support heterogeneous networks, with the machines fixed at run time.

Because of the inflexibility of MPI in the area of starting up tasks, the SPMD (Single Program Multiple Data) model is just about the only option. Multiple identical copies of the same program run on each processor. The basic code structure of a SPMD program is in outline (not in MPI format):

```
myid=Initialize();
if(myid==master) {
      /* Master Code */
      }
else {
      /* Slave Code */
      }
```

UNIX programmers will recognize the similarity to the **fork()** system call. The major difference is that the UNIX fork creates one additional copy of the program, while in a SPMD program there will be any number of "slaves."

There will be synchronization barriers as appropriate in the above code. For example, each Receive in "**loop over slaves: Receive(Result)** " cannot be executed until the corresponding slave has completed its task. Hence, a Barrier might be included before this statement, with a corresponding statement before the **Send(Result)** for the slaves to announce their arrival at the synchronization point. Alternatively, the sends and receives may be used to effect synchronization by having the Receive wait ("block") until the corresponding Send has been executed. A more detailed outline of a typical SPMD model code would be:

```
if(myid==master){
      loop over slaves: Send(TaskAssignment);
      loop over slaves: Receive(Result);
      ProcessResults();
      exit(0);
      }
else  {/* slave */
      Receive(TaskAssignment);
      DoWork();
      Send(Result);
      exit(0);
      }
```

For MPI, the initialization section of the code will look something like:

```
int myid, numprocs, argc;
char *argv[];

MPI_Init(&argc, &argv);
MPI_Comm_size(MPI_COMM_WORLD,&numprocs);
MPI_Comm_rank(MPI_COMM_WORLD,&myid);
```

The **argc** and **argv** variables are the usual command-line arguments sent to the main program by the UNIX system. They are sent to **MPI_Init**, which is not obligated to use them. In an earlier version of **MPI_Init**, **argc** and **argv**, not their addresses, were sent to **MPI_Init**. Unless **MPI_Init** is going to change them, there is no need to send pointers to these variables, and it is unlikely that most MPI implementations will want to alter these parameters, but the option is there should they wish to do so. The previous version of the MPI standard specified **MPI_Init(argc,argv)** instead of pointers to these arguments in the current version, so if you encounter "legacy" MPI code that fails early on a "segmentation violation" or similar error, this might be the cause. The standard does not appear to address the issue of how these arguments are to be used. As with the UNIX **fork** process, the **myid** variable, set by the **MPI_Comm_rank** call, should be different for each process, running from 0 to numprocs-1. The **MPI_COMM_WORLD** is a predefined constant denoting the "global" communications handle. This handle can be used to communicate between all processors. It is possible under MPI to create your own communications handles that specify a certain subset of the set of processors. The user can then designate one process, e g., with myid equal to 0, as the "master" and the rest as "slaves." (If you prefer the terminology "client" and "servers," please feel free to make the substitution in your mind whenever these terms arise. Here, we use the master/slave terminology, as the client/server terminology typically implies a single server.)

The receives in the above example are obviously synchronization points, i.e., they should not return, and execution should not continue, until the data has been received. This is accomplished with blocking receives discussed below. The slaves cannot proceed until they receive their assigned tasks, and the master must then wait until the slaves have returned their results before it can put all the results together to produce the overall result.

Message Passing Primitives

Initialization and Termination

The three calls discussed above, to **MPI_Init**, **MPI_Comm_size** and **MPI_Comm_rank,** will generally occur at or near the beginning of the program. Note that **MPI_Comm_size** does not set the size (number of processors); it obtains that information. MPI does not specify how to tell the system how many processors are desired. As MPI does not support adding new processors to your set, specifying the processor count cannot be done after the program begins execution. Normally, environmental variables are set and the program is loaded onto the processors. Notice that, because the SPMD process model is employed, the same program is running on each node.

Upon completion of execution, **MPI_Finalize()** should be called to do the usual cleanup functions. This constitutes good-neighborliness to other users.

Simple synchronization can be implemented using the **MPI_Barrier(MPI_Comm comm)** call. This call effects a global synchronization point. No processor will proceed beyond this point until all processors have reached it.

Sends and Receives

MPI supports a plethora of sends. The principal ones are shown in Table 6.1. Blocking sends do not return control until the buffer area has been read completely and is free to be overwritten. Note that on some implementations this may not occur until the message is actually received by the receiver. It will be seen that there are three "modes": standard, synchronous, and ready. Synchronous is a mode in which the send does not return control to the caller until the receiver has acknowledged receipt. Note that this doubles the message traffic count, and increases the risk of a deadlock situation where two processes are each waiting for acknowledgments from the other. Synchronous mode is of most interest in situations with very limited buffer space on some or all machines, and perhaps in debugging. Ready mode requires the receive to be posted before the send. The standard documentation states that the results of a ready-mode send are undefined if the receive has not been posted at the time of the send! It also states that the ready mode send may be implemented as a normal send. Blocking sends do not return control until the buffer area is ready for reuse, while blocking receives do not return until the buffer contains the received data.

Table 6.1 MPI message send calls		
Name	**Mode**	**Remarks**
MPI_Send	standard	blocking
MPI_Bsend	standard	buffered, blocking
MPI_Ibsend	standard	buffered, nonblocking
MPI_Irsend	ready	nonblocking
MPI_Isend	standard	nonblocking
MPI_Isend	synchronous	nonblocking
MPI_Rsend	ready	nonblocking
MPI_Ssend	synchronous	blocking

The standard syntax for the various sends is:

int MPI_Send(void* buf, int count, MPI_Datatype datatype, int dest, int tag, MPI_Comm comm);

Here **buf** is a pointer to the buffer containing the data to be sent, count is a count of the number of data items to be sent, datatype is the type of data (e. g., **MPI_FLOAT**, **MPI_LONG**, **MPI_DOUBLE**, **MPI_INT**, etc.). The integer **dest** specifies the destination process, and hence runs between 0 and **numprocs-1** inclusive. The tag is employed to specify the user-defined category of the message. It may be desirable for the user to define a number of such categories for different types of messages. The variable **comm** is typically **MPI_COMM_WORLD**, meaning the entire set of processors for the particular problem. However, it may be desirable to limit the set of allowed processors to a subset, called a group in MPI argot, and that is where other values of **comm** might be defined. This will be discussed shortly.

The analogous blocking receive is:

int MPI_Recv(void* buf, int count, MPI_Datatype datatype, int source, int tag, MPI_Comm comm), MPI_Status* status);

Here the variable **source** specifies the allowed source for the message; in addition to specifying a specific originator for the sent data, the **MPI_ANY_SOURCE** may be specified here. Similarly, the tag value may be specified as **MPI_ANY_TAG**, which will match any tag. The variable **status** specifies a data structure. For example, **status.MPI_TAG** would contain the tag value of the message, and status.**MPI_SOURCE** would contain the source id. These values are obviously of use when **MPI_ANY_TAG** or **MPI_ANY_SOURCE** have been used.

Note that in using the receive, a buffer must be supplied which is large enough to contain the received data. Hence, it may be necessary to determine how much data has been received, before **MPI_Recv** is called. Also, as the call blocks until appropriate data is received, it may be necessary to first check to see if any data has been received. This is done with the non-blocking call:

int MPI_IProbe(int source, int tag, MPI_Comm comm, int flag, MPI_Status * status);

Note that we use **MPI_IProbe**, not the blocking version **MPI_Probe**; the **I** in **Iprobe** stands for immediate. This function returns **True** if there is a received message which matches the values specified by the variables **source**, **tag**, and **comm**. If **flag** is **True**, then the status variable returns information about the message. It is guaranteed that the next call to **MPI_Recv** with the same **source**, **tag**, and **comm** values will recover that message. A call to:

int MPI_Get_Count(MPI_Status *status, MPI_Datatype datatype, int *count);

with the pointer to the status structure returned by **MPI_IProbe** will return the count of elements in the message.

It should be obvious from the foregoing that MPI is easiest to use if the data is passed in messages of a homogeneous data type. It is possible to define user-specified types and structures, but this complicates the usage of MPI. In the past, this has been a trap for implementers of MPI, with bugs in the processing of user-defined types common.

Buffered Message Passing

To maximize the potential for overlapping communications and computation, MPI provides a number of functions in which the data transfer is deferred. For example, **MPI_Recv** is equivalent to **MPI_Recv_init(...)**, **MPI_Request(*request)** followed by **MPI_Start(request)** . At the conclusion of the operation, which may be determined by **MPI_Wait(request)** , a call to the function **MPI_Request_Free(request)** will free the memory resources. A virtue of this approach is that the buffer need not be reallocated and freed, reducing overhead.

Structured Message Passing

Many years ago, the concept of "structured programming" caught hold and reshaped programming. The idea was that the most general, flexible, and "closest-to-hardware" control structures, involving the use of the "goto" and "conditional goto" constructs, were actually too flexible, giving the programmer too much opportunity to go wrong. The solution was to limit the programmer to more strictly-defined control structures, such as while(), until(), and if..then..else. Most languages (Ada and Pascal, for example) retained the goto for special cases, although at least one, Modula-2, eliminated the goto entirely (although it enforced the "short-circuited" if requirement, which lessened the need for gotos).

Similar considerations apply to message-passing communications. If the communications can be performed in a particular pattern, it is likely that specialized system calls for that operation could be done more reliably and more efficiently. MPI supports a number of such operations. I have not heard a term such as "structured message passing" in use, but it seems natural and appropriate. Notice that we make no claim to inventing the concept. Where possible, these structured operations provided by MPI should be utilized. Most other message-passing systems, such as PVM have only limited support for these "structured" operations.

The **MPI_Reduce** function is a good example. The requisite syntax is:

int MPI_Reduce(void* sendbuf, void* recbuf, int count, MPI_Datatype datatype, MPI_Op op, int root, MPI_Comm comm);

This function will perform the operation specified by **op** on all of the processors. For example, if **op** is given the value **MPI_SUM**, then the variable recbuf on the processor specified by root will contain the sum of all of the values pointed to by the variable sendbuf on all of the processors in the group defined by comm. A variety of built-in operations, such as **MPI_MAX**, logical and bitwise-logical operations, and **MPI_MAXLOC** and **MPI_MINLOC**, which return both a value and a pointer to the location of that value, are supported. The user can also define operations. In defining the operation, the user specifies an external function. The user also specifies if the operation is commutative; if so, MPI has the option of reordering evaluations for maximum efficiency. We refer you to Gropp et al. (1994) and the MPI specification for details. Note that PVM supports the reduce operation, as well as barrier, broadcast, and has a multicast operation as well. See also Sunderam et al. (1994) for background.

There are a number structured messaging operations (Table 6.2). It is often necessary to broadcast the same information from one processor (typically the master) to all others, or for that processor to obtain information from all the others. It also may be desirable to send information from every processor to all the others. There are structured broadcast and scatter/gather operations for these needs in MPI. In many books on parallel algorithms (see chapters 1 and 10, Suppliers), these "structured" operations, such as the reduce, scan, and scatter/gather operations, are frequently discussed and employed.

One valuable feature of using the "structured" messaging calls for such purposes is that they will most likely be optimized for the computer architecture, without any user effort necessary. For example, consider the broadcast operation. This can be done naively with a simple loop in which the root processor sends the information to each other processor in sequence. However, a divide-and-conquer approach may be used. The root sends the information to, say, two processors, say one in the "left" half of the processor array and the other in the "right" half. (The root might be one of these two processors.) Then, each of these processors sends the data to two processors, representing say the "upper" and "lower" halves of their regions. This process continues recursively, as in the orthogonal recursive bisection method (See chapter 4). The result would be a time delay that is logarithmic in the number of processors rather than linear, due to the simultaneous communications.

Table 6.2: Collective communication operations in MPI	
MPI_Allgatherv	Vector data version of Allgather.
MPI_Allgather	All processors form the same vector of 1 element each from each processor.
MPI_Allreduce	Reduce over all processors.
MPI_Alltoallv	vector data version of Alltoall.
MPI_Alltoall	All processors form different vectors of 1 element from each processor. Each processor specifies data for each destination.
MPI_Bcast	Send same data to all processors.
MPI_Gatherv	Vector data version of Gather.
MPI_Gather	Collect data from processors (forming vector).
MPI_Reduce_scatter	Collective operation & scatter result.
MPI_Reduce	Collective reduction (e. g., max, or sum).
MPI_Scatterv	Vector data version of Scatter.
MPI_Scatter	Distribute a vector of elements 1 each to processors
MPI_Scan	Like reduce but processor r gets result of operation on data from processors 0, 1, r.

Collective Communications

MPI permits the user to define groups, which are subsets of the "world" of communicating processors. This can be a useful simplification and debugging aid. For example, if a recursive bisection approach is taken for load-balancing purposes (see chapter 4), one might define two groups, "right" and "left," which might be further subdivided each into "upper" and "lower" groups, or explicitly into four groups: "upper_right" etc., and so forth. It might also be desirable to define as groups the levels; i.e., there might be one group of the two highest-level processors, the next two groups those plus their direct children, etc. There are two reasons for creating such groups. First, once a group has been defined, collective operations may be done on that group alone, simplifying programming and possibly resulting in more efficient communications. In addition, some errors might be detected at compile time rather than run time, resulting in faster debugging.

For each group there are two associated data items. One, the *communicator*, we have already encountered as **MPI_COMM_WORLD**, the communicator for the entire set of processors. Think of it as a handle or identifier for the group. The other is the **MPI_Group** data structure, which defines the group membership. At the start of the program, the communicator for the world is given. You can then form the associated group data structure via:

MPI_Group world_group;
MPI_Comm_Group(MPI_COMM_WORLD,&world_group);.

Once you have the world_group data structure initialized, it can be modified to form other groups. For example, a call to:

int MPI_Group_excl(MPI_Group start, int count, int ranks[],MPI_Group * result);

where **start** would be world_group in our example, and **ranks** would be a vector of length count listing the ranks of the processors we wished to exclude from the group, and **result** would the new group resulting from the execution of the exclusion function. MPI supplies a number of constructors of groups, including functions to exclude (delete) processors, to take the union and intersection of groups, and to include or exclude certain ranges of ranks. It does not seem to allow constructing groups by adding processors (except through the union of previously formed groups). Instead, it appears much easier to start with the world and remove processors.

MPI Implementations

There are a number of implementations of MPI. In addition to proprietary implementations on various hardware, there are a number of portable implementations intended to run on a variety of architectures. Please note that all are evolving. It is not possible to compare these, as they are all moving targets subject to change.

LAM

The LAM implementation of MPI has been developed and supported by the Ohio Supercomputer center at Ohio State University. See chapter 10, Suppliers, for the Internet site for source code and documentation. LAM runs on the IBM RS/6000 AIX system, Sun 4 Sparc machines under SunOS, DEC AXP, and HP 9000's.

CHIMP

CHIMP was developed at the University of Edinburgh. It operates on the same machines as Lam, as well as the Sequent Symmetry and Meiko Computing Surface.

MPICH

MPICH was developed at Argonne National Laboratory. It includes a number of support tools, including **mpirun** to execute jobs and **upshot** which can analyze a logfile produced by a program. These logging operations are performed by an extension to MPI called MPE. MPE provides facilities for profiling the execution.

UNIFY

UNIFY is a subset of the MPI standard, under development at Mississippi State University.

OTHER IMPLEMENTATIONS

WinMPI

A version of MPICH was ported to Windows 3.1 See chapter 10 for sources, and chapter 9 for an example of its employment.

MPI on the Maui SP-2

In addition to MPICH, CHIMP, and LAM, a native implementation of MPI developed by IBM is available on the Maui SP-2. IBM participated in drafting the MPI standard, and the early MPL library for the SP-2 was close to the MPI standard. At the time this book is written (late 1995), it appears that this implementation is the fastest of the MPI and PVM messaging systems. Normally, a multiprocessor MPI job is run using the LoadLeveler system. This system will automatically distribute a SPMD job among a set of processors.

PVM Services

PVM message passing	Debugger scripts
PVM shell	XPVM - graphical shell

Figure 6.3: PVM provides more than simple message passing services. It also includes a shell interface for configuring and monitoring machines, as well as provisions to run your local machine's debugger in parallel.

PVM

PVM stands for Parallel Virtual Machine. PVM provides an environment for running a number of jobs in parallel on a single machine, a network, or a parallel machine. In contrast to MPI, PVM is much more than a massage-passing interface specification. Using PVM, one can emulate a parallel system and debug a parallel program on a single processor. The PVM interface should be virtually identical on all machines. PVM can dynamically add new processes or spawn jobs, something that is beyond the scope of MPI. In summary, the ability to run under PVM greatly increases the flexibility of a program during development as well as during production runs.

PVM and MPI are complementary in many ways. PVM provides a number of development environments, including XPVM (Geist et al. 1994) and PADE (Devaney et al. 1995). Experience with PVM (White et al. 1995, Reale 1994) suggests that PVM is reasonably effective on a wide range of platforms and heterogeneous networks. MPI has turned in good performance on many systems (e.g., Gropp and Lusk 1995); it is to be expected that optimized implementations of MPI would be somewhat more efficient than PVM, due to PVM's higher overhead, simpler interface, and its focus on portability and the need for the ability to operate on heterogeneous systems. PVM also has a much simpler feature set than MPI, which can be an advantage if you are a beginner. Unfortunately it can also be a disadvantage if you are an advanced programmer trying to eke the last few percent of performance out of your application.

PVM Message Passing Primitives

Initialization

As PVM is more comprehensive than MPI in its support for parallel task control; the initialization and housekeeping functions are somewhat more complicated, but much more powerful. A PVM programmer is not limited to the SPMD model. The function

int pvm_spawn(char *task, char **arg, int flag, char *where, int ntask, int *tids);

may be used in either SPMD or MPMD modes. This can be a real advantage in environments where different programs might want to communicate, such as a real time visualization program communicating with a parallel scientific computation. For SPMD, the program name specified by **task** is the same as that of the spawning process. The integer variable **ntask** specifies how many tasks to spawn. The **flag** variable specifies the significance of the where string. If its value is **PvmTaskDefault**, for example, then the system determines where to begin the other tasks, and the where variable is ignored. The where variable could contain either host names or host architecture names. Note that the integer array tid is returned. It contains the task ids of the processes that are spawned. The call

tid= pvm_mytid();

may be used to obtain the task id of the calling process. This call will generally be the very first call in a program. The call **tid = pvm_parent()** returns the tid of the process which spawned the caller; the value **PvmNoParent** is returned if there is no parent. If there is no parent, the caller is the "master" or "client." This function call is often used in SPMD programs to effect the if...else... block for the master/slave execution.

Sends and Receives

PVM supports the **pvm_recv**, **pvm_send**, and **pvm_probe** operations, which are analogs of the MPI operations. The syntax is

int pvm_send(int tid, int msgtag);

int pvm_recv(int tid, int msgtag);

int pvm_probe(int tid, int msgtag);

where tid specifies the source or destination and the **msgtag** functions as it does in MPI. As in MPI, there are wildcards for the **tid** and **msgtag** values; the wildcard value for either is the integer -1. The function value returned is 0 if successful, and is negative if not. The msgtag integer should be non-negative. The **probe** operation returns 0 if there is no corresponding message; otherwise it returns an identifier structure that can be processed using **pvm_bufinfo** to determine the size (in bytes, unlike MPI) of the received message, the **tag**, and the **tid**. In short, the procedure is very similar to MPI. As PVM predates MPI, it is likely that the committee that developed MPI chose to use a scheme similar to that of PVM. This, of course, makes the layering of MPI over PVM that much easier.

To send data, a number of function calls are required. Obviously, the system has to be told of a buffer region, and its size, which contains the data, for anything useful to happen. A three-step process is typically used. First, the buffer to be used by the **send** is initialized. Then, the data is packed into this buffer. Finally, the data is actually sent, and any cleanup is done.

The sender might first invoke **int bufid=pvm_initsend(int encoding)** where encoding is **PvmDataDefault** (0), for the XDR standard, **PvmDataRaw** (1) for no encoding (less overhead, but unsafe except on homogenous networks), and **PvmDataInPlace** (2) where only pointers to data and their sizes are passed for items to be sent, the items being copied directly by the send operation. Alternately, if the user wishes to manage multiple message buffers himself, the call **int bufid = pvm_mkbuf(encoding)** can be used. There is the analogous routine to free the buffer. To use this buffer for the send data, invoke **pvm_setsbuf(bufid)** , and similarly set the receive buffer using **pvm_setrbuf(bufid)**. Data is then packed by function calls such as: **int pvm_pkint(int *np, int cnt, int stride)** where **np** points to an array of integers (because our example uses **pvm_pkint** for integers), **cnt** is the count of items to be packed, and **stride** is the distance between items in the array to be sent; a **stride** of 1 would send each element, a **stride** of two would send every other element, etc.

Finally, **int pvm_send(int tid, int msgtag)** would send the data on its way. The function **pvm_freebuf(bufid)** would free the buffer if desired. **pvm_getsbuf()** returns the currently active send buffer.

There is no "**pvm_initrecv**" call. The receiver will unpack the received data with **int pvm_upint (int *np, int cnt, int stride)**, the received data being placed into the array np. If desired, the receive buffer can be managed by the user, but this is not necessary. Instead, the call **int bufid= pvm_recv(int tid, int msgtag)** is used. For a non-blocking receive, call **pvm_nrecv**. It will return 0 if there is no matching message. Or use the probe function. The function **int pvm_bufinfo (int bufid, int *bytes, int *msgtag, int *tid)** will return information on the received data, analogous to the information in the MPI_Status structure.

Thus, PVM handles data structures somewhat more naturally than MPI. However, the overhead of the buffer packing and unpacking will generally result in greater latency for communications operations. (Latency is defined as the minimum time for an operation from start to completion. It includes the startup time due to overhead.)

Using PVM

Introduction

The Parallel Virtual Machine (PVM) set of libraries and utilities is a very powerful tool for exploiting virtually any network of computers or parallel computers. It lets the user create and control a virtual parallel machine from any heterogeneous set of computers connected via a network. For example, the following parallel virtual machine was constructed from a large set of workstations connected by a standard network:

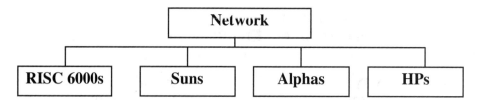

Figure 6.4: A Parallel Virtual Machine may be created from any collection of UNIX computers connected by a network. You can control PVM from any machine.

PVM lets you do essentially the same thing on parallel machines, creating a single Parallel Virtual Machine from a set of parallel computing nodes on a massively parallel machine. PVM gives you a standard way of connecting these computers together, and running and controlling your programs.

The PVM Daemon

To let different nodes of our Parallel Virtual Machine communicate, PVM uses a communication daemon called *pvmd3*. You may see this daemons running when you use the Unix **ps** command. The PVM daemon is nothing more than a program you start that runs continuously. It negotiates the communications between different computers on your network, so that you can start a single job on one computer and have it run across the entire network.

What's important to know about the daemon is that you need one running on each computer in your parallel virtual machine. If for some reason one of your computers is powered down or rebooted, you may need to restart the PVM daemon and any jobs you had running before continuing. Fortunately, you can perform all of these operations from the PVM console.

Building a Virtual Machine

Before you can run on multiple machines in your network, you need to perform the following steps:

1. Make sure you have PVM and your application installed and compiled on each computer on which you wish to run. If you have PVM and your application on a shared file system, it may not be necessary to recompile on every system, but you will need to recompile for different types of computers. For example, if you have a SUN and ALPHA sharing the same file system, you do need to compile PVM and your application on the SUN, and then recompile it for the ALPHA.

2. Configure your .cshrc file as previously described to run PVM. Test PVM on each of your computers to make sure that it is installed properly. Halt all PVM daemons after testing them by typing *halt* at the PVM prompt.

3. Create or edit the *.rhosts* file in your home directory so that each machine you want to use is in this file. Its important that your .rhosts file exists on each machine, and names every other machine. For example if you want to use computers named *jake, joker.plk.af.mil, roy,* and *elwood*, your .rhosts file might look like:

```
jake
joker.plk.af.mil
roy
elwood
```

1. Make sure that there are no PVM daemons running on any of the machines you wish to configure. You can check this by running a *ps -fa* on each machine you might have had PVM running on.

2. Start the PVM console by typing *pvm* on one of the machines.

3. Add new machines from the *PVM>* prompt by typing *add {machine name}* where *{machine name}* is the name of the machine you wish to add. For example, you might type *add elwood* to add a machine named *elwood* to the configuration.

4. Type *conf* to view the virtual machine you have created. Type *quit* to exit the PVM console. Once your virtual machine is

configured, if you run your application it will be run across the set of computers in your virtual machine.

5. If you have problems, see the section on common PVM problems below.

Running the PVM console

You can access the PVM console from any computer in your virtual machine by typing the *pvm* command. This will give you the *PVM>* prompt. From the PVM console you can view your current virtual machine configuration, view and kill jobs running on your virtual machine, and change your PVM configuration. Commands are detailed below:

PVM Commands

The following commands may be accessed from the *PVM>* prompt on any configured computer in your virtual machine.

- To view your current virtual machine configuration: *conf*

- To add a computer called *{hostname}* to your virtual machine: *add {hostname}*

- To delete a computer called *{hostname}* from your virtual machine: *delete {hostname}*

- To view jobs running on any of your virtual machines: *ps -a*

- To kill jobs running (use the *{TaskIds}* from the **ps** command): *kill {TaskIds}*

- To kill all of your PVM tasks on all machines in your virtual machine: *reset*

- To halt all PVM daemons on all machines in your virtual machine: *halt*

- To quit the PVM console, leaving all PVM daemons running: *quit*

Automating PVM Configuration

Rather than having to manually add hosts to your virtual machine each time you wish to restart the PVM daemons, you can use a *hostfile* listing the hosts you want configured in your virtual machine, and then run ***pvm {hostfile}*** where *{hostfile}* is the name of the file you have created listing computers you want in your virtual machine. For example, if you want computers named *roy, jake,* and *elwood* configured in your PVM on startup, you could create a *hostfile* with the following entries (note that the line beginning with the pound sign # is a comment):

```
#My Host File
roy
jake
elwood
```

Typing ***pvm {hostfile},*** where *{hostfile}* is the name of the file with these entries in it, would start the PVM console and daemons with these computers configured. You can also use a hostfile to configure machines you optionally want to include, and computers that may have a different login name or require a password to ***rlogin*** into. To configure a machine that you may want to add later, simply put an ampersand (&) character in front of the hostname. This will tell PVM to reserve that host name and options for adding the machine later. If you want to use a different login name on the remote host, include the ***lo={mylogin}*** option on the same line as the machine name, where *{mylogin}* is your login id on the remote host. Similarly adding the letters ***so=pw*** after the hostname will make PVM look for a password when trying to add the new host. Therefore an optional machine called ***batman, that*** you may want to add later, that has a login id of ***smithb*** and requires a separate password, might appear in your hostfile as:

&batman lo=smithb so=pw

Optimizing PVM on Networks

PVM running over a network can communicate in either "normal" and "direct" modes (Chang et al. 1995). The former routes all communications through the PVM daemon; the latter allows the task to communicate directly through the socket interface to other processes accross the network. Chang et al. (1995) have found significant performance benefits accruing to the direct mode. However, this mode may not work on some machines if the number of file descriptors is limited. Therefore, if PVM is to be run on a network, it would be a good idea to attempt to run in direct mode if possible.

Common Problems with PVM Installations

Can't Start PVM on Remote Host

This is usually caused by one of three problems:

1. You already have a PVM daemon running on the computer you are trying to add. Try logging into it, typing *pvm* to bring up the PVM console, and type *halt* to kill off the daemon. Then go back to your original host and try to add the computer again.

2. Its possible that a PVM daemon died on the remote machine when it was brought down at some point in the past. If this happened you will get a "Unable to contact daemon" message when you try running PVM on the remote host. The dead daemon leaves a file called */tmp/pvmd.{uid}* where uid is your numerical user id. You can get your user id by typing the *id* command at the prompt, then remove the file */tmp/pvmd.{uid}* from the computer you could not add and try to add this machine again.

3. A third common cause is that you can't *rlogin* to the remote host. This can be caused by a variety of problems. The most common causes are: errors in your *.rhosts* file, and the need to specify a password or different user id (possibly requiring a PVM *hostfile* to be set up). Another common problem that can cause difficulty for PVM is the presence of items in your *.cshrc* file that print output to your terminal. These cause problems because PVM is looking to log in and run a command without this extra output. It is usually best to eliminate these items in your *.cshrc* or enclose them in a conditional such as:

```
if ( { tty -s } && $?prompt ) then
{ PUT YOUR INTERACTIVE COMMANDS HERE... }
endif
```

PVM Troubleshooting

General Comments

Above all, be aware of the many resources available to help you. For example, if there are problems at the Maui SP-2, you can direct e-mail to the consultants there, as well as to the Albuquerque Resource Center (ARC). Telephone discussions with ARC personnel can also be helpful. Problems with PVM, etc., can often be resolved by sending e-mail to the groups at Oak Ridge National Laboratories, etc. that support these products. Also, keep in touch with the computer center at which you are running your application. Often, changes in operating systems, "upgrades" etc., are not backward-compatible with previous versions of libraries, shell scripts, and so on.

If problems arise with compiling, linking, or running, first make sure that all versions and options are consistent. Thus, if your application was linked to one version of PVM, it will generally need the same version number to run with at execution time. If different, incompatible options are specified in the command line and config.h files, all manner of problems can arise. Be sure you are not specifying one option for, say, neighbor searching in one place and another option somewhere else. Pay attention to the error and warning messages. Hydrocodes are not black boxes, and an understanding of the program and problem are necessary to successful operation!

Program Halts Suddenly on One Machine

Occasionally, because of heavy network traffic or machine loads on one of your computing nodes, one of the PVM daemons may time out and lose touch with the others. When this happens your PVM run will stop because the affected machine will lose contact with the other machines on which you are running. When this happens it is usually best to halt PVM, start

PVM again on desired machines, and then restart your from the last available dump file. The pvm header file ddpro.h contains a parameter DDMINTIMEOUT, which in release 3 has a value of 3 minutes. It may be desirable to increase this value for your system, depending on the problems being run. Problems with a great deal of computation can cause timeouts due to the long duration of the computation between interrogations of the pvm daemon.

PVM Can't Start PVMD on Remote Host

This is probably the most common PVM problem. Here's a comprehensive list of possible causes we have experienced. Note that you can often narrow down the exact cause by looking at the */tmp/pvml.{uid}* log file for your user id. This file usually contains a message saying why PVM could not start the daemon on the remote host:

- Be sure that the PVM daemon (pvmd3) is not already running on the remote host under your user id. If it is, halt the daemon on the host, and try to add the remote host again.

- Be sure that there is no file named */tmp/pvmd.{uid}* where *{uid}* is your numerical user id on the remote host. This file is a lock file that indicates to PVM that the daemon is already running. Typically if the system is rebooted before you halt your daemons, this file is left on the system even though no *pvmd3* daemon is running. If this file exists on the remote host and no daemon is running, simply remove it before continuing.

- Another common problem is no ability to **rlogin** to the remote host. You can test your **rlogin** ability by typing **rlogin hostname.** You should be able to rlogin to the remote host with no password. Check your *.rhosts* file on all hosts in your parallel virtual machine to verify that each file contains all of the hosts you want in your virtual machine. If the machine requires a password, make sure you have the so=pw option set in your hostfile.

- A less common problem occurs when you have PVM installed in different locations on different machines. In particular, if you have it installed in your HOME directory on one machine, and a shared directory on another machine, you may encounter a conflict because PVM tries to start *pvmd3* with the full path from one machine or another. The best way to resolve this problem is to use the dx= option in the host file. Another simple way to resolve this problem is to link the shared pvm3 directories to a directory called pvm3 in your home directory, and then modify your PVM environment variables and path to use the linked copy in your home directory. For example, the following will link appropriate libraries to your pvm3 directory. Note you will still need to remove your PVM_ROOT definition and path to use these linked copies:

mkdir pvm3

ln -s /usr/local/pvm3/lib pvm3

ln -s /usr/local/pvm3/include pvm3

Running PVM and MPI Jobs under LoadLeveler

Subject to the usual caveats concerning the ephemeral nature of such information, we present here LoadLeveler scripts suitable for use at the Maui Supercomputer Center for the IBM SP-2.

First, the LoadLeveler script for using pvm, version 3:

```
#!/bin/csh
#  FOR FOUR PROCESSORS
#@ numproc = 4
#@ job_name = myjob
#@ intialdir = /u/lbaker/myplace
#@ parallel_path = /u/lbaker/myplace
#@ environment = PVMEPATH=/u/lbaker/mypvm
```

```
#@ job_type = pvm3
#@ notification = complete
#@ notify_user = lbaker@mhpcc.edu
#  SMALL SHORT JOB QUEUE:
#@ class = Small_Short
#@ min_processors = $(numproc)
#@ max_processors = $(numproc)
#@ requirements = (Adapter == "hps_ip")
#@ output = $(job_name.).$(numproc).out
#@ errror = $(job_name.).$(numproc).err
#@ queue

echo 'Using these processors...'
echo $LOADL_PROCESSOR_LIST
echo ' '

/u/lbaker/myplace/myprogram

# Save the execution logs
set myid='id -u'
foreach a ('echo $ $LOADL_PROCESSOR_LIST')
      echo $a
      rsh $a cat /tmp/mpvl.$myid
end
```

Fig. 6.5: A LoadLeveler script for using pvm on SP-2 at Maui.

Most of the items in this script should be obvious. Comments have a # in column 1. The name of the SPMD program to be executed is myprogram, found in the directory specified as shown. Some items, such as the specification that the high-performance switch (Adapter== hps_ip), are obviously specific to the implementation. Figure 6.6 shows the corresponding script for using MPI. Indeed, LoadLeveler is AIX-specific, so beyond the SP-2 there is little interest in LoadLevler scripts. Expect magic incantations such as these to be subject to the whims of the systems programmers and to change with little notice.

```
#!/bin/csh
#  FOR FOUR PROCESSORS
#@ numproc = 4
#@ job_name = myjob
#@ intialdir = /u/lbaker/myplace
#@ parallel_path = /u/lbaker/myplace
#@
environment=MPIEUILIB=us;MP_INFOLEVEL=9;MP_LABELIO=
yes;MP_PROC=32
#@ job_type = parallel
#@ notification = complete
#@ notify_user = lbaker@mhpcc.edu
#  SMALL SHORT JOB QUEUE:
#@ class = Small_Short
#@ min_processors = $(numproc)
#@ max_processors = $(numproc)
#@ requirements = (Adapter == "hps_user")
#@ output = $(job_name.).$(numproc).out
#@ errror = $(job_name.).$(numproc).err
#@ queue

/u/lbaker/myplace/myprogram
```

Fig. 6.6: A LoadLeveler script for using the native MPI
implementation on SP-2 at Maui.

References

Chang, S.L., Du, D. H.-C., Hsieh, J., Tsang, R. P., Lin, M., "Enhanced PVM Communications over a High-Speed LAN," *IEEE Parallel & Distributed Technlogy*, **3** (3), pp. 20-32,Fall 1995.

Devaney, J. E., Lipman, R., Lo, M., Mitchell, W. F., Edwards, M., Clark, C. W., "The Parallel Applications Development Environment (PADE)

User's Manual," available via anonymous ftp from ftp://gams.nist.gov/pub/pade. May 1 1995.

Geist, A., Beguelin, A., Dongarra, J., Jiang, W., Manchekc, R., Sunderam, V., *PVM: Parallel Virtual Machine*, Cambridge, M. A.: MIT Press, 1994.

Grant, B. K., Skjellum, A., "The PVM Systems: An In-Depth Analysis and Documenting Study-Concise Edition," available via anonymous ftp from ftp://aurora.cs.msstate.edu/pub/reports/Message-Passing.

Gropp, W., Lusk, E., Skjellum, A., *Using MPI*, Cambridge, M. A.: MIT Press, 1994.

Gropp, W., Lusk, E., "Some Early Performance Results with MPI on the IBM SP1," available via anonymous ftp from ftp://aurora.cs.msstate.edu/pub/reports/Message-Passing.

Reale, F., Bocchino, F., Sciortino, S., "Parallel computing on Unix workstation arrays," *Computer Physics Communications*, **83**, 130-140 (1994).

Skjellum, A., Grant, B. K., "Message Passing in the 1990's: Performance, Safety, Correctness," available via anonymous ftp from ftp://aurora.cs.msstate.edu/pub/reports/Message-Passing.

Skjellum, A., Lusk, E., Gropp, W., "Early Applications in the Message-Passing Interface (MPI)," available via anonymous ftp from ftp://aurora.cs.msstate.edu/pub/reports/Message-Passing.

Still, C. H., "Portable Parallel Computing via the MPI1 Message-Passing Standard," *Computers in Physics*, **8** (5) 533-539, Sept./Oct. 1994.

Sunderam, V. S., Geist, G. A., Dongarra, J., Manchek, R., "The PVM Concurrent Computing System:: Evolution, Experiences, and Trends," *Parallel Computing*, **20**, pp. 531-545, (1994).

Walker, D. W., "The design of a standard message passing interface for distriuted memory concurrent computers," *Parallel Computing*, **20**, 657-673, 1994.

White, S., Alund, A., Sunderam, V. S., "Performanceof the NAS Parallel Benchmarks on PVM-Based Networks," *J. of Parallel and Distrib. Computing*," **26**, 1-71 (1995).

Chapter 7

Implementing Message Passing

The previous chapter discussed the basics of message passing, including the syntax and semantics of the MPI and PVM message-passing systems. In this chapter we discuss the details of putting together a viable message-passing system, with code examples.

Layered Message Passing

In preceding chapters, we have advocated an approach of layering MPI calls over PVM. This provides significant advantages for portability, debugging, detailed message tracing and ease of use. The main disadvantage is the need to create and maintain such a library. Here we show explicitly how to do this. The MPI calls are implemented by a collection of three files. Figure 7.1 shows the calling sequence.

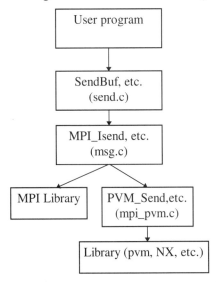

Fig. 7.1: Layering of message passing code.

The user writes code that invokes the highest-level routines, which ship data to and from the communications buffers, via calls to routines contained in file send.c. If an MPI library is in use, those routines will be called. If pvm or a proprietary library, such as NX on the Intel Paragon, are used, then the MPI-syntax calls in msg.c are used. The actual pvm calls are supported by the code in file mpi_pvm.c. For example, the function PVM_Send in this file will create or select the buffer, as appropriate, call pvm_send or pvm_mcast as appropriate, and free the buffer, if appropriate.

The first file listed here is called msg.c and contains the "pseudo-MPI" call interface. It provides support only for the most necessary routines, listed in 7.1. The prototypes for this code is contained in file send.h along with the prototpes for send.c.

Table 7.1: Implemented MPI routines in layered MPI/PVM	
Function	Purpose
MPI_Init	Initialize
MPI_Comm_size	Return number of processors in group
MPI_Comm_rank	Return processor "id" of self
MPI_Abort	Terminate process
MPI_Finalize	Terminate parallel job
MPI_Send	Send
MPI_Recv	Send
MPI_Isend	Immediate send
MPI_Irecv	Immediate send
MPI_Wait	Wait until buffer available
MPI_Test	Return result: is buffer available?
MPI_Iprobe	Return result: message received?
MPI_Get_source	Return rank of sender for received message
MPI_Get_tag	Return tag of received message
MPI_Get_count	Return size of received message
MPI_Barrier	Synchronize group
MPI_Reduce	Perform parallel reduction operation
_MPI_Op	Operation for MPI_Reduce

The header file *msg.h*, containing the interface definition and function prototypes for msg.c and mpi_pvm.c, mpl.c, and pgon.c, is:

```
/*
Copyright 1994, 1995 Louis Baker, Bradley Smith, Anthony
Giancola. All rights reserved.
*/

/* Message passing library - generic
*/

#ifdef MYMPI
/* My MPI Implementation */

/* Typedefs */
typedef int MPI_Datatype;
typedef int MPI_Comm;
typedef int MPI_Op;

typedef struct tagMPI_Status
       {
       int source, tag;
       int count;
       } MPI_Status;

typedef struct tagMPI_Request
       {
       MPI_Status status;
       MPI_Datatype datatype;
       int is_send;
       char *buf;
       int msgid;
       } MPI_Comm_request;

/* Defines */
#if defined(MYMPI)
#define MPI_CHAR                      (MPI_Datatype) 1
```

```
#define MPI_SHORT                    (MPI_Datatype) 2
#define MPI_INT                      (MPI_Datatype) 3
#define MPI_LONG                     (MPI_Datatype) 4
#define MPI_UNSIGNED_CHAR            (MPI_Datatype) 5
#define MPI_UNSIGNED_SHORT           (MPI_Datatype) 6
#define MPI_UNSIGNED        (MPI_Datatype) 7
#define MPI_UNSIGNED_LONG            (MPI_Datatype) 8
#define MPI_FLOAT                    (MPI_Datatype) 9
#define MPI_DOUBLE                   (MPI_Datatype) 10
#ifndef PVM        /* PVM LONG DOUBLE not supported */
#define MPI_LONG_DOUBLE              (MPI_Datatype) 11
#endif
#define MPI_BYTE            (MPI_Datatype) 12
#endif


/* Reduction operations - only a handful implemented under
PVM */
#define MPI_MAX   (MPI_Op) 1
#define MPI_MIN    (MPI_Op) 2
#define MPI_SUM (MPI_Op) 3
#define MPI_PROD (MPI_Op) 4

#ifndef PVM
#define MPI_BAND (MPI_Op) 5
#endif
/* Note - other reduction opss are defined but we don't use
them! */

/* Error returns */
#define MPI_SUCCESS 0
#define MPI_FAILURE -1

/* Random source/tags for receives */
#define MPI_PROCNULL (-2)     /* No send */
#define MPI_ANY_SOURCE       (-1)
```

```
#define MPI_ANY_TAG    (-1)

#define MPI_SYS_TAG 16300
#define BARRIER_MSG_TAG (MPI_SYS_TAG+1)
#define REDUCE_MSG_TAG (MPI_SYS_TAG+2)

/* Default universal communications channel */
#define MPI_COMM_WORLD (MPI_Comm) 0


void _MPI_Op(void *b1, void *b2, int count,MPI_Datatype
datatype, MPI_Op op);

/* Basic environment operations */
int MPI_Init(int* argc, char*** argv);
int MPI_Comm_size(MPI_Comm comm, int *size);
int MPI_Comm_rank(MPI_Comm comm, int *rank);
int MPI_Abort(MPI_Comm comm, int errcode);
int MPI_Finalize(void);

/* Basic send and receive */
int MPI_Send(void *buf, int count, MPI_Datatype datatype,
      int dest, int tag, MPI_Comm comm);
int MPI_Recv(void *buf, int count, MPI_Datatype datatype,int
source,
      int tag, MPI_Comm comm, MPI_Status *status);

/* Non-blocking send and receive */
int MPI_Isend(void *buf, int count, MPI_Datatype datatype,
      int dest, int tag, MPI_Comm comm, MPI_Comm_request
*request);
int MPI_Irecv(void *buf, int count, MPI_Datatype datatype,
      int source, int tag, MPI_Comm comm,
MPI_Comm_request *request);
int MPI_Wait(MPI_Comm_request *request, MPI_Status
*status);
```

```
int MPI_Test(MPI_Comm_request *request, MPI_Status
*status);

/* Probes */
int MPI_Iprobe(int source, int tag, MPI_Comm comm, int *flag,
     MPI_Status *status);

/* Trivial comm status */
int MPI_Get_source(MPI_Status status, int *source);
int MPI_Get_tag(MPI_Status status, int *tag);
int MPI_Get_count(MPI_Status* status, MPI_Datatype datatype,
     int *count);

/* Fundamental Synchronization */
int MPI_Barrier(MPI_Comm comm);
int MPI_Reduce(void *sendbuf, void *recvbuf, int count,
     MPI_Datatype datatype, MPI_Op op, int root,
     MPI_Comm comm);


#ifdef PVM

#include "pvm3.h"

/* MPI - to PVM interface */
#define PVM_SOURCE(source)
     ((source==MPI_ANY_SOURCE)?-1:PVM_tid[source])

int PVM_Init(char *name, int n);          /* Spawns n processes */
int PVM_Nproc(void);     /* Returns number of processors */
int PVM_Rank(void);      /* Returns this proc's id */
void PVM_Abort(int errcode);   /* Prints message and kills
              everyone */
int PVM_Send(void *buf, int count, MPI_Datatype data_type,
     int *dests, int ndest,int tag);  /* Generic blocking send */
int PVM_Receive(void *buf, int count, MPI_Datatype data_type,
```

```
        int source, int tag, MPI_Status *status, int *bufid);
                /* Generic blocking receive */
int PVM_Unpack(int buf_id,void *buf, int count,
        MPI_Datatype data_type,int source, MPI_Status *status);
                /* Unpacks PVM buffer */
int PVM_Pack(void *buf, int count, MPI_Datatype data_type);
void PVM_GetStatus(int buf_id,  int count,
        MPI_Datatype datatype, int source, MPI_Status *status);
                /* Grab status on buffer */
int PVM_Isend(void *buf, int count, MPI_Datatype data_type,
        int dest, int tag, MPI_Comm_request *request);
                /* Non blocking send (fake) */
int PVM_Irecv(void *buf, int count, MPI_Datatype datatype,
        int source, int tag, MPI_Comm_request *request);
int PVM_Wait(MPI_Comm_request *request,
        MPI_Status *status);
int PVM_Test(MPI_Comm_request *request,
        MPI_Status *status);
int PVM_Probe(int source, int tag, int *flag,
        MPI_Status *status);
int PVM_SizeDataType(MPI_Datatype dt);

#endif /* PVM */

#ifdef PGON_MSG
/* Paragon message passing calls (native) */
/* Initialize n copies of the named process */
int PGON_Init(int n, int argc, char **argv);
int PGON_Rank();
int PVM_Nproc();
void PGON_Abort(int errcode);
int PGON_Send(void *buf, int count, MPI_Datatype data_type,
        int *dest, int ndest, int tag);
int PGON_Receive(void *buf, int count, int data_type,
        int source, int tag, MPI_Status *status);
int PGON_Isend(void *buf, int count, MPI_Datatype data_type,
```

```
        int dest, int tag, MPI_Comm_request *request);
int PGON_Irecv(void *buf, int count, MPI_Datatype data_type,
        int source, int tag, MPI_Comm_request *request);
int PGON_Wait(MPI_Comm_request *request,
        MPI_Status *status);
int PGON_Test(MPI_Comm_request *request,
        MPI_Status *status);
int PGON_Probe(int source, int tag, int *flag,
        MPI_Status *status);
#endif /* PGON_MSG */

#ifdef MPL_MSG
/* Paragon message passing calls (native) */
/* Initialize n copies of the named process */
int MPL_Init(int n, int argc, char **argv);
int MPL_Rank();
int PVM_Nproc();
void MPL_Abort(int errcode);
int MPL_Send(void *buf, int count, MPI_Datatype data_type,
        int *dest, int ndest, int tag);
int MPL_Receive(void *buf, int count, int data_type, int source,
        int tag, MPI_Status *status);
int MPL_Isend(void *buf, int count, MPI_Datatype data_type,
        int dest, int tag, MPI_Comm_request *request);
int MPL_Irecv(void *buf, int count, MPI_Datatype data_type,
        int source, int tag, MPI_Comm_request *request);
int MPL_Wait(MPI_Comm_request *request,
        MPI_Status *status);
int MPL_Test(MPI_Comm_request *request,
        MPI_Status *status);
int MPL_Probe(int source, int tag, int *flag,
        MPI_Status *status);
#endif /* MPL_MSG */

#else  /* MYMPI */
```

```
#include "mpi.h"
#define MPI_Comm_request MPI_Request

#endif /* MYMPI */
```

Figure 7.2: msg.h.

The user specifies in a configuration header file his choice of message-passing system via a define statement. Thus **#define MYMPI** is included to specify the use of the layered implementation over another message-passing system; otherwise it will be assumed an MPI library is directly used. In the former case, define **PVM**, **PGON_MSG**, or **MPL_MSG** depending upon the lower-level messaging scheme used: PVM, the Intel Paragon's NX system, or the IBM MPL library for the SP-2.

The executable code in file *msg.c* consists of "wrappers" that support the MPI calling syntax, and invoke the appropriate programs in PVM, NX, etc. Most of the functions are therefore rather simple and require little comment. The **MPI_Barrier** function, which performs the synchronization of all processes, is implemented simply by having all nodes report their arrival at the synchronization point to the rank zero (root or "master") node, which then instructs them to proceed after it has received messages from all. Note that the **MPI_Reduce** uses the barrier function for synchronization; "slave" nodes cannot proceed until informed by the master, via the barrier, that it has finished the Reduce operation. Furthermore, the initiation of parallel programs on the CM-5, Intel Paragon, and Cray T3D is different from other machines, as these machines have a "front-end" or host machine which distributes the tasks to the processor nodes; on other architectures, e. g., the IBM SP-2, the program begins execution as a single task on one of the nodes. **MPI_Init** takes care of this. The include file *all.h* is simply a set of include statements for all the header files. The file *msg.c* is:

```
/*
Copyright 1994,1995 Louis Baker, Bradley Smith, Anthony
Giancola. All rights reserved.
```

```
*/
/* Message passing routines -
 * Operating System Dependent!
 */

#include "all.h"

#ifdef LAST_COMM
extern int LastSendDest, LastSendTag, LastRecvSource,
LastRecvTag;
#endif

#if defined(MYMPI)
int
MPI_Init(int* argc, char*** argv)
{

#if defined(PVM) || defined(PGON_MSG) || defined(MPL_MSG)
 int nproc;
 /* Determine number of processes to spawn, and start PVM */
 nproc = ParseSpawnArg(*argc, *argv);

 /* CM5 and PGON use slaves */
#ifdef PVM
#ifdef USE_SLAVE
 return(PVM_Init("slave", nproc));
#else
 return(PVM_Init((*argv)[0],nproc));
#endif
#endif /* PVM */

#ifdef PGON_MSG
 return(PGON_Init(nproc, *argc, *argv));
#endif

#ifdef MPL_MSG
```

```
 return(MPL_Init(nproc, *argc, *argv));
#endif

#else
 return(MPI_SUCCESS);
#endif
}


int
MPI_Comm_size(MPI_Comm comm, int *size)
{
#ifdef PVM
 *size = PVM_Nproc();
#else
#ifdef MPL_MSG
 *size = MPL_Nproc();
#else
#ifdef PGON_MSG
 *size = PGON_Nproc();
#else
 *size = 1;
#endif /* PGON_MSG */
#endif /* MPL_MSG */
#endif /* PVM */
 return(MPI_SUCCESS);
}

int
MPI_Comm_rank(MPI_Comm comm, int *rank)
{
#ifdef PVM
 *rank = PVM_Rank();
#else
#ifdef PGON_MSG
 *rank = PGON_Rank();
```

```
#else
#Ifdef MPL_MSG
 *rank = MPL_Rank();
#else
 *rank = 0;
#endif /* PGON_MSG */
#endif /* MPL_MSG */
#endif /* PVM */
 return(MPI_SUCCESS);
}

int
MPI_Abort(MPI_Comm comm, int errcode)
{
#ifdef LAST_COMM
 UserMessage("Last send was to dest=%d tag=%d\nLast recv
was from=%d tag=%d\n", LastSendDest, LastSendTag,
       LastRecvSource, LastRecvTag);
#endif
#ifdef PVM
 PVM_Abort(errcode);
#endif
#ifdef PGON_MSG
 PGON_Abort(errcode);
#endif
#ifdef MPL_MSG
 MPL_Abort(errcode);
#endif
 return(MPI_SUCCESS);
}

int
MPI_Finalize()
{
#ifdef LAST_COMM
```

```
 UserMessage("Last send was to dest=%d tag=%d\nLast recv
was from=%d tag=%d\n",  LastSendDest, LastSendTag,
       LastRecvSource, LastRecvTag);
#endif
#ifdef TRACE
 EndTrace();
#endif
#ifdef PVM
 pvm_exit();
#endif
 return(MPI_SUCCESS);
}

int
MPI_Send(void *buf, int count, MPI_Datatype datatype,
       int dest, int tag, MPI_Comm comm)
{
 int ret;

#ifdef TRACE
StartSendTrace(tag,count,1);
#endif

#ifdef PVM
 ret = PVM_Send(buf, count, datatype, &dest, 1, tag);
#else
#ifdef PGON_MSG
 ret = PGON_Send(buf, count, datatype, &dest, 1, tag);
#else
#ifdef MPL_MSG
 ret = MPL_Send(buf, count, datatype, &dest, 1, tag);
#else
 ret = MPI_SUCCESS;
#endif /* MPL_MSG */
#endif /* PGON_MSG */
#endif /* PVM */
```

```
#ifdef TRACE
StopSendTrace(tag);
#endif

 return(ret);
}

int
MPI_Recv(void *buf, int count, MPI_Datatype datatype,
        int source, int tag, MPI_Comm comm,
        MPI_Status *status)
{
 int ret, bufid;

#ifdef TRACE
StartRecvTrace(tag);
#endif

#ifdef PVM
 ret = PVM_Receive(buf, count, datatype, source, tag,
        status, &bufid);
#else
#ifdef PGON_MSG
 ret = PGON_Receive(buf, count, datatype, source, tag, status);
#else
#ifdef MPL_MSG
 ret = MPL_Receive(buf, count, datatype, source, tag, status);
#else
 ret = MPI_SUCCESS;
#endif
#endif
#endif

#ifdef TRACE
StopRecvTrace(tag,status->count);
```

```
#endif

 return(ret);
}

int
MPI_Isend(void *buf, int count, MPI_Datatype datatype, int
dest,
        int tag, MPI_Comm comm, MPI_Comm_request *request)
{
#ifdef PVM
 return(PVM_Isend(buf, count, datatype, dest, tag, request));
#else
#ifdef MPL_MSG
 return(MPL_Isend(buf, count, datatype, dest, tag, request));
#else
#ifdef PGON_MSG
 return(PGON_Isend(buf, count, datatype, dest, tag, request));
#else
 return(MPI_SUCCESS);
#endif
#endif
#endif
}

int
MPI_Irecv(void *buf, int count, MPI_Datatype datatype,
        int source, int tag, MPI_Comm comm,
            MPI_Comm_request *request)
{
#ifdef PVM
 return(PVM_Irecv(buf, count, datatype, source, tag, request));
#else
#ifdef MPL_MSG
 return(MPL_Irecv(buf, count, datatype, source, tag, request));
#else
```

```
 return(MPI_SUCCESS);
#endif
#endif
}

int
MPI_Wait(MPI_Comm_request *request, MPI_Status *status)
{
 int ret;

#ifdef PVM
 ret = PVM_Wait(request,status);
#else
#ifdef MPL_MSG
 ret = MPL_Wait(request,status);
#else
#ifdef PGON_MSG
 ret = PGON_Wait(request,status);
#else
 ret = MPI_SUCCESS;
#endif
#endif
#endif

 return(ret);
}

int
MPI_Test(MPI_Comm_request *request, MPI_Status *status)
{
#ifdef PVM
 return(PVM_Test(request,status));
#else
#ifdef MPL_MSG
 return(MPL_Test(request,status));
#else
```

```
#ifdef PGON_MSG
 return(PGON_Test(request,status));
#else
 return(TRUE);
#endif
#endif
#endif
}

int
MPI_Iprobe(int source, int tag, MPI_Comm comm, int *flag,
       MPI_Status *status)
{
#ifdef PVM
 return(PVM_Probe(source, tag, flag, status));
#else
#ifdef PGON_MSG
 return(PGON_Probe(source, tag, flag, status));
#else
#ifdef MPL_MSG
 return(MPL_Probe(source, tag, flag, status));
#else
 *flag = FALSE;
 return(MPI_SUCCESS);
#endif
#endif
#endif
}

int
MPI_Get_source(MPI_Status status, int *source)
{
 return(*source = status.source);
}

int
```

```
MPI_Get_tag(MPI_Status status, int *tag)
{
 return(*tag = status.tag);
}

int
MPI_Get_count(MPI_Status* status, MPI_Datatype datatype,
        int *count)
{
 return(*count = status->count);
}

int
MPI_Barrier(MPI_Comm comm)
{
 int rank, nproc, dummy,i;
 MPI_Status status;


 /* For right now - do this with generic sends and receives */
 MPI_Comm_size(comm, &nproc);
 MPI_Comm_rank(comm, &rank);
 if(nproc <= 1)
        return(MPI_SUCCESS);

 /* Everyone send to rank zero */
 if(rank > 0)
        {
        MPI_Send(&rank, 1, MPI_INT, 0, BARRIER_MSG_TAG,
                comm);
        MPI_Recv(&dummy,1,MPI_INT, 0, BARRIER_MSG_TAG,
                comm, &status);
        }
 else
        {
        /* Zero'th processor collects messages */
```

```
        for(i=1; i<nproc; i++)
                MPI_Recv(&dummy,1, MPI_INT,
                MPI_ANY_SOURCE, BARRIER_MSG_TAG,
                    comm, &status);
        /* Now let everyone proceed */
        for(i=1; i<nproc; i++)
                MPI_Send(&rank, 1, MPI_INT, i,
                        BARRIER_MSG_TAG, comm);
        }

 return(MPI_SUCCESS);
 }



/* A very limited implementation ! - only a few ops */
int
MPI_Reduce(void *sendbuf, void *recvbuf, int count,
MPI_Datatype datatype,
        MPI_Op op, int root, MPI_Comm comm)
{
 int rank, nproc, i;
 void *buf;
 MPI_Status status;

 /* For right now - do this with generic sends and receives */
 MPI_Comm_size(comm, &nproc);
 MPI_Comm_rank(comm, &rank);
 if(nproc <= 1)
        return(MPI_SUCCESS);
 if(rank != root)
        {
   MPI_Send(sendbuf, count, datatype, root,
REDUCE_MSG_TAG, comm);
        }
 else
        {
```

```
        /* Master */
        buf = New(count * _MPI_SizeDataType(datatype));
        memcpy(recvbuf, sendbuf, count,
               _MPI_SizeDataType(datatype));

        for(i=1; i<nproc; i++)
                {
                MPI_Recv(buf,count, datatype,
                MPI_ANY_SOURCE, REDUCE_MSG_TAG,
                      comm, &status);
                _MPI_Op(recvbuf, buf, count, datatype,op);
                }
    free(buf);
        }
/* Need to wait for master before continuing */
MPI_Barrier(comm);
return(MPI_SUCCESS);
}


void
_MPI_Op(void *b1, void *b2, int count,MPI_Datatype datatype,
MPI_Op op)
{
 int i;
 float *f1,*f2;
 double *d1, *d2;
 int *i1,*i2;

 f1 = (float *) b1;    f2 = (float *) b2;
 d1 = (double *) b1;       d2 = (double *) b2;
 i1 = (int *) b1;          i2 = (int *) b2;

 for(i=0; i<count; i++)
        {
        switch(datatype)
```

```
            {
        case MPI_FLOAT:
            switch(op)
                {
                case MPI_MAX:
                    f1[i] = MAX(f1[i], f2[i]);
                    break;
                case MPI_MIN:
                    f1[i] = MIN(f1[i], f2[i]);
                    break;
                case MPI_SUM:
                    f1[i] += f2[i];
                    break;
                case MPI_PROD:
                    f1[i] *= f2[i];
                    break;
                default:
                    ReportError("MPI:Unsupported
MPI_FLOAT reduction operation\n",FALSE);
        break;
                }
    break;
    case MPI_DOUBLE:
                switch(op)
                {
                case MPI_MAX:
                    d1[i] = MAX(d1[i], d2[i]);
                    break;
                case MPI_MIN:
                    d1[i] = MIN(d1[i], d2[i]);
                    break;
                case MPI_SUM:
                    d1[i] += d2[i];
                    break;
                case MPI_PROD:
                    d1[i] *= d2[i];
```

```
                                        break;
                            default:
                                    ReportError("MPI:Unsupported
MPI_DOUBLE reduction operation\n",FALSE);
                                    break;
                        }
                break;
        case MPI_INT:
        case MPI_UNSIGNED:
                switch(op)
                        {
                        case MPI_MAX:
                                i1[i] = MAX(i1[i], i2[i]);
                                break;
        case MPI_MIN:
                                i1[i] = MIN(i1[i], i2[i]);
                                break;
                        case MPI_SUM:
                                i1[i] += i2[i];
                                break;
                        case MPI_PROD:
                                i1[i] *= i2[i];
                                break;
                        default:
                                ReportError("MPI:Unsupported
MPI_INT reduction operation\n",FALSE);
                                break;
                        }
                break;
        default:
                ReportError("MPI: Unsupported type in
MPI_Reduce()\n", FALSE);
                break;
    } /* End switch */
  }
}
```

#endif /* MYMPI */

Figure 7.3: msg.c.

The variables **TRACE** and **LAST_COMM** are defined for debugging purposes as required.

Support routines are contained in two files, send.c and mpi_pvm.c Send.c contains a number of the higher-level support routines. The variable **PVM_BUF** is used for machine-dependent optimization. If it is defined, then routines **PVM_Pack** and **PVM_Unpack** are used; otherwise, memcpy is used to move data between buffers. The variable **NB_SEND**, if defined, invokes the use of nonblocking sends, via the routines **NBSend**, **NBFree**, **GetNBBuf**. This too may be set as appropriate for best system performance. The variable **PRINTROOT** is for the diagnostic printing functions. If defined, all printing is routed to the root processor, which prints to a single file. Otherwise, the diagnostic information is printed locally for each processor.

Send.c contains a set of high-level routines to manage data buffers, as well as a number of other utility functions are contained in the file. As will be illustrated later in this chapter, a message buffer is first created with **NewMsgBuf**, data is packed into it by the appropriate calls (**PackBuf**, and **PackString**), then **SendBuf** and **RecBuf** are used to communicate the data. The receiver then uses **UnPackBuf** or **UnPackString** as appropriate. These buffer managment functions simplify sending large blocks of data; their use is illustrated in the section of this chapter titled: *Example of the Use of Buffered Messaging Routines*. **ParseSpawnArg** is used to determine the number of tasks to spawn, given the command line input. If one of the arguments is of the form, say, -16, then sixteen processors (including the root) are to be used. The functions **OnePrintString** and **PrintToLog** are useful for printing diagnostics. The function **GetCurDirectory** is used to determine the directory (path) name for log files.

The header file *send.h* is given :

```c
/* Our own message passing functions - based on mpi
 * Brad Smith
 */

#define PRINTROOT        /* Only print from the root node */

/* Code to manage non-blocking sends */
#ifdef NB_SEND
#define NB_BUF_SIZE 128
typedef struct tagNBSend{
        char *buf;
        MPI_Comm_request request;
        struct tagNBSend *next;
        char smallbuf[NB_BUF_SIZE];
        } NBSend;

typedef NBSend *PNBSend;
extern PNBSend NBPending, NBFree;

void FlushAllPending();
PNBSend GetNBBuf(void *buf, int count,
        MPI_Datatype datatype);
#endif /* NB_SEND */


/* Global variables and functions - Communications */
extern int Rank, NProc;
extern MPI_Comm Comm;
extern int *AllDest;
extern int *AllDestButMe;

/* Define Our FLOAT type */
#ifdef DOUBLE_PRECISION
#define MPI_MYFLOAT MPI_DOUBLE
#else
#define MPI_MYFLOAT MPI_FLOAT
```

```
#endif

/* Initialize MPI */
void InitMPISystem(int argc, char **argv, char *logfile, int
quiet);
void ExitMPISystem(void);

/* Extensions - used to parse -s spawn argument */
int ParseSpawnArg(int argc, char **argv);

#if !defined(MYMPI)
  int _MPI_SizeDataType(MPI_Datatype datatype);
#endif

/* Message buffers */
#define BUF_ALLOC 4096          /*BUFFER ALLOCATION
INCREMENT */
typedef struct tagMsgBuffer
        {
        int count, nalloc;    /* Number of items, and number
allocated */
        int nused;            /* Number used - on receive */
        char *buf;            /* Buffer */
        MPI_Datatype datatype;  /* Datatype */
        int datasize;         /* Datasize */
        BOOL is_send;         /* Send or receive buffer */
#define SEND_BUF 1
#define RECV_BUF 0

        int bufid;               /* Buf id for using direct PVM
                                    buffering of data */
        }MsgBuf;

typedef MsgBuf *PMsgBuf;

/* Global buffers */
```

```
extern PMsgBuf GSendBuf, GRecvBuf;

/* Buffer allocation/destruction */
PMsgBuf NewMsgBuf(BOOL is_send, int size);
void DeleteMsgBuf(PMsgBuf mbuf);
void SizeMsgBuf(PMsgBuf mbuf, int new_size);

/* Global (default) buffers! */

/* Buffered send and receive operations */
int PackBuf(PMsgBuf msgbuf, void *buf, int count,
      MPI_Datatype datatype);          /* Returns actual count */
int PackString(PMsgBuf msgbuf, char *string);
int SendBuf(PMsgBuf mbuf, int *destarray, int destcount,
      int tag, MPI_Comm comm);
int BroadcastBuf(PMsgBuf mbuf, int tag, MPI_Comm comm);

/* Buffered receive operations */
int UnPackBuf(PMsgBuf msgbuf, void *buf, int count);
      /* Returns actual count */
int UnPackString(PMsgBuf msgbuf, char *string, int max_len);
int RecvBuf(PMsgBuf msg_buf, int count,
      MPI_Datatype datatype, int source, int tag,
          MPI_Comm comm, MPI_Status *status);

/* Simple defines */
#define PackIVector(mbuf,pivec) PackBuf(mbuf,pivec, DIM,
      MPI_INT)
#define PackVector(mbuf,pvec) PackBuf(mbuf,pvec, DIM,
      MPI_MYFLOAT)
#define UnPackIVector(mbuf,pivec) UnPackBuf(mbuf,pivec,
      DIM)
#define UnPackVector(mbuf,pvec) UnPackBuf(mbuf,pvec, DIM)
#define PackTensor(mbuf, ptens) PackBuf(mbuf, ptens, 2*DIM,
      MPI_MYFLOAT)
#define UnPackTensor(mbuf, ptens) UnPackBuf(mbuf, ptens,
```

    2*DIM)

```
/* Single print */
void OnePrintString(char *str);
void PrintToLog(char *s, int rank);
void GetCurDirectory(char *s);
```

Figure 7.4: Send.h.

Table 7.2 lists the functions contained in file send.c.

| Table 7.2: Principal functions in send.c ||
Function	Purpose
ExitMPISystem	flush pending messages, finalizeMPI
InitMPISystem	initialize SPMD mode
NewMsgBuf	create message buffer
SizeMsgBuf	allocate/reallocate message buffer
DeleteMsgBuf	delete message buffer
SendBuf	send data in a buffer
RecvBuf	receive data
PackBuf	put data into a buffer for sending
UnPackBuf	unpack received data
FlushAllPending	flush pending messages at end
GetNBBuf	allocate buffer for non-blocking send
Pack String	pack string into buffer
UnPackString	get received string
ParseSpawnArg	parse command line
OnePrintString	print string at single location
PrintToLog	print string to log file
GetCurDirectory	get directory for log file at master proc.

ExitMPISystem and **InitMPISystem** support clean termination and initiation. The latter allocates buffers and creates a logfile if appropriate. The former will flush pending sends (if non-blocking sends are used), and then calls **MPI_Finalize**.

ParseSpawnArg is used to determine the number of processes requested by the user in the command line. If the (SPMD) program is named bob, then running: bob -s 32 may be used to request that 32 processors be used. The standard C command line arguments **argc** and **argv** are supplied to the main program, which can use **ParseSpawnArg** to return the requested count. Other command line arguments may be present, and, if so, are ignored by this function.

OnePrintString and **PrintToLog** may be used to maintain a log file; the former uses the latter to print strings. The variables **PRINT_FROM_ROOT** and **SPLIT_LOG** control the operation. The former variable is defined to instruct processors to print by sending messages to the root, which writes the strings to the file. The latter variable, if defined, instructs processors to maintain individual log files. Obviously, both should not be defined; **PrintToLog** will do nothing if they are.

The function **GetCurDirectory** uses the UNIX system call **getcwd()** to determine the current directory.

The variable **NB_SEND**, if defined, causes the buffered messaging routines to use non-blocking sends. In this case, the responsibility is on the code in send.c to ensure that the buffered data has been sent before the buffer is overwritten. **SendBuf** does so by allocating buffers via **GetNBBuf**, one per recipient. The code makes use of broadcast functions if appropriate and available. The various buffer management routines are otherwise straightforward, and use **New**, **ReAlloc**, etc., as defined in *os.c*, which is presented later in this chapter.

The *send.c* file, which implements these functions, is:

```
/*
Copyright 1994,1995 Louis Baker, Bradley Smith, Anthony
Giancola. All rights reserved.
*/
/* Buffered send and receive functions */

#include "all.h"
```

```c
/* Global variables */
int Rank, NProc;
MPI_Comm Comm;
int *AllDest;
int *AllDestButMe;
int Quiet=FALSE;

char LogFile[256];
static int OutFile;

#ifdef LAST_COMM
/* Record status of last communication and report it on
        break */
int LastSendDest, LastSendTag;
int LastRecvSource, LastRecvTag;
#endif

/* Global message buffers */
PMsgBuf GSendBuf, GRecvBuf;

void
ExitMPISystem()
{
#ifdef NB_SEND
 FlushAllPending();
#endif
 MPI_Finalize();
}

void
InitMPISystem(int argc, char **argv, char *logfile, int quiet)
{
 int i,j=0;
 char curdir[256];
 Quiet = quiet;
```

```
 fprintf(stderr, "Hello World\n");
 {
   int i;
   for(i=0; i<argc; i++) {
     fprintf(stderr, "i=%d argv=%s\n", i, argv[i]);
   }
 }
 fprintf(stderr, "Hello World\n");
 if(MPI_Init(&argc,&argv) != MPI_SUCCESS)
        ReportError("Can't initialize MPI!\n", TRUE);
 Comm = MPI_COMM_WORLD;
 MPI_Comm_size(Comm, &NProc);
 MPI_Comm_rank(Comm, &Rank);

 /* Set up an array that is all destinations */
 AllDest = (int *) New(sizeof(int)*NProc);
 AllDestButMe = (int *) New(sizeof(int)*NProc);
 j=0;
 for(i=0; i<NProc; i++)
        {
        AllDest[i] = i;
        if(i != Rank)
                AllDestButMe[j++] = i;
        }

 /* Allocate our own send and receive buffers - global */
 GSendBuf = NewMsgBuf(SEND_BUF, BUF_ALLOC);
 GRecvBuf = NewMsgBuf(RECV_BUF, BUF_ALLOC);

 if(logfile)
        {
        GetCurDirectory(curdir);
        sprintf(LogFile, "%s/%s", curdir, logfile);
        OutFile = -1;
#ifndef SPLIT_LOG
```

```
        if(Rank == 0 )
                {
                if(access(logfile, 0) == 0)
                        unlink(logfile);
                OutFile = open(logfile, O_APPEND | O_CREAT |
                        O_WRONLY, 0440);
                }
#endif
#ifdef SPLIT_LOG
        sprintf(LogFile, "%s/%s.%d", curdir, logfile, Rank);
        OutFile = open(LogFile, O_CREAT | O_WRONLY, 0440);
#endif
        }
 else
        LogFile[0] = NULLC;
}


PMsgBuf
NewMsgBuf(BOOL is_send, int nalloc)
{
 PMsgBuf mbuf;
 mbuf = (PMsgBuf) New(sizeof(MsgBuf));
 mbuf->count = mbuf->nused = 0;
 mbuf->nalloc = 0;
 mbuf->is_send = is_send;
 mbuf->datatype = MPI_INT;
 mbuf->datasize = sizeof(int);
 mbuf->buf = NULL;
#ifndef PVM_BUF
 SizeMsgBuf(mbuf, nalloc);
#else
 mbuf->bufid = -1;
#endif
 return(mbuf);
}
```

```
void
SizeMsgBuf(PMsgBuf mbuf, int nalloc)
{
 if(mbuf->nalloc <= 0)
        {
        mbuf->nalloc = nalloc;
        mbuf->buf = (char *) New(nalloc);
        return;
        }
 mbuf->buf = (char *) ReAlloc(mbuf->buf, nalloc);
 mbuf->nalloc = nalloc;
}

void
DeleteMsgBuf(PMsgBuf mbuf)
{
#ifndef PVM_BUF
 if(mbuf->nalloc > 0)
        Delete(mbuf->buf);
#else
 if(mbuf->bufid >= 0)
        pvm_freebuf(mbuf->bufid);
#endif
 Delete(mbuf);
}

int
PackBuf(PMsgBuf mbuf, void *buf, int count,
        MPI_Datatype datatype)
{

 if(!mbuf)
        mbuf = GSendBuf;
 if(!mbuf->is_send)
        {
```

```
        ReportError("Packbuf called on Receive type buffer!-
ignored\n", FALSE);
        return(0);
        }
 if(mbuf->count > 0 && mbuf->datatype != datatype)
        {
            ReportError("PackBuf called with bad datatype -
ignoring Pack call!\n", FALSE);
            Debug("mbuf->datatype = %d, datatype = %d\n",
                mbuf->datatype, datatype );
            return(0);
            }


 if(mbuf->count <= 0)
        {
        mbuf->datatype = datatype;
        mbuf->datasize = _MPI_SizeDataType(datatype);
#ifdef PVM_BUF
        /* Free and create a new buffer */
        if(mbuf->bufid >= 0)
                pvm_freebuf(mbuf->bufid);
        mbuf->bufid = pvm_mkbuf(PvmDataDefault);
        pvm_setsbuf(mbuf->bufid);
#endif
        }

#ifdef PVM_BUF /* Set our pvm-buffer! */
 if(pvm_getsbuf() != mbuf->bufid)
        {
        pvm_setsbuf(mbuf->bufid);
        }
#endif

#ifdef PVM_BUF
 PVM_Pack(buf, count, datatype);
#else
```

```
/* Check for enough room in buffer */
if(mbuf->nalloc < (mbuf->count + count) * mbuf->datasize)
        {
        /* Enlarge send buffer */
        SizeMsgBuf(mbuf, MAX(mbuf->nalloc+BUF_ALLOC,
                (mbuf->count + count) * mbuf->datasize) );
        }
/* Copy the data over */
memcpy(&mbuf->buf[mbuf->count * mbuf->datasize], buf,
        count*mbuf->datasize);
#endif
 mbuf->count += count;
 return(count);
}

#ifdef NB_SEND
PNBSend NBFree=NULL;
PNBSend NBPending = NULL;
#endif

/* Actually send the buffer */
int
SendBuf(PMsgBuf mbuf, int *destarray, int destcount, int tag,
        MPI_Comm comm)
{
 int i,ret;
 char errmsg[120];
#ifdef NB_SEND
 PNBSend nbs;
#endif
 if(!mbuf)
        mbuf = GSendBuf;
 if(!mbuf->is_send)
        {
        ReportError("SendBuf called on Receive type buffer!-
ignored\n", FALSE);
```

```
        return(0);
        }
  if(mbuf->count <= 0)
            {
            sprintf(errmsg,"Send with count=0?: count=%d
type=%d dest=%d tag=%d\n",
                mbuf->count, mbuf->datatype, destarray[0],
tag);
            ReportError(errmsg, TRUE);
            }

/* Code to manage non-blocking sends */
#ifdef NB_SEND
 for(i=0; i<destcount; i++)
        {
        nbs=GetNBBuf(mbuf->buf, mbuf->count,
            mbuf->datatype);
        ret=MPI_Isend(nbs->buf, mbuf->count,
            mbuf->datatype, destarray[i], tag,
                comm,&nbs->request);
        if(ret != MPI_SUCCESS)
            {
            sprintf(errmsg,"Send failed: count=%d type=%d
dest=%d tag=%d\n",
                mbuf->count, mbuf->datatype,
                    destarray[i], tag);
            ReportError(errmsg, TRUE);
            }
        }
#else /* NOT NB_SEND */
#ifdef PGON_MSG
 /* Optimization - take advantage of the PGON
 * multicast operation by using the mult-send features
 * of the PGON interface */
 ret= PGON_Send(mbuf->buf, mbuf->count, mbuf->datatype,
        destarray, destcount, tag);
```

```
#else
#ifndef PVM
 /* Under normal MPI - do multiple sends */
 for(i=0; i<destcount; i++)
        {
        ret=MPI_Send(mbuf->buf,mbuf->count,mbuf->datatype,
                destarray[i], tag, comm);
        if(ret != MPI_SUCCESS)
                {
                sprintf(errmsg,"Send failed: count=%d type=%d
dest=%d tag=%d\n",
                        mbuf->count, mbuf->datatype,
                                destarray[i], tag);
                ReportError(errmsg, TRUE);
                }
        }
#else
 /* Optimization - take advantage of the PVM
  * multicast operation by using the mult-send features
  * of the PVM interface */
#ifdef TRACE
 StartSendTrace(tag, mbuf->count, destcount);
#endif

#ifdef PVM_BUF
 ret = PVM_Send(NULL, mbuf->bufid, mbuf->datatype,
destarray, destcount, tag);
#else
 ret= PVM_Send(mbuf->buf, mbuf->count, mbuf->datatype,
destarray, destcount, tag);
#endif

#ifdef TRACE
 StopSendTrace(tag);
#endif
#endif
```

```
#endif /* PGON_MSG */
#endif /* NOT NB_SEND */
#ifdef LAST_COMM
 LastSendDest = destarray[0];
 LastSendTag = tag;
#endif

 mbuf->count = 0;
 return(ret);
}

#ifdef NB_SEND
void
FlushAllPending()
{
 PNBSend p;
 MPI_Status status;
 int count=0;

 for(p = NBPending; p!= NULL; p=p->next)
        {
#ifdef PGON
        MPI_Wait(&p->request, &status);
#endif
        ++count;
        }
 Debug("Count of leftover sends is %d\n", count);
}

PNBSend
GetNBBuf(void *buf, int count, MPI_Datatype datatype)
{
 int n;
 PNBSend p,last;
 MPI_Status status;
```

```
n = count * _MPI_SizeDataType(datatype);

if(NBPending)
      {
      /* Free the pending requests */
      last = NULL;
      for(p=NBPending; p!= NULL; p = p->next)
              {
              if(MPI_Test(&p->request, &status))
                      {
                      /* Remove it from our list */
                      if(last)
                              last->next = p->next;
                      else
                              NBPending = p->next;
                      /* Add it to the free list */
                      p->next = NBFree;
                      NBFree = p;
                      /* Free the buffer if required */
                      if(p->buf != p->smallbuf)
                              Delete(p->buf);
                      }
              else
                      last = p;
              }
      }

/* Now find a free request */
if(NBFree)
      {
      p = NBFree;
      NBFree = p->next;
      }
else
      p = (PNBSend) New(sizeof(NBSend));
```

```c
/* Create our buffer */
if(n > NB_BUF_SIZE)
        {
        p->buf = New(n);
        }
else
        p->buf = p->smallbuf;

/* Copy it */
memcpy(p->buf, buf, n);

/* Put in the pending list */
p->next = NBPending;
NBPending = p;

/* Return it */
 return(p);
}
#endif


/* Convenience function */
int
PackString(PMsgBuf mbuf, char *s)
{
 return(PackBuf(mbuf, s, strlen(s)+1, MPI_CHAR));
}

int
UnPackBuf(PMsgBuf mbuf, void *buf, int count)
{
 MPI_Status status;
 if(!mbuf)
        mbuf = GRecvBuf;
 if(mbuf->is_send)
        {
```

```
      ReportError("FATAL: UnpackBuf called on Send type
buffer!\n", TRUE);
      return(0);
      }

#ifdef PVM_BUF
 /* Set the buffer under PVM */
 if(pvm_getrbuf() != mbuf->bufid)
      {
      pvm_setrbuf(mbuf->bufid);
      }
#endif

 if(mbuf->count-mbuf->nused <= 0)
      {
      ReportError("FATAL: UnPackBuf called on empty
buffer!\n", TRUE);
      return(0);
      }

 count = MIN(mbuf->count-mbuf->nused, count);

#ifdef PVM_BUF
 PVM_Unpack(mbuf->bufid, buf, count, mbuf->datatype, Rank,
&status);
#else
 memcpy(buf, &mbuf->buf[mbuf->nused * mbuf->datasize],
count*mbuf->datasize);
#endif

 mbuf->nused += count;
 return(count);
}

int
RecvBuf(PMsgBuf mbuf, int count, MPI_Datatype datatype,
```

```
        int source, int tag, MPI_Comm comm,
        MPI_Status *status)
{
 char errmsg[120];

 if(!mbuf)
        mbuf = GRecvBuf;
 if(mbuf->is_send)
        {
        ReportError("RecvBuf called on Send type buffer!-
ignored\n", FALSE);
        return(0);
        }
 if(count <= 0)
                {
                sprintf(errmsg,"Recv with count=0?: count=%d
type=%d dest=%d tag=%d\n",
                        count, datatype, source, tag);
                ReportError(errmsg, TRUE);
                }
 mbuf->datasize = _MPI_SizeDataType(datatype);
 mbuf->datatype = datatype;
#ifdef LAST_COMM
 LastRecvSource = source;
 LastRecvTag = tag;
#endif

#ifdef PVM_BUF
 /* Do the receive from here */
 PVM_Receive(NULL, count, datatype, source, tag, status,
        &mbuf->bufid);
#else
 if(mbuf->datasize * count > mbuf->nalloc)
        {
        /* Need bigger buffer */
        SizeMsgBuf(mbuf, MAX(mbuf->nalloc + BUF_ALLOC,
```

```
                    count * mbuf->datasize));
        }

 /* Actually do a receive */
 if(MPI_Recv(mbuf->buf, count, datatype, source, tag, comm,
status) != MPI_SUCCESS)
                {
                sprintf(errmsg,"Recv Failed: count=%d type=%d
dest=%d tag=%d\n",
                        count, datatype, source, tag);
                ReportError(errmsg, TRUE);
                }
#endif
 MPI_Get_count(status, datatype,&mbuf->count);
 mbuf->nused = 0;

 return(mbuf->count);
}

int
UnPackString(PMsgBuf mbuf, char *string, int max_len)
{
 int i;
 if(!mbuf)
        mbuf = GRecvBuf;
 if(mbuf->is_send)
        {
        ReportError("UnpackBuf called on Send type buffer!-
ignored\n", FALSE);
        return(0);
        }

 for(i=mbuf->nused; i<mbuf->nused+max_len &&
        i<mbuf->count && mbuf->buf[i] != NULLC; i++)
        *string++ = mbuf->buf[i];
```

```
/* Increment by one if we have used NULLC character */
if(i<mbuf->count && mbuf->buf[i] == NULLC)
        i++;
*string = NULLC;
mbuf->nused+= i;

return(i); /* Return the string length */
}


#if defined(MYMPI)
int
_MPI_SizeDataType(MPI_Datatype datatype)
{
switch(datatype)
        {
        default:
        case MPI_INT:
        return(sizeof(int));
        case MPI_UNSIGNED:
        return(sizeof(unsigned));
        case MPI_SHORT:
        return(sizeof(short));
        case MPI_UNSIGNED_SHORT:
                return(sizeof(unsigned short));
        case MPI_LONG:
        return(sizeof(long));
        case MPI_UNSIGNED_LONG:
                return(sizeof(unsigned long));
        case MPI_BYTE:
        case MPI_CHAR:
                return(sizeof(char));
        case MPI_DOUBLE:
                return(sizeof(double));
        case MPI_FLOAT:
                return(sizeof(float));
```

```c
        }
}
#endif

int
ParseSpawnArg(int argc, char **argv)
{
 int i,n=1;

 for(i=1; i<argc; i++)
        {
        if(*argv[i] == '-' && isdigit(argv[i][1]))
                n = MAX(n, atoi(&argv[i][1]));
        if(strncmp(argv[i],"-s",2) == 0)
                {
                /* Found -s spawn argument */
                if(strlen(argv[i]) == 2)      /* Number is in
                                                    next space */
                        {
                        if(++i >= argc)
                                {
                                ReportError("Error: -s argument
should be followed by number to spawn.\n",FALSE);
                                ReportError("Defaulting to one
task.\n",FALSE);
                                }
                        else
                                n=MAX(1,atoi(argv[i]));
                        }
                else
                        n=MAX(1,atoi(&argv[i][2]));
                }
        }
 return(n);
}
```

```
/* Extension - to print a single string at a location */
void
OnePrintString(char *str)
{
 int rank,flag,nproc;
 int count;
 MPI_Status status;
 char s[1024];
 static int out;

 flag = TRUE;
 MPI_Comm_rank(MPI_COMM_WORLD, &rank);
 MPI_Comm_size(MPI_COMM_WORLD, &nproc);

#ifdef PRINT_FROM_ROOT
 if(rank != 0)
        {
        /* Write to the message */
        sprintf(s,"[%2d] %s", rank,str);
        MPI_Send(s, strlen(s)+1, MPI_CHAR, 0, STRING_TAG,
                MPI_COMM_WORLD);
#ifdef SPLIT_LOG
        PrintToLog(s,rank);
#endif
        return;
        }
 else
        {
        /* Print stuff out */
        while(flag && nproc > 1)
                {
                MPI_Iprobe(MPI_ANY_SOURCE, STRING_TAG,
                        MPI_COMM_WORLD, &flag, &status);
                if(!flag)
                        break;
```

```
                MPI_Recv(s, 1023,MPI_CHAR,
                        MPI_ANY_SOURCE,STRING_TAG,
                            MPI_COMM_WORLD, &status);
                MPI_Get_count(&status, MPI_CHAR, &count);
                s[count] = NULLC;
#ifndef SPLIT_LOG
                PrintToLog(s,rank);
#endif
                if(!Quiet)
                        printf("%s",s);
                }
        }
#endif
 sprintf(s,"[%2d] %s", rank,str);
 PrintToLog(s,rank);
 if(!Quiet)
        printf("%s", s);
}

void
PrintToLog(char *s, int rank)
{
#if defined(PRINT_FROM_ROOT) && !defined(SPLIT_LOG)
 if(rank != 0)
        return;
#endif

 if(LogFile[0] == NULLC)
        return;
#ifndef PRINT_FROM_ROOT
 /* May need to open file each time to avoid concurrent writes */
 if(OutFile <= 0)
        OutFile = open(LogFile, O_APPEND | O_WRONLY,
                0440);
#endif
 if(OutFile > 0)
```

```
        {
        write(OutFile, s, strlen(s));
        }
}

void
GetCurDirectory(char *dir)
{
 MPI_Status status;

/* Use the proc 0 directory as the master */
if(Rank == 0)
    {
    getcwd(dir, 120);
    if(NProc > 1)
        {
        PackString(NULL,dir);
        SendBuf(NULL,&AllDest[1], NProc-1,
            CUR_DIR_TAG, Comm);
        }
    }
 else
    {
    RecvBuf(NULL,120, MPI_CHAR, 0, CUR_DIR_TAG, Comm,
            &status);
    UnPackString(NULL,dir, 120);
    }
}
```

Figure 7.5: send.c.

The file *mpi_pvm.c* contains the lowest-layer support routines. Instead of directly calling the pvm_ routines, for convenience and portability we call our own routines, named **PVM_Init**, **PVM_Send**, etc. These perform diagnostic tests, alternative buffering, and other functions. For example, **PVM_Send** will call either **pvm_send** or **pvm_mcast** as appropriate, after calling **pvm_mkbuf**, **pvm_setsbuf**, **pvm_initsend**, and **pvm_freebuf** as required. Table 7.3 lists these routines.

Table 7.3: Principal functions in mpi_pvm.c	
Function	Purpose
PVM_Init	initialize pvm
PVM_Rank	returns processor rank. 0=master
PVM_Send	send data
PVM_Abort	abort job
PVM_Receive	receive data
PVM_Pack	pack data into buffer
PVM_Unpack	get data from buffer
PVM_GetStatus	get info. about received message
PVM_Isend	immediate send
PVM_Irecv	immediat receive
PVM_Test	buffer free?
PVM_Probe	received message?
PVM_Wait	block until ready

PVM_Init, for example, must process the invocation of pvm differently for the Cray T3D than other machines. The pvm_parent function is used by processes to determine whether they are the root or slaves; this works well, is backward compatible to earlier versions of pvm, and is the method used in Geist et al. (1994), p. 70. These routines are relatively simple "wrappers" which encapsulate the pvm calls in error checking and reporting, along with the processing of the information structures returned by pvm receives (see chapter 6) containing the source, type, and amount of data received..

```
/*
Copyright 1994,1995 Louis Baker, Bradley Smith, Anthony
Giancola. All rights reserved.
*/
/* MPI Implementation for PVM */

#include "all.h"

/* Some compilers require at least one external reference */
extern int NProc;

#ifdef PVM
static int *PVM_tid; /* Task id array */
static int PVM_nproc,PVM_proc;
static int *PVM_dests;

/* Initialize n copies of the named process */
int
PVM_Init(char *name, int n)
{
 int i;
 int tid;
 tid=pvm_mytid();  /* Initializes PVM */

#ifdef T3D /* T3D has funky PVM setup!!! */
 /* Need to do some special setup since T3D auto
        spawns everything */
 pvm_tasks(0, &n, NULL);
 PVM_tid = (int *) New((SIZETYPE) n * sizeof(int));
 for(i=0; i<n; i++)
     PVM_tid[i] = i;
 PVM_nproc = n;
 PVM_proc = pvm_get_PE(tid);
#else
```

```
tid = pvm_parent();        /* Check if we are children or
                                    the parent */
if(tid < 0)     /* Parent */
      {

      /* Set number of processors */
      PVM_nproc = n;

      /* Allocate the list */
      PVM_tid = (int *) New((SIZETYPE) n * sizeof(int));
      PVM_tid[0] = pvm_mytid();

      if(n<=1)
            {
            PVM_proc = 0;
            return(MPI_SUCCESS);
            }

      /* Spawn other tasks */
      if(pvm_spawn(name, NULL, 0, "", n-1, &PVM_tid[1]) < 0)
            return(MPI_FAILURE);

      /* Send number and tids of tasks to each */
      pvm_initsend(PvmDataDefault);
      pvm_pkint(&n,1,1);
      pvm_pkint(PVM_tid, n, 1);
      if(pvm_mcast(&PVM_tid[1], n-1, 0) < 0)
            return(MPI_FAILURE);
      }
else
      {
      /* Children */
      if(pvm_recv(tid,0) < 0)
            return(MPI_FAILURE);
      /* Recieve number of tasks */
      pvm_upkint(&PVM_nproc, 1,1);
```

```
        /* Allocate list */
        PVM_tid = (int *) New((SIZETYPE) PVM_nproc *
              sizeof(int));

        /* Get the rest of the stuff */
        pvm_upkint(PVM_tid, PVM_nproc, 1);
        }

 /* Now we need to identify ourselves */
 tid = pvm_mytid();
#ifdef PVM_DIRECT
 /* Try out direct routing */
 pvm_setopt(PvmRoute, PvmRouteDirect);
#endif

 for(i=0; i<PVM_nproc; i++)
        {
        if(tid == PVM_tid[i])
                {
                PVM_proc = i;
                break;
                }
        }
#endif
 /* Create a dest array for multicasts */
 PVM_dests = (int *) New((SIZETYPE) PVM_nproc * sizeof(int));

 return(MPI_SUCCESS);
}

int
PVM_Rank()
{
 return PVM_proc;
}
```

```
int
PVM_Nproc()
{
 return(PVM_nproc);
}

void
PVM_Abort(int errcode)
{
 char s[80];
 int i;

 if(!PVM_tid)
        PVM_Init("",1);

 sprintf(s, "Fatal error=%d rank=%d task=%xd - signalling PVM
abort!\n",errcode, PVM_proc,
        PVM_tid[PVM_proc]);
 ReportError(s,FALSE);

 /* Kill everyone */
 for(i=0; i<PVM_nproc; i++)
        if(i != PVM_proc)
                pvm_kill(PVM_tid[i]);
 /* Kill ourselves */
 pvm_exit();
}

/* Now capable of doing a multisend */
int
PVM_Send(void *buf, int count, MPI_Datatype data_type, int
*dest, int ndest, int tag)
{
 int i;
 int self_send=FALSE;
```

```
#ifdef PVM_BUF
 int newbuf=-1, old_buf=-1;
#endif


 /* Begin send */
 for(i=0; i<ndest && i < PVM_nproc; i++)
        {
        if(dest[i] < 0 || dest[i] >= PVM_nproc)
                {
                UserMessage("PVM_Send: Error - attempt to send
to bad address '%d'\n",dest[i]);
                return(MPI_FAILURE);
                }
        if(dest[i] == PVM_proc)
                {
                self_send=TRUE;
                }
        /* Copy real address to destination array */
        PVM_dests[i] = PVM_tid[dest[i]];
        }

 /* Simply select appropriate PVM buffer ! */
 /* Note - count is overloaded -> actually the message id */
#define MY_BUFID count
 if(buf == NULL && MY_BUFID != pvm_getsbuf())
        {
        pvm_setsbuf(MY_BUFID);
        }
 else if(buf != NULL)
        {
        /* Otherwise pack it up */
#ifdef PVM_BUF
        newbuf = pvm_mkbuf((data_type == MPI_BYTE)?
                PvmDataRaw: PvmDataDefault);
        if(newbuf < 0)
                return(MPI_FAILURE);
```

```
        old_buf = pvm_setsbuf(newbuf);
#else
        if(pvm_initsend((data_type ==
        MPI_BYTE)?PvmDataRaw:PvmDataDefault) < 0)
                return(MPI_FAILURE);
#endif
        if(PVM_Pack(buf, count, data_type) < 0)
                return(MPI_FAILURE);
        }

 if(ndest == 1)
        {
        if(pvm_send(PVM_dests[0], tag) < 0)
                return(MPI_FAILURE);
        }
 else
        {
        /* Broadcast to all !! */
        if(pvm_mcast(PVM_dests, ndest, tag) < 0)
                return(MPI_FAILURE);
        if(self_send)
                if(pvm_send(PVM_tid[PVM_proc], tag) < 0)
                        return(MPI_FAILURE);
        }
#ifdef PVM_BUF
        if(old_buf >= 0)
                pvm_setsbuf(old_buf);
        if(newbuf >= 0)
                pvm_freebuf(newbuf);
#endif

 return(MPI_SUCCESS);
}


int
PVM_Receive(void *buf, int count, int data_type, int source,
```

```
        int tag, MPI_Status *status, int *buf_id)
{

 if(source >= PVM_nproc || source < MPI_ANY_SOURCE)
        {
        UserMessage("PVM_Receive: Attempt to receive on bad
source=%d\n", source);
        return(MPI_FAILURE);
        }
 *buf_id=pvm_recv(PVM_SOURCE(source),tag);
 if(*buf_id < 0)
        return(MPI_FAILURE);

 PVM_GetStatus(*buf_id,count, data_type, source, status);

 if(buf)
        return(PVM_Unpack(*buf_id,buf, status->count,
data_type, source, status));

 return(MPI_SUCCESS);
}

int
PVM_Pack(void *buf, int count, MPI_Datatype data_type)
{
 int i;
 int ret;

 switch(data_type)
        {
     default:
       case MPI_BYTE:
       case MPI_UNSIGNED_CHAR:
       case MPI_CHAR:
            ret=pvm_pkbyte((char *)buf, count, 1);
            break;
```

```
        case MPI_INT:
                ret=pvm_pkint((int *)buf, count, 1);
                break;
        case MPI_UNSIGNED:
                ret=pvm_pkuint((unsigned int *)buf, count, 1);
                break;
        case MPI_LONG:
                ret=pvm_pklong((long *) buf, count, 1);
                break;
        case MPI_UNSIGNED_LONG:
                ret=pvm_pkulong((unsigned long *) buf, count, 1);
                break;
        case MPI_UNSIGNED_SHORT:
                ret=pvm_pkushort((unsigned short *) buf,
                        count, 1);
                break;
        case MPI_SHORT:
                ret=pvm_pkshort((short *)buf, count,1 );
                break;
        case MPI_FLOAT:
                ret=pvm_pkfloat((float *) buf, count, 1);
                break;
        case MPI_DOUBLE:
                ret=pvm_pkdouble((double *) buf, count, 1);
                break;
        }

 return((ret < 0)? MPI_FAILURE: MPI_SUCCESS);
}

int
PVM_Unpack(int buf_id,void *buf, int count, MPI_Datatype
data_type, int source,
        MPI_Status *status)
{
  int i;
```

```
int ret;

switch(data_type)
    {
  default:
    case MPI_BYTE:
    case MPI_UNSIGNED_CHAR:
    case MPI_CHAR:
          ret=pvm_upkbyte((char *)buf, count, 1);
          break;
    case MPI_INT:
          ret=pvm_upkint((int *)buf, count, 1);
          break;
    case MPI_UNSIGNED:
          ret=pvm_upkuint((unsigned int *)buf, count, 1);
          break;
    case MPI_LONG:
          ret=pvm_upklong((long *) buf, count, 1);
          break;
    case MPI_UNSIGNED_LONG:
          ret=pvm_upkulong((unsigned long *) buf,
                  count, 1);
          break;
    case MPI_UNSIGNED_SHORT:
          ret=pvm_upkushort((unsigned short *) buf,
                  count, 1);
          break;
    case MPI_SHORT:
          ret=pvm_upkshort((short *)buf, count,1 );
          break;
    case MPI_FLOAT:
          ret=pvm_upkfloat((float *) buf, count, 1);
          break;
    case MPI_DOUBLE:
          ret=pvm_upkdouble((double *) buf, count, 1);
          break;
```

```
        }

  return((ret < 0)?MPI_FAILURE:MPI_SUCCESS);
}

void
PVM_GetStatus(int buf_id,  int count, MPI_Datatype datatype,
int source, MPI_Status *status)
{
 int i;
 pvm_bufinfo(buf_id, &status->count, &status->tag,
       &status->source);

 /* get the id of the sender */
 if(source == MPI_ANY_SOURCE)
       {
       for(i=0; i<PVM_nproc; i++)
              if(status->source == PVM_tid[i])
                     {
                     status->source = i;
                     break;
                     }
       }
  else
       status->source = source;

 /* Determine the real count */
 status->count = MIN(count, status->count /
PVM_SizeDataType(datatype));
}

int
PVM_Isend(void *buf, int count, MPI_Datatype data_type, int
dest,
       int tag, MPI_Comm_request *request)
{
```

```
/* Actually do the send */
if(PVM_Send(buf,count, data_type, &dest,1, tag) < 0)
        return(MPI_FAILURE);
 request->status.source = dest;
 request->status.tag = tag;
 request->status.count = count;
 request->is_send = TRUE;
 return(MPI_SUCCESS);
}

int
PVM_Irecv(void *buf, int count, MPI_Datatype data_type, int
source,
        int tag, MPI_Comm_request *request)
{
 request->status.source = source;
 request->status.tag = tag;
 request->status.count = count;
 request->is_send = FALSE;
 request->datatype = data_type;
 request->buf = buf;
 return(MPI_SUCCESS);
}

int
PVM_Wait(MPI_Comm_request *request, MPI_Status *status)
{
 int bufid;

 if(request->is_send)
        {
        *status = request->status;
        return(MPI_SUCCESS);
        }
 else
        return(PVM_Receive(request->buf,
```

```
                    request->status.count, request->datatype,
                    request->status.source, request->status.tag,
                        status, &bufid));
}

int
PVM_Test(MPI_Comm_request *request, MPI_Status *status)
{
 int buf_id;
 if(request->is_send)
        {
        *status = request->status;
        return(TRUE);
        }
  else
        {
        if((buf_id=pvm_nrecv(PVM_SOURCE(
                request->status.source), request->status.tag))
                    <= 0)
                return(FALSE);
         PVM_Unpack(buf_id,request->buf,
                request->status.count, request->datatype,
                    request->status.source, status);
         return(TRUE);
        }
}

int
PVM_Probe(int source, int tag, int *flag, MPI_Status *status)
{
 int buf_id;

 buf_id = pvm_probe(PVM_SOURCE(source), tag);
 if(buf_id <=0)
        {
        *flag = FALSE;
```

```c
        return(MPI_SUCCESS);
        }
 PVM_GetStatus(buf_id,  1, MPI_CHAR, source, status);
 *flag = TRUE;
 return(MPI_SUCCESS);
}

int
PVM_SizeDataType(MPI_Datatype datatype)
{
#if !defined(ALPHA) && !defined(CRAY) && !defined(T3D)
        return(_MPI_SizeDataType(datatype));
#else
switch(datatype)
        {
        default:
        case MPI_INT:
                return(4);
        case MPI_UNSIGNED:
                return(4);
        case MPI_SHORT:
        return(sizeof(short));
        case MPI_UNSIGNED_SHORT:
                return(sizeof(unsigned short));
        case MPI_LONG:
                return(4);
        case MPI_UNSIGNED_LONG:
                return(4);
        case MPI_BYTE:
        case MPI_CHAR:
                return(sizeof(char));
        case MPI_DOUBLE:
                return(sizeof(double));
        case MPI_FLOAT:
                return(4);
        }
```

```
#endif
}

#endif /* PVM */
```

Figure 7.6: mpi_pvm.c.

Example of the Use of Buffered Messaging Routines

The following code was taken from a parallel application developed by the authors. It demonstrates the typical use of these libararies:

```
/* Exchange restart information */
if(Rank == 0)
      {
      if(restart_file)
              sprintf(rfile_name, "%s/%s", CurDir, restart_file);
      else
              strcpy(rfile_name, "");
      /* Send restart file name to others */
      PackString(NULL, rfile_name);
      SendBuf(NULL, &AllDest[1], NProc-1, RESTART_TAG,
              Comm);
      PackBuf(NULL, &SharedFileSys, 1, MPI_INT);
      SendBuf(NULL, &AllDest[1], NProc-1,
              SHARED_FILE_TAG, Comm);
      }
  else
      {
      RecvBuf(NULL, 120, MPI_CHAR, 0, RESTART_TAG,
              Comm, &status);
      /* Receive restart file name */
      UnPackString(NULL, rfile_name, 119);
      RecvBuf(NULL, 1, MPI_INT, 0, SHARED_FILE_TAG,
              Comm, &status);
      UnPackBuf(NULL, &SharedFileSys, 1);
```

```
        if(rfile_name[0] == NULLC)
                restart_file = NULL;
    else
                restart_file = rfile_name;
  }
```

Figure 7.7: Example of the use of buffered messaging.

The four routines **PackBuf**, **SendBuf**, **RecvBuf**, and **UnPackBuf**, are, along with the initialization and finalization routines, all that is needed. These are contained in send.c. They call routines in mpi_pvm.c and msg.c to effect the necessary data transmission.

Finally, some potentially system-dependent routines are in file *os.h*. This includes the diagnostic reporting functions **Debug**, which prints out a message to the logfile, **PPrintString**, a parallel string print command, and **UserMsg**, which is a more general parallel print command that employs the ANSI-C variable-number-of-arguments support. The three functions **ReportError**, **LogFatalError**, and **Exit** support aborting programs. The utilities **New**, **Delete**, and **ReAlloc** are intended to provide portable memory management. File *os.h* is:

```
/*
Copyright 1994, 1995 Louis Baker, Bradley Smith, Anthony
Giancola. All rights reserved.
*/
/* Operating System Specific Functions
*/

/* Message Functions */
/* Parallel print */
void Debug(char *fmt, ...); /* Debugging output */
void PPrintString(char *s); /* Actual parallel print */

/* Pop-up style user messages */
void UserMessage(char * s,...);
/* Major error */
```

```
void ReportError(char * s, int fatal);
/* Normal Messages */
void Report(char * s);
/* Exit program */
void Exit(int status);
/* Log errors */
void LogFatalError(char *s);

/* Memory Allocation Functions */
void *New(SIZETYPE size);
void *ReAlloc(void *old, SIZETYPE newsize);
void Delete(void *ptr);

#ifdef DEBUG
extern int DebugFlag;
#endif
```

Figure 7.8: os.h.

The file *os.c* contains the executable code to implement these functions. The code is fairly straightforward. The function **OnePrintString**, which is used here, is implemented in *send.c*, which is covered previously in this chapter.

```
/*
Copyright 1994,1995 Louis Baker, Bradley Smith, Anthony
Giancola. All rights reserved.
*/
/* Potentially Operating System Specific Stuff
*/

#include "all.h"

#ifdef DEBUG
int DebugFlag = FALSE;
#endif

void
```

```
PPrintString(char *s)
{
#ifdef PRINTROOT
 OnePrintString(s);
#else
 printf("%s",s);
#endif
}

static char out_str[1024];

void
Debug(char *fmt, ...)
{
#ifdef DEBUG
 va_list args;
 va_start(args,fmt);
 vsprintf(out_str,fmt,args);
 PPrintString(out_str);
 va_end(args);
#else
#endif
}

void
UserMessage(char * fmt,...)
{
 va_list args;
 va_start(args,fmt);
 vsprintf(out_str,fmt,args);
 PPrintString(out_str);
 va_end(args);
}

void
ReportError(char * s, int status_fatal)
```

```
{
 PPrintString(s);
 if(status_fatal)
        {
        LogFatalError(s);
        Exit(status_fatal);
        }
}

void
LogFatalError(char *s)
{
 /* Attempt to open a fatal error log */
 FILE *f;
 char fatal_log[120];
 char *home;

 if((home = getenv("HOME")) == NULL)
#ifdef WINDOWS
        home = "\\";
#else
        home = "/tmp";
#endif

 sprintf(fatal_log, "%s/program.log", home);

 if((f=fopen(fatal_log,"a")) != NULL)
        {
#ifdef PVM
        fprintf(f,"[%d] [%x] %s", Rank, pvm_mytid(), s);
#else
        fprintf(f,"[%d] %s", Rank, s);
#endif
        fclose(f);
        }
}
```

```
void
Exit(int status)
{
 char msg[80];
 if(status == 0)
        ExitMPISystem();
  else
        {
        sprintf(msg, "Proc %d is abnormally exiting MPI
(status=%d)\n", Rank, status);
        PPrintString(msg);
        LogFatalError(msg);
#ifdef PVM
        pvm_perror("PVM Error ");
#endif
        MPI_Abort(MPI_COMM_WORLD, status);
        }
 exit(status);
}

void
Report(char * s)
{
 PPrintString(s);
}

void *
New(SIZETYPE size)
{
 void *p;
#ifdef DEBUG
 if(size == 0)
        Debug("New() called with size == 0!\n");
#endif
 if((p=malloc(size)) == NULL)
```

```
        ReportError("Out of memory\n",TRUE);
 return p;
}

void *
ReAlloc(void *old, SIZETYPE size)
{
 void *p;
  char str[256];
#ifdef DEBUG
 if(size == 0 || old == NULL)
        Debug("ReAlloc called with size == 0 or old
ptr==NULL\n");
#endif
 if((p=realloc(old, size)) == NULL)
        ReportError("Out of memory in ReAlloc\n", TRUE);
 return(p);
}

void
Delete(void *p)
{
#ifdef DEBUG
 if(p== NULL)
        Debug("WARNING - Delete(NULL) called in os.c\n");
#endif
 free(p);
}
```

Figure 7.9: os.c.

MPMD Example

As examples of SPMD programming are all too common, we include an example of the use of PVM to effect the MPMD model for communications. Because MPI does not support MPMD, we do not recommend using it in general. Furthermore, it is fairly easy to implement the same method either way, because the structure of any SPMD program is of the form: **if(root){/*master*/...} else {/*slave*/...}**. Such a program may be separated into two programs, a master and a slave, relatively easily. However, the SPMD processes will be larger than they need be, because they will contain code that is never executed (code for the master in the slave and vice versa). Consequently, there are some circumstances in which it is desirable to use MPMD if possible.

The purpose of these two programs is to transfer a datafile from one machine to another, effecting whatever data conversions are necessary. The master causes the startup of the slave on the specified machine. The data is read from and send to the appropriate machine for writing the file based on the command-line arguments. This code was written for the transfer of application dumpfiles. The routines specific to this code are not included here, as they are not of general interest.

The code for the client or master is in file *mdump.c*:

```
/*
 * mdump.c: routines for processing dumpfiles
 * ReadSPHDumpFile the opposite of WriteSPHDumpFile
 * in io.c may be used with restart or with loading of file
 * to transmit data
 *
 * use PVM to read dumpfile and send across network
 */

/* static char sccs_id[]="%Z% %P% %I% %D%"; */

#define DEBUG
#include "all.h"
/* ultimately, move below to tag.h! */
#define DUMP_CSPTAG (TAG_BASE + 17)
#define DUMP_FSPTAG (TAG_BASE + 18)
#define DUMP_ISPTAG (TAG_BASE + 19)
```

```
#define DUMP_CMATTAG (TAG_BASE + 20)
#define DUMP_IMATTAG (TAG_BASE + 21)

extern int *PVM_tid;
/* MASTER */

FILE *fn;
#ifdef DEBUG
FILE *diagn;
#endif

main(int argc,char **argv)
{
int From, numt,mytid,flag;
char **sargv,where[20],direction, name[20];
if(argc <4)
        {
        fprintf(stdout," usage: mdump fromfilename where
tofilename [r|s]\n");
        exit(0);
        }
#ifdef DEBUG
diagn=fopen("master.dia","w");
fprintf(diagn," master starting\n");
printf(" direction=%s where=%s
ffilename=%s\n",argv[4],argv[2],argv[1]);

#endif
        flag=1;/* specific host*/
        strncpy(where,argv[2],20);
        if(strlen(where)<=0) flag=0;
        /* above defaults to "most appropriate" host for
                spawn this will NOT in general be useful */
        strncpy(name,"sdump",20);
        sargv = (char **)malloc( 4* sizeof( char *));
        sargv[0]=(argv[1]);
```

```
        sargv[1]="s";/*default*/
        sargv[2]=NULL;
        direction = *(argv[4]);
        if(direction == 'r')
        {
        /*get other guy to send */
#ifdef DEBUG
        printf(" master receiving\n");
#endif
        numt=PVM_GInit(name,sargv,flag,where,2);

#ifdef DEBUG
        printf(" master after PVM_GInit=%d %d %d\n",
               numt, PVM_tid[0],PVM_tid[1]);
#endif
        /*From=PVM_tid[1]; slave tid */
        From=1;
        /* From=1 used to look up PVM_tid[From]
                    by SendBuf/RevBuf*/
        printf(" tid of spawned task %d\n",From);
        if((fn=fopen(argv[3],"wb"))==NULL)
                {
                fprintf(stderr," cant open output dump file
        %s\n",argv[3]);exit(0);
                }
        RecvDumpFile(fn, From);
        }
        else
        {       /* get other guy to receive */
#ifdef DEBUG
        printf(" master sending spawning=%s at %s flag%d\n",
        name,where,flag);
#endif
        sargv[0]=(argv[3]);            /* needs to know name of
                                            file to create*/

        sargv[1]="r";
```

```
        numt=PVM_GInit(name,sargv,flag,where,2);
#ifdef DEBUG
        printf(" master after PVM_GInit=%d %d %d\n",numt,
                PVM_tid[0],PVM_tid[1]);
#endif
        From=1;
        printf("  tid of spawned task=%d\n",From);
        if((fn=fopen(argv[1],"r"))==NULL)
                {
                fprintf(stderr," cant open dump file %s to
        send\n",argv[1]);exit(0);
                }
        SendDumpFile(fn, From);
        }
        fclose(fn);
        pvm_exit();
}
```

Figure 7.10: mdump.c.

The corresponding code for the server or slave, in file *sdump.c*, is :

```
/* Parallel Dump Transfer Program
 * Brad Smith & Lou Baker, Dagonet Software
 * dump.c: routines for processing dumpfiles
 * ReadSPHDumpFile the opposite of WriteSPHDumpFile
 * in io.c may be used with restart or with loading of file
 * to transmit data
 *
 * use PVM to read dumpfile and send across network
*/

/* static char sccs_id[]="%Z% %P% %I% %D%"; */
#define DEBUG
#include "all.h"


 /* ultimately, move below to tag.h! */
```

```
#define DUMP_CSPTAG (TAG_BASE + 17)
#define DUMP_FSPTAG (TAG_BASE + 18)
#define DUMP_ISPTAG (TAG_BASE + 19)
#define DUMP_CMATTAG (TAG_BASE + 20)
#define DUMP_IMATTAG (TAG_BASE + 21)

/* SLAVE */

FILE *fn,*diagn;
extern int NProc,NRank;
extern  int *PVM_tid;

main(int argc,char **argv)
{
int mytid,From,tid[4];
/* init pvm */
char direction;
diagn=fopen("slave.dia","w");
fprintf(diagn," SLAVE started\n");
fflush(diagn);
PVM_GInit(NULL,NULL,0,NULL,1);
/* do pvm_mytid , set Rank, etc. */
fprintf(diagn," SLAVE after PVMGInit in main\n");
fflush(diagn);
/* I assume argv[1]=sargv[0], etc, with argv[0]=program
      name=sdump*/
From = atoi(argv[2]);
#ifdef DEBUG
fprintf(diagn," SLAVE %d [1]=%s\n",argc,argv[1]);
fflush(diagn);
#endif
if(argv[0]==NULL)
      {
      fprintf(diagn," slave got argv[0]=NULL\n");
      Debug(" slave got argv[0]=NULL\n");
      exit(0);
```

```
        }
if(argv[1]==NULL)
        {
        fprintf(diagn," slave got argv[1]=NULL\n");
        Debug(" slave got argv[1]=NULL\n");
        exit(0);
    }
if(argv[2]==NULL)
        {
        fprintf(diagn," slave got argv[2]=NULL\n");
        Debug(" slave got argv[2]=NULL\n");
        }
direction = *(argv[2]);
fprintf(diagn," direction %c\n",direction);
fprintf(diagn," NProc=%d\n",NProc);
fprintf(diagn," tid=%d %d\n",PVM_tid[0],PVM_tid[1]);
From=0;       /* from needs parent id PVM_tid[0]  for
                        SendBuf/RecvBuf*/
if(direction=='s')
        {
#ifdef DEBUG
        Debug(" Slave Sending tidparent=%d\n",From);
#endif
        if((fn=fopen(argv[1],"rb"))==NULL)
                {
                /* use msg.c stuff to report error back to master*/
                Debug(" Slave cant open dump file %s to send
%s\n",argv[0],argv[1]);
                exit(0);
                }
        SendDumpFile(fn, From);
        }
else if(direction=='r')
        {       /* receive file from master */
#ifdef DEBUG
        fprintf(diagn," slave receiving\n");
```

```
            fflush(diagn);
            Debug(" Slave Receiving\n");
#endif
        if((fn=fopen(argv[1],"wb"))==NULL)
                {
                /* use msg.c stuff to report error back to master*/
                Debug(" Slave cant open receive dump file %s
%s\n",argv[0],argv[1]);
                exit(0);
                }
#ifdef DEBUG
        fprintf(diagn," slave  before RecvDumpfile\n");
        fflush(diagn);
        Debug(" Slave before RecvDumpfile\n");
#endif
        RecvDumpFile(fn, From);
#ifdef DEBUG
        fprintf(diagn," slave  after RecvDumpfile\n");
        fflush(diagn);
        Debug(" Slave after RecvDumpfile\n");
#endif
        }
else
        {
        Debug(" Slave cant understand args=%s %s
%s\n",argv[0],argv[1],argv[2]);
        fprintf(diagn," Slave cant understand args=%s %s
%s\n",argv[0],argv[1],argv[2]);
        fflush(diagn);
        exit(0);
    }
 fclose(fn);
 fclose(diagn);
#ifdef DEBUG
 Debug(" Slave Exiting\n");
#endif
```

```
 pvm_exit();
}
```

Figure 7.11: sdump.c

A generalized version of **PVM_Init** is used with the MPMD program. It is necessary, as the version used for the SPMD programs does not need to be passed the name of the program to be started; it is not different from that of its initiator. This code is contained in the file *d.c*:

```
/* Generalized Spawn PVM */

#include "all.h"
#include "pvm3.h"

#define DEBUG

/* Global variables */
extern int Rank, NProc;
extern MPI_Comm Comm;
extern int *AllDest;
extern int *PVM_tid;
extern int PVM_proc, PVM_nproc;
/* Global message buffers */
PMsgBuf GSendBuf, GRecvBuf;


/* Initialize process similar to PVM_Init of mpi_pvm.c
        but generalized!  */
int
PVM_GInit(char *name, char **sargv,int flag,char *where,int n)
{
 int i,tid,myid,ntospawn,numt=-100;
 Comm = MPI_COMM_WORLD;
 myid= pvm_mytid();        /* Initializes PVM */
```

```
tid = pvm_parent();          /* Check if we are children or
                                        the parent */
#ifdef DEBUG
 Debug(" entered PVM_GInit myid %d,
      tid(parent)=%d\n",myid,tid);
 printf(" id's= %d %d n=%d\n",myid,tid,n);
#endif
 if(n>0)
      ntospawn=n-1;/ * for compatibility, count n
                            includes parent itself! */
 else
      ntospawn= -n;
 if(tid < 0)     /* Parent */
      {

      /* Set number of processors */
      PVM_nproc = (n>0)?n: 1+ntospawn;
      /* Allocate the list */
      if(n<=0) n=2;
#ifdef DEBUG
      Debug(" Parent calling New n=%d\n",n);
#endif
      PVM_tid = (int *) New((SIZETYPE) n * sizeof(int));
#ifdef DEBUG
      Debug(" PVM_GInit n= %d\n",n);
#endif
      PVM_tid[0] = myid;
      if(!n)
          {
          Debug(" bad spawn n=0\n");
          }
      if(n==1)
          {
          PVM_proc = 0;
          return(MPI_SUCCESS);
          }
```

```
        /* Spawn n-1 other tasks */
        if(n>0)
                numt=pvm_spawn(name, sargv, flag,where,
                        ntospawn, &PVM_tid[1]);
        printf(" spawn numt=%d of %d\n",numt,ntospawn);
                        /* we are master so printf ok*/
        printf(" tid(child)=%d\n",PVM_tid[1]);
        /* Send number and tids of tasks to each */
        pvm_initsend(PvmDataDefault);
        pvm_pkint(&n,1,1);
        pvm_pkint(PVM_tid, n, 1);
        pvm_mcast(&PVM_tid[1], n-1, 0);
        }
 else
        {
        /* Children */
        pvm_recv(tid,0);
        /* Recieve number of tasks */
        pvm_upkint(&PVM_nproc, 1,1);

        /* Allocate list */
        PVM_tid = (int *) New((SIZETYPE) PVM_nproc *
                sizeof(int));

        /* Get the rest of the stuff */
        pvm_upkint(PVM_tid, PVM_nproc, 1);
        }

/* Now we need to identify ourselves */
MPI_Comm_size(Comm, &NProc);
MPI_Comm_rank(Comm, &Rank);
tid = myid;
for(i=0; i<PVM_nproc; i++)
        {
        if(tid == PVM_tid[i])
                {
```

```
                    PVM_proc = i;
                    break;
                }
        }
/* following code borrowed from InitMPISystem in send.c*/
/* Set up an array that is all destinations */
AllDest = (int *) New(sizeof(int)*NProc);
for(i=0; i<NProc; i++)
        AllDest[i] = i;

/* Allocate our own send and receive buffers - global */
GSendBuf = NewMsgBuf(SEND_BUF, BUF_ALLOC);
GRecvBuf = NewMsgBuf(RECV_BUF, BUF_ALLOC);
/* preceeding code borrowed from InitMPISystem in send.c*/

return(MPI_SUCCESS);
}
```

Figure 7.12: d.c.

Naive Implementation of Broadcast, etc.

We present here a naive implementation of the basic MPI structured message-passing routines, layered over the pvm calls. For parallel supercomputers, there will undoubtedly be systems routines to perform these functions. These routines would only be of interest in environments that do not support MPI, such as distributed heterogeneous networks. Note that our version of broadcast would not generally meet the MPI standard requirements as it would be a simple, order N implementation on N processors, whereas the standard would require a more sophisticated implementation if possible, which would be an order $log(N)$ operation. On the other hand, this implementation should be completely portable, albeit inefficient. We leave a better implementation to the reader as an exercise. An order $log(N)$ multicast would have the sender delegate half of the sending to each of two processors. These would recursively subdivide the sending tasks. The true level of improvement would depend on the network architecture. The code in file *msg2.c* is:

```
/* Message passing routines - Collective
 *(see also MPI_Reduce and MPI_Barrier in msg.c)
 */

#include "all.h"

#define BCAST_MSG_TAG  16382
#define SCATTER_MSG_TAG  16383
/* assumes GATHER tag etc biggest tags
        so proc# can be low-order bits */
#define GATHER_MSG_TAG 16384

/* one(root) to all broadcast */

int
MPI_Bcast(void *buf,  int count, MPI_Datatype datatype,
        int root, MPI_Comm comm)
{
 int rank, nproc, i;
 void *buff;
 MPI_Status status;

 /* For right now - do this with generic sends and receives */
 MPI_Comm_size(comm, &nproc);
 MPI_Comm_rank(comm, &rank);
 if(nproc <= 1)
        return(MPI_SUCCESS);
 if(rank != root)/*Recv */
        {
        MPI_Recv(buf, count, datatype,root,
                BCAST_MSG_TAG, comm, &status);
        }
 else
        {
        /* root sends */
        for(i=0; i<nproc; i++)
```

```
                {
                if(i==root) continue;/* no need to send to self*/
                MPI_Send(buf,count, datatype, i,
                        BCAST_MSG_TAG, comm);
                }
        }
 return(MPI_SUCCESS);
}


/* all send to root */
int
MPI_Gather(void *sendbuf,  int sendcount,
        MPI_Datatype sendtype,  void *recvbuf,
        int recvcount, MPI_Datatype recvtype,
        int root, MPI_Comm comm)
{
 int rank, nproc, i;
 void *buff;
 MPI_Status status;

 /* For right now - do this with generic sends and receives */
 MPI_Comm_size(comm, &nproc);
 MPI_Comm_rank(comm, &rank);
 if(nproc <= 1)
        return(MPI_SUCCESS);
 if(rank == root) /* recv */
        {
        for(i=0;i<nproc;i++)
                {
                buff = &(recvbuf[i*recvcount*
                        _MPI_SizeDataType(recvtype) ]);
                if(i==root)
                        {
                        memcpy(buff, sendbuf, recvcount *
                                _MPI_SizeDataType(recvtype));
```

```
                }
            else
                    MPI_Recv(buff, recvcount,
                            recvtype,MPI_ANY_SOURCE,
                            (GATHER_MSG_TAG|i), comm,
                            &status);
                }
        }
    else
        {
        /* Not root-send to root. */
        MPI_Send(sendbuf,sendcount, sendtype, root,
                (GATHER_MSG_TAG | rank) , comm);
        }
    return(MPI_SUCCESS);
}




/* root sends to all */
int
MPI_Scatter(void *sendbuf,int sendcount,
        MPI_Datatype datatype, void *recvbuf,int recvcount,
        MPI_Datatype recvtype, int root, MPI_Comm comm)
{
 int rank, nproc, i;
 void *buff;
 MPI_Status status;

 /* For right now - do this with generic sends and receives */
 MPI_Comm_size(comm, &nproc);
 MPI_Comm_rank(comm, &rank);
 if(nproc <= 1)
        return(MPI_SUCCESS);
 if(rank != root)
        {
```

```
            MPI_Recv(recvbuf, recvcount, datatype,
                 MPI_ANY_SOURCE, (SCATTER_MSG_TAG)
                 , comm, &status);
        }
    else
        {
        /* root-send.*/
        /* send to self! */
        for(i=0; i<nproc; i++)
                {
                buff=(char*)( ((int)sendbuf)+i*
                    _MPI_SizeDataType(datatype));
                if(i==root)memcpy(recvbuf, buff,
                    _MPI_SizeDataType(datatype));
                else MPI_Send(buff,sendcount, datatype, i,
                    (SCATTER_MSG_TAG ) , comm);
                }
        }
 return(MPI_SUCCESS);
}

/* all send same data to each other */
int
MPI_Allgather(void *sendbuf,  int sendcount,
        MPI_Datatype datatype, void *recvbuf,
                int recvcount, MPI_Datatype recvtype,
                int root, MPI_Comm comm)
{
 int rank, nproc, i;
 void *buff;
 MPI_Status status;

 /* For right now - do this with generic sends and receives */
 MPI_Comm_size(comm, &nproc);
 MPI_Comm_rank(comm, &rank);
 if(nproc <= 1)
```

```
        return(MPI_SUCCESS);
/* everyone send to everyone else */
for(i=0; i<nproc; i++)
    {
    if(i==rank) continue;/* skip send to self*/
            MPI_Send(sendbuf,sendcount, datatype, i,
                (GATHER_MSG_TAG I rank) , comm);
    }
/* ALL Recv-including root! */
{
/*        buff = New();*/
/* receive from each other proc in order! */
for(i=0;i<nproc;i++)
    {
    buff= &(recvbuf[i*recvcount *
            _MPI_SizeDataType(datatype)]);
    if(i==rank)
            {
            /* memcpy = send to self */
            memcpy(buff,sendbuf, recvcount *
                _MPI_SizeDataType(datatype));
            }
    else
            MPI_Recv(buff, recvcount, datatype,
            MPI_ANY_SOURCE, (GATHER_MSG_TAGIi)
                , comm, &status);
    }
 free(buff);
 }
 return(MPI_SUCCESS);
}
```

Figure 7.13: msg2.c.

A test driver for the above is in file *spmd2.c*:

```
/* Parallel Program
 * Brad Smith, & Lou Baker, Dagonet Software
 * test of Scatter, Gather, etc. SPMD
 */

/* static char sccs_id[]="%Z% %P% %I% %D%"; */

#define DEBUG
#include "all.h"
/* ultimately, move below to tag.h! */
#define DUMP_CSPTAG (TAG_BASE + 17)
#define DUMP_FSPTAG (TAG_BASE + 18)
#define DUMP_ISPTAG (TAG_BASE + 19)
#define DUMP_CMATTAG (TAG_BASE + 20)
#define DUMP_IMATTAG (TAG_BASE + 21)

int *PVM_tid,PVM_proc,PVM_nproc;
char LogFile[128];
/* MASTER */

FILE *fn;
#ifdef DEBUG
FILE *diagn;
#endif

main(int argc,char **argv)
{
int From, numt,mytid,flag,halfrank,i,comm,reckt;
char **sargv,where[20],direction, name[20];
char buf[100]; int recbuf[100],sendbuf[100];
#ifdef DEBUG
diagn=fopen("master.dia","w");
fprintf(diagn," master starting\n");
#endif
        halfrank=atoi(argv[1]);
```

```
numt=atoi(argv[2]);
printf(" halfrank=%d\n",halfrank);
sargv = (char **)malloc( 4* sizeof( char *));
sargv[0]=(argv[1]);
sargv[1]=argv[2];
sargv[2]=NULL;
fprintf(diagn," REQUESTED number of
processes=%d\n",numt);
if(numt<=1)
        {
        fprintf(diagn," Bad numberof processes
requested\n",TRUE);
         exit(1);
        }
strcpy(name,"spmd2");
where[0]='\0';/*if flag=0, where not used?*/
flag=0;/* no specific host*/

reckt=PVM_GInit(name,sargv,flag,where,numt);

Debug(" number of SPAWNED processes=%d Rank=%d
halfrank=%d\n",numt,Rank,halfrank);
/* do the scatters and the gathers and Bcasts  */
/*       halfrank= numt/2;*/
/* halfrank=0 */
comm=Comm;
if(Rank==halfrank)
        {
        /* copy hafrank to buf */
        memcpy(recbuf,&halfrank,sizeof(int));
        Debug(" packed buffer with %d\n",halfrank);
        }
Debug(" Before broadcast\n");
/* halfrank here is root of bcast*/
MPI_Bcast(recbuf, 1,MPI_INT, halfrank, comm);
/* root->all*/
```

```
/* report*/
Debug(" BCAST Rank=%d got: %d half=%d\n",
      Rank,recbuf[0],halfrank);

/* all send SAME kind of data to root */
memcpy(sendbuf,&Rank,sizeof(int));
  for(i=0;i<numt;i++)recbuf[i]=-1;
        reckt=1;
  MPI_Allgather(sendbuf,1,MPI_INT,recbuf,reckt,
        MPI_INT,halfrank,comm);
if(Rank==halfrank)
   {
  Debug(" reckt=%d\n",reckt);
   for(i=0;i<numt;i++)
        Debug(" got %d as %d data\n",recbuf[i],i);
   }
  /* root takes in report from each*/
  for(i=0;i<numt;i++)recbuf[i]=-1;
        sendbuf[0]=Rank*10;

  MPI_Gather(sendbuf,1,MPI_INT,recbuf,reckt,MPI_INT,
        halfrank,comm);/* all->root*/
if(Rank==halfrank)
        for(i=0;i<numt;i++)
                Debug("Gather got %d from
        %d\n",recbuf[i],i);
  /* root sends a different message to each */
  for(i=0;i<numt;i++)
        recbuf[i]=-1;
if(Rank==halfrank)
        for(i=0;i<numt;i++)
                sendbuf[i]=i*10-5;

  MPI_Scatter(sendbuf,1,MPI_INT,recbuf,reckt,MPI_INT,
        halfrank,comm);/* root->all*/
  Debug(" SCATTER:Rank=%d got: %d\n",
```

```
                Rank,recbuf[0]);
        if(!Rank)
                Debug(" root flushing messages\n");
        pvm_exit();
}
```

Figure 7.14: spmd2.c (test driver).

Message Passing Performance

Latency

Latency is the total time between the beginning and the completion of an operation. It therefore is the most complete or the most pessimistic measure of performance, depending on your point of view. It includes all start-up and systems overhead costs, such as allocating buffers, moving data, and so on. Usually, there is an overhead cost almost independent of the quantity of data for each message. As a consequence, it becomes attractive to pack a buffer with as much information as possible, in order to minimize the message traffic count and amortize the fixed overhead per message over the largest amount of data.

Bandwidth

Bandwidth is the data transfer rate, typically given in terms of Megabytes per second or some similar unit. It should include latency effects, resulting in increased bandwidth with larger-size messages. The increase in bandwidth with message size is rarely monotonic, however. Typically, some "glitches" occur at multiples of system buffer sizes, which are often determined by the hardware, and result in a decrease in efficiency when the message requires only slightly more than an integral number of buffers, resulting in the last buffer being inefficiently utilized. Gropp and Lusk (1995) present performance comparisons for three message-passing systems on the SP-1 (predecessor of the SP-2). There is a large, narrow glitch for one of these systems - a sharp decrease in performance from approximately 8.7 MB/s down to 8.2 MB/s, at a message size of 200,000 bytes. Performance for that message-passing system varies from about 8.5 MB/s for 100,000 byte messages up to 8.8 MB/s, which remains roughly constant for messages from approximately 400,000 bytes to 1 MB. The mpich implementation reported on has slightly lower bandwidth, typically about 8.7 MB/s, with more substantial variation. For messages shorter than 100KB, the trend seems to be toward smaller bandwidths, approximately 7.5 MB/s for 16KB messages. The performance variation between the three systems compared (mpich, IBM's mpi-f, and IBM's euih) is relatively small, and even for the large variation in message size the bandwidth is not large.

Very often, the "bisection bandwidth" is used to specify machine performance. This is the bandwidth based on half of the processors communicating with the other half. Manufacturers will choose the precise pattern to show the best result.

Performance

Depending on the user's problem, it may not be possible to take advantage of bandwidth improvements for huge data transfers if more modest data transfers are appropriate. Similarly, the pattern of user data transfers may not be such as to approach the bisection bandwidth ideal. Zhiwei Xu (zxu@aloha.usc.edu) posted to comp.parallel.mpi interesting statistics for the performance of the SP-2, using the native MPL library.

Table 7.4: SP-2 Communications Performance, MPL	
Operation	**Time (usec for m bytes, N nodes)**
pingpong/2	46+.035m
pingpong/2, IBM code	39+.028m
barrier	10+ 94 logN
reduce	23+ 20 logN
prefix	25+ 60 logN
broadcast	(10+ 16 logN)+(.025logN)m
gather/scatter	(15+ 17 logN)+(.025logN-.02)m
index	(0+ 80 logN)+(.03 $N^{1.29}$)m
shift	(60+ 6 logN)+(.04+.003 logN)m

We have previously discussed the barrier, reduce, prefix, broadcast, and gather/scatter operations as "structured message passing" operations. Pingpong sends a message from a to b and back to a. Index is basically a sorting operation; given a set of N processors, each with a "key," indexing would order these according to the key, assigning an index to each. For example, given a binary tree, some of whose leaves contain a "packet," the index of any packet is the number of packets to the left of it in the tree (Leighton, 1992); in this case, the key is effectively the position of the node in the tree as well as the existence or nonexistence of the packet on the node. Shift is an operation in which processor i sends a message to processor $(i+N) \bmod N$.

Experiments done by personnel of the Albuquerque Resource Center (ARC) of the Maui High Performance Computer Center showed significantly higher bandwidth and lower latency for the native MPI implementation than for PVM; performance was on the order of 20% higher for MPI. The paper by Saphir (1994) cites the following results for MPL, MPI, and PVMe, version 3.2, which is a version of PVM optimized by IBM for the SP2:

Table 7.5: Performance of MPL., MPI, PVMe on SP-2 (Saphir 1994)		
Library	Latency (microsec)	Bandwidth (MBytes/sec)
MPL	45	34
MPI	58	33
PVMe	220	27

The high overhead of PVMe is evident in both the latency and bandwidth statistics. Clearly, MPI is a better choice for this machine. Al Geist (private communication) reports that for PVM 3.3.9, a latency of 50 microseconds with a bandwidth of 34 MB/sec was achieved on an SP-2.

Building High-Level Services

Adding Parallel I/O and Logging Services

Parallel I/O is at the moment a controversial topic, as no one knows the "right" way to do it. See Feitelson (1995) for a review on the subject.

The situation on the SP-2 is fairly typical for massively parallel machines. There is a universal directory, **/scratch**, that all users have access to. Each node has a directory, **/localscratch**, that is similar. Files have a limited lifetime in these directories. A user can write to a single file in **/scratch**, or have each node write its results to the **/localscratch**. Often, both is done. The root/master process writes summary information to a single file, while each node writes its own data to the local storage. This data can be collected later. Our SPH code has each processor dump its particle values to local files. These are collected together in a single dump file as a post-processing step. We have already discussed in this chapter one situation in which it may be desirable to join split files: When the variable **SPLIT_LOG** is defined for use with the logging feature.

The program joindump.c uses the UNIX rcp function to copy the individual files to the single node executing the code, which assembles the unified file. The files are copied over one at a time, to minimize the disk space required; the UNIX unlink function is used to delete the files after they have been copied. The file host is assumed to contain the names of these nodes.

```
/* Program to join split files */
#include <stdio.h>

void
main(int argc, char **argv)
{
FILE *f, *out, *hf;
int i;
char name[256];
char tmp[256], host[256];
int n;
```

```
char buf[4096];

if(argc != 2 && argc != 3 && argc != 4)
        {
        fprintf(stderr, "Usage: joindump <filename> [hosts]\n");
        exit(1);
        }

if((out=fopen(argv[1],"w")) == NULL)
        {
        fprintf(stderr, "Can't open output file '%s' for write\n",
                argv[1]);
        exit(1);
        }
if(argc >= 3)
        {
        if((hf = fopen(argv[2], "r")) == NULL)
                {
                fprintf(stderr,"Can't open host file %s\n", argv[2]);
                exit(1);
                }
        }
else
        hf = NULL;
if(argc == 4)
        i=atoi(argv[3]);
else
        i=0;
for(; i<2048; i++)
        {
        sprintf(name, "%s.%d", argv[1], i);
        if(hf)
                {
                if(fgets(host,sizeof(host),hf) == NULL)
                        break;
                if(host[strlen(host)-1] == '\n')
```

```
                    host[strlen(host)-1] = '\0';
                sprintf(tmp,"rcp %s:/tmp/%s %s", host, name,
                        name);
                if(system(tmp) != 0)
                        {
                        fprintf(stderr,"Joindump failed in RCP:
%s\n",
                                tmp);
                        exit(1);
                        }
                sprintf(tmp,"rsh %s 'rm -f /tmp/%s'", host,name);
                if(system(tmp) != 0)
                        fprintf(stderr,"Warning: RM failed: %s\n",
                                tmp);
                }

        printf("Joining %s\n", name);
        if((f=fopen(name,"r")) == NULL)
                break;
        while((n=fread(buf, 1, sizeof(buf), f)) > 0)
                fwrite(buf, 1, n, out);
        fclose(f);
        unlink(name);
        }

#ifdef NOTDEF
 for(i=0; i<2048; i++)
        {
        sprintf(name, "%s.%d", argv[1], i);
        if(access(name,0) == 0)
                unlink(name);
        else
                break;
        }
#endif
```

```
fclose(out);
}
```

Figure 7.15: joindump.c.

The layered message-passing libraries presented above support basic parallel I/O and logging services, primarily for debugging and performance tuning. We have also implemented similar code that supports tracing in a manner similar to the PICL (portable instrumented communications library; see below). It does not produce output compatible with the ParaGraph program which is a part of the PICL system, however. There are two formats, *compact* and *verbose*, both ASCII, for the ParaGraph trace file; see Geist et al. (1990). We refer readers to this document as the specification of the tracing functions interface as well as the ParaGraph file format. We were concerned about the overhead cost of formatting data for such files, so we use a binary file format. This output is then post-processed into a readable form. It should not be very difficult to make the output compatible with ParaGraph, however, perhaps by slightly modifying the post-processor file. The function names are compatible with PICL. See Heath et al. (1995a,b) for a discussion of the use of ParaGraph for performance analysis. ParaGraph may be obtained through netlib by e-mailing "send paragraph.shar" to a netlib site such as netlib@ornl.gov. See also the other articles in the Winter 1995 issue *of IEEE Parallel and Distributed Technology*, which is devoted to the topic of "Performance Evaluation Tools." The file trace.h is:

```
/* routines to implement a picl-style tracing feature
   NOT compatible with ParaGraph!
   L. Baker
*/
/* boolean: 1: trace enabled, 0: do not trace */
/* not enabled until trace enable called*/

#define TRACE
```

```
void traceenable( char *tracefile, int format);
void traceexit(void);
void traceflush(void);
void tracehost(int tracesize, int flush);
void traceinfo(int *remaining, int *event, int *compstats, int
*commstats);
void tracelevel(int event, int compstats, int commstats);
void tracemark(int marktype);
void tracemsg(char *message);
void tracenode(int tracesize,int flush, int sync);
void traceon(void);
void traceoff(void);
void traceclose(void);


void sync0(void);

/* event types: */

typedef int Event; /* use int or char? save a byte? */

#define TraceSTART_SEND 1
#define TraceFINISH_SEND 2
#define TraceWAIT_RECV 3
#define TraceFINISH_RECV 4
#define TraceOPEN 5
#define TraceCLOSE 6
#define TraceTRACE_FLUSH 7
#define TraceTRACE_FLUSHD 8
#define TraceTRACE_LEVEL 9
#define TraceTRACE_START 10
#define TraceTRACE_FINISH 11
#define TraceWAIT_BARRIER 12
#define TraceWAIT_OVER 13
#define TraceUSR_MSG 14                /*pack msg in CurDir? */
#define TraceWAIT_START 15             /* for MPI_Wait */
```

#define TraceWAIT_DONE 16

#define TraceNULLEVENT 15

#define TraceMAXEVENT TraceNULLEVENT

Event traceMaxEvent(void);

/* USER-DEFINED EVENTS (MARKS) IF ANY SHOULD EXCEED
MAXEVENT!!!!!!*/

/* Definitions and structures */

#define NAMESIZE 60

#define MaxCurDirS 20

typedef time_t Time; /* UNIX time: good to milliseconds */

```
typedef int MSGTYPE;
struct traceitem
      {
      Time  when;
      Event what;
      int   who;/*rank*/
      char  where[MaxCurDirS];
      };
```

#define SAFTEY 1

Figure 7.16: trace.h.

PIC- Style Trace

We provide here simple "wrapper" functions to support the PICL syntax
for tracing functions. These functions perform simple tasks such as turning

tracing on and off, and maintaining and reporting statistics. The functions in msg.c will have to be modified as well (see next listing). The code to perform the PICL-style trace is in *trace.c*:

```
/* Brad Smith, and Lou Baker, Dagonet Software */
/* routines to implement a picl
* -style tracing feature
*   NOT compatible with ParaGraph!
*
* L. Baker     DAGONET SOFTWARE 11/93
*
* assumes an external  char *CurDir;
*
* HOST = MASTER  in Master/Slave model (assumed)
*
* caveat: recv has only 1023 bytes for msg! might have to
* up this.
* Also, potential problems if "host" does not generate traces
* often to recover trace messages from other slave nodes.
*/
#define TRACE
#ifdef TRACE

#define PICLCODE

#include "all.h"

/* Generic rank */
static int MyRank;

/* below only for node zero. wasted space otherwise. Not much
though*/

static char TraceFileName[NAMESIZE];
static FILE *TraceFileP=NULL;
static long int tracekt= 0l;
```

```
static struct traceitem *TraceBuffer;
static int TraceBufferHolds=0,TraceBufferSize=0, FlushSize;

/* Definitions */
#define Host() (MyRank == 0)

static tracewrite(int mark,Time *t,char * msg);
void MPI_WriteTrace(struct traceitem *str, int bytecount);

int traceon_picl=0,tracelevel_picl;/* do not make static */

void traceon(){traceon_picl=1;
tracemark(TraceTRACE_START);}
void traceoff(){
tracemark(TraceTRACE_FINISH);traceon_picl=0;}

void sync0()
{
MPI_Barrier(MPI_COMM_WORLD);
}

void TraceInit( char *tracefile, int format)
{
 /* Get my rank */
 MPI_Comm_rank(MPI_COMM_WORLD, &MyRank);

 /* open trace file. format ignored, similar to keywd(verbose)
NOT ParaGraph(=0) */
if(Host())
        {
        strncpy(TraceFileName,tracefile,NAMESIZE-1);

        /* no translation CR/LF */
        TraceFileP=fopen(tracefile,"wb");
        if(TraceFileP==NULL)
                {
```

```
                ReportError("TraceInit:  Open Failed\n",FALSE);
                return;
                }
        }
return;
}

void TraceExit()
{
 traceflush();
 traceoff();
 /* do not close file (if host) as children might not have
 all responded yet */
 return;
}

void traceenable(char *tracefile,int
format){TraceInit(tracefile,format);}
void traceexit(){TraceExit();}

void traceclose()
{
/* close trace file if Host */
if(Host())
    fclose(TraceFileP);
}


void traceflush()
{
 /* flush buffer*/
 /* need to account for time tracing, particularly when sending
    data! time filling buffers, etc. probably negligible
 */
 Time start,st,end,ed;
 st=time(&start);
```

```
/*send data!*/
MPI_WriteTrace(TraceBuffer,sizeof(struct
        traceitem)*TraceBufferHolds);
tracekt += TraceBufferHolds;
TraceBufferHolds=0;
ed=time(&end);
/* this recursion should be allowed but may be dangerous*/
tracewrite(TraceTRACE_FLUSH,&start,NULL);
tracewrite(TraceTRACE_FLUSHD,&end,NULL);
return;
}

void tracehost(int tracesize, int flush)
{
tracenode(tracesize,flush, FALSE);/* DO NOT SYNC*/
return ;/* DUMMY- Delta, etc not Host/Node machine*/
}

void traceinfo(int *remaining, int *event, int *compstats, int
*commstats)
{
int hold;
hold=tracelevel_picl;
*event= hold & 0x7;
hold>>=3;
*compstats=hold & 0x7;
hold>>=3;
*commstats=hold;
*remaining= (TraceBufferHolds-TraceBufferSize -SAFTEY);
return;
}

void tracelevel(int event, int compstats, int commstats)
{
if(commstats>3)
        commstats=3;
```

```
 if(event>4)
      event=4;
 if(compstats>4)
      commstats=4;
 tracelevel_picl = event |(compstats<<3)|(commstats<<6);
 return;
 /* DUMMY ParaGraph only wants (4,4,0) anyway! 4
      should behave same as 3*/
}


static tracewrite(int mark,Time *t, char * msg)
{
 int len;
 Time timer;
 struct traceitem *event;
 if(TraceBuffer==NULL)
      return;
 event= &(TraceBuffer[TraceBufferHolds]);
 if(t==NULL)
      timer= time(&(event->when));    /*return value stored
                                              in  timer */
else
      {
      event->when= *t;
      /* CAVEAT: this assumes Time ie time_t is
              atomic variable!!!!!!!!!!!!!*/
      }
 event->who= MPI_COMM_WORLD;
 event->what= mark;
 if( msg==NULL)
      {
      if(CurDir!=NULL)strncpy(event->where,
              CurDir,MaxCurDirS);
      }
else
```

```
        {
        strncpy(event->where,msg,MaxCurDirS);
        }
TraceBufferHolds++;
if(TraceBufferHolds >= FlushSize)
        traceflush();
 return 0;
}


void tracemark(int marktype)
{
 /* system or user-defined event */
 /*write to buffer*/
 int rv;
if(!traceon_picl)
        return;
rv=tracewrite(marktype,NULL,NULL);
}

void tracemsg(char *message)
{
 /* user msg */
 if(!traceon_picl)
        return;
tracewrite(TraceUSR_MSG, NULL,message);
 return;
}

void tracenode(int tracesize,int flush, int sync)
{
 int need_size;
 /* establish buffer. flush automatically=1 <=0 immediate.
        if sync=1 synchronize first */
 need_size = tracesize;
 TraceBufferSize=tracesize;
```

```
 FlushSize=TraceBufferSize;
 TraceBufferHolds=0;
 if(flush <=0)
        FlushSize=3;/* flush each msg along with its
                              FLUSH msgs */
if(FlushSize<3)
        FlushSize=3;
TraceBuffer=(struct traceitem *)malloc(need_size *
        sizeof(struct traceitem ));
if(TraceBuffer==NULL)
        {
        /* send error message */
        ReportError("tracenode msg buffer malloc
               falied\n",FALSE);
        exit(1); /* abort? */
        }
if(sync)
        {
        sync0();
        }
traceon();
return;
}

Event traceMaxEvent(){return TraceMAXEVENT;}

static FILE *out=NULL;

void MPI_WriteTrace(struct traceitem *str, int bytecount)
{
 int rank,flag;
 int count,i;
 MPI_Status status;
 struct traceitem *ti;
 char s[1024];
#define TRACE_TAG 4095
```

```
#ifdef DEBUG
if(Host())printf(" WriteTraceEntered Host %d %d\n",
        bytecount, sizeof(struct traceitem));
#endif

 flag = TRUE;
 MPI_Comm_rank(MPI_COMM_WORLD, &rank);

#ifdef DEBUG
if(rank > 0)
        {
        /* temporary since str is struct traceitem
        sprintf(s,"[%2d] %s", rank,str);
        str = s;
        */
        }

if(!out)/* && Host added by Baker */
        out=fopen("~/program.trc","a");
if(out  && Host())
    {
    count = bytecount/sizeof(struct traceitem);
    ti=str;
    for(i=0;i<count;i++,ti++)
    fprintf(out,"host:Id=%d event=%d\n",ti->who,ti->what);
    }
if(!out && !rank)
        {
        printf(" cannot open program.trc\n");
        fflush(stdout);
        }
#endif

 if(rank == 0)
        {
        /* Print stuff out */
```

```
        while(flag)
                {
                /* printf(" TOP TRACE DEBUG: tracemsg
count=%ld\n",tracekt);
                fflush(stdout);
                */
                MPI_Iprobe(MPI_ANY_SOURCE, TRACE_TAG,
                        MPI_COMM_WORLD, &flag,
                        &status);
                if(!flag)
                        break;
                MPI_Recv(s, 1023,MPI_CHAR, MPI_ANY_SOURCE,
                        TRACE_TAG,MPI_COMM_WORLD,&status);
                MPI_Get_count(status, MPI_CHAR, &count);
                fwrite(s,count,1,TraceFileP);
                fflush(TraceFileP);
                tracekt += count/sizeof(struct traceitem) ;
        /*      printf(" TRACE DEBUG: tracemsg
count=%ld\n",tracekt);
                fflush(stdout);
                */
                count = bytecount/sizeof(struct traceitem);
                ti=s;
                for(i=0;i<count;i++,ti++)
                        fprintf(out,"slave:ld=%d event=%d\n",ti-
>who,ti->what);

                }
        fwrite(str,bytecount,1,TraceFileP);
        fflush(TraceFileP);
        }
 else
        MPI_Send(str, bytecount, MPI_CHAR, 0, TRACE_TAG,
                MPI_COMM_WORLD);

#ifdef DEBUG
```

```
/* Debug(" WriteTrace Exiting Rank=%d %d\n",MyRank,
bytecount);  */
#endif
}

#endif /* TRACE */
```

Figure 7.17: trace.c.

The code in file msg.c needs to be modified to call **tracemark** as needed to record to the tracefile the information on the initiation of sends, receives, and other operations. This code is in file *msgtr.c*:

```
/* Message passing routines -
 * Operating System Dependent!
 */

#include "all.h"

#ifdef MPI  /* Generic message passing interface */
#include "mpi.h"
#endif

#if defined(MYMPI)
int
MPI_Init(int *argc, char ***argv)
{

#if defined(PVM)
 int nproc;
 /* Determine number of processes to spawn, and start PVM */
 nproc = ParseSpawnArg(*argc, *argv);
#ifdef CM5  /* CM5 has a host program that spawns others */
 return(PVM_Init("slave", nproc));
#else
```

```c
  return(PVM_Init(*argv[0],nproc));
#endif
#else
 return(MPI_SUCCESS);
#endif
}

int
MPI_Comm_size(MPI_Comm comm, int *size)
{
#ifdef PVM
 *size = PVM_Nproc();
#else
 *size = 1;
#endif
 return(MPI_SUCCESS);
}

int
MPI_Comm_rank(MPI_Comm comm, int *rank)
{
#ifdef PVM
 *rank = PVM_Rank();
#else
 *rank = 0;
#endif
 return(MPI_SUCCESS);
}

int
MPI_Abort(MPI_Comm comm, int errcode)
{
#ifdef PVM
 PVM_Abort(errcode);
#endif
 return(MPI_SUCCESS);
```

```
}

int
MPI_Finalize()
{
#ifdef PVM
 pvm_exit();
#endif
 return(MPI_SUCCESS);
}

int
MPI_Send(void *buf, int count, MPI_Datatype datatype,
         int dest, int tag, MPI_Comm comm)
{
 int ret;

#ifdef TRACE
tracemark(TraceSTART_SEND);
#endif

#ifdef PVM
 ret = PVM_Send(buf, count, datatype, dest, tag);
#else
 ret = MPI_SUCCESS;
#endif

#ifdef TRACE
tracemark(TraceFINISH_SEND);
#endif

 return(ret);
}

int
MPI_Recv(void *buf, int count, MPI_Datatype datatype,
```

```c
        int source, int tag, MPI_Comm comm,
            MPI_Status *status)
{
 int ret;

#ifdef TRACE
tracemark(TraceWAIT_RECV);
#endif

#ifdef PVM
 ret = PVM_Receive(buf, count, datatype, source, tag, status);
#else
 ret = MPI_SUCCESS;
#endif

#ifdef TRACE
tracemark(TraceFINISH_RECV);
#endif

 return(ret);
}

int
MPI_Isend(void *buf, int count, MPI_Datatype datatype,
      int dest, int tag, MPI_Comm comm,
            MPI_Comm_request *request)
{
#ifdef PVM
 return(PVM_Isend(buf, count, datatype, dest, tag, request));
#else
 return(MPI_SUCCESS);
#endif
}

int
```

```
MPI_Irecv(void *buf, int count, MPI_Datatype datatype, int
source,
        int tag, MPI_Comm comm, MPI_Comm_request *request)
{
#ifdef PVM
 return(PVM_Irecv(buf, count, datatype, source, tag, request));
#else
 return(MPI_SUCCESS);
#endif
}

int
MPI_Wait(MPI_Comm_request *request, MPI_Status *status)
{
 int ret;

#ifdef TRACE
 tracemark(TraceWAIT_START);
#endif

#ifdef PVM
 ret = PVM_Wait(request,status);
#else
 ret = MPI_SUCCESS;
#endif

#ifdef TRACE
 tracemark(TraceWAIT_DONE);
#endif
 return(ret);
}

int
MPI_Test(MPI_Comm_request *request, MPI_Status *status)
{
#ifdef PVM
```

```
 return(PVM_Test(request,status));
#else
 return(TRUE);
#endif
}

int
MPI_Iprobe(int source, int tag, MPI_Comm comm, int *flag,
      MPI_Status *status)
{
#ifdef PVM
 return(PVM_Probe(source, tag, flag, status));
#else
 *flag = FALSE;
 return(MPI_SUCCESS);
#endif
}

int
MPI_Get_source(MPI_Status status, int *source)
{
 return(*source = status.source);
}

int
MPI_Get_tag(MPI_Status status, int *tag)
{
 return(*tag = status.tag);
}

int
MPI_Get_count(MPI_Status status, MPI_Datatype datatype,
      int *count)
{
 return(*count = status.count);
}
```

```
int
MPI_Barrier(MPI_Comm comm)
{
 int rank, nproc, dummy,i;
 MPI_Status status;

#ifdef TRACE
 tracemark(TraceWAIT_BARRIER);
#endif


 /* For right now - do this with generic sends and receives */
 MPI_Comm_size(comm, &nproc);
 MPI_Comm_rank(comm, &rank);
 if(nproc <= 1)
        return(MPI_SUCCESS);

 /* Everyone send to rank zero */
 if(rank > 0)
        {
        MPI_Send(&rank, 1, MPI_INT, 0, BARRIER_MSG_TAG,
                   comm);
        MPI_Recv(&dummy,1,MPI_INT, 0, BARRIER_MSG_TAG,
                   comm, &status);
        }
  else
        {
        /* Zero'th processor collects messages */
        for(i=1; i<nproc; i++)

        MPI_Recv(&dummy,1,MPI_INT,MPI_ANY_SOURCE,
             BARRIER_MSG_TAG, comm, &status);
        /* Now let everyone proceed */
        for(i=1; i<nproc; i++)
                MPI_Send(&rank, 1, MPI_INT, i,
```

```
                            BARRIER_MSG_TAG, comm);
        }

#ifdef TRACE
 tracemark(TraceWAIT_OVER);
#endif

  return(MPI_SUCCESS);
 }


/* A very limited implementation ! - only a few ops */
int
MPI_Reduce(void *sendbuf, void *recvbuf, int count,
       MPI_Datatype datatype,MPI_Op op, int root,
              MPI_Comm comm)
{
 int rank, nproc, i;
 void *buf;
 MPI_Status status;

 /* For right now - do this with generic sends and receives */
 MPI_Comm_size(comm, &nproc);
 MPI_Comm_rank(comm, &rank);
 if(nproc <= 1)
        return(MPI_SUCCESS);
 if(rank != root)
        {
        MPI_Send(sendbuf, count, datatype, root,
             REDUCE_MSG_TAG, comm);
        }
 else
        {
        /* Master */
        buf = New(count * _MPI_SizeDataType(datatype));
        memcpy(recvbuf, sendbuf, count *
```

```
                    _MPI_SizeDataType(datatype));

        for(i=1; i<nproc; i++)
                {
                MPI_Recv(buf,count, datatype,MPI_ANY_SOURCE
                    , REDUCE_MSG_TAG, comm, &status);
                _MPI_Op(recvbuf, buf, count, datatype,op);
                }
        free(buf);
        }
/* Need to wait for master before continuing */
MPI_Barrier(comm);
return(MPI_SUCCESS);
}


void
_MPI_Op(void *b1, void *b2, int count,MPI_Datatype datatype,
MPI_Op op)
{
int i;
float *f1,*f2;
double *d1, *d2;
int *i1,*i2;

f1 = (float *) b1;
f2 = (float *) b2;
d1 = (double *) b1;
d2 = (double *) b2;
i1 = (int *) b1;
i2 = (int *) b2;

for(i=0; i<count; i++)
        {
        switch(datatype)
                {
```

```
          case MPI_FLOAT:
             switch(op)
                {
                case MPI_MAX:
                      f1[i] = MAX(f1[i], f2[i]);
                      break;
                case MPI_MIN:
                      f1[i] = MIN(f1[i], f2[i]);
                      break;
                case MPI_SUM:
                      f1[i] += f2[i];
                      break;
                case MPI_PROD:
                      f1[i] *= f2[i];
                      break;
                default:
                      ReportError("MPI:Unsupported
MPI_FLOAT reduction operation\n",FALSE);
          break;
                }
     break;
   case MPI_DOUBLE:
             switch(op)
                {
                case MPI_MAX:
                      d1[i] = MAX(d1[i], d2[i]);
                      break;
                case MPI_MIN:
                      d1[i] = MIN(d1[i], d2[i]);
                      break;
                case MPI_SUM:
                      d1[i] += d2[i];
                      break;
                case MPI_PROD:
                      d1[i] *= d2[i];
                      break;
```

```
                        default:
                                ReportError("MPI:Unsupported
MPI_DOUBLE reduction operation\n",FALSE);
                                break;
                        }
                break;
            case MPI_INT:
            case MPI_UNSIGNED:
                switch(op)
                    {
                    case MPI_MAX:
                            i1[i] = MAX(i1[i], i2[i]);
                            break;
                    case MPI_MIN:
                            i1[i] = MIN(i1[i], i2[i]);
                            break;
                    case MPI_SUM:
                            i1[i] += i2[i];
                            break;
                    case MPI_PROD:
                            i1[i] *= i2[i];
                            break;
                    default:
                            ReportError("MPI:Unsupported
MPI_INT reduction operation\n",FALSE);
                            break;
                    }
                break;
            default:
                    ReportError("MPI: Unsupported type in
MPI_Reduce()\n", FALSE);
                    break;
    } /* End switch */
  }
}
```

```
#endif /* MYMPI */
```

A test driver for the tracing feature is:

```
/*  testbed for trace(PICL)
L. Baker Dagonet Software
Copyright 1993 L. Baker
*/

#define TESTMPI

#include "all.h"

#ifdef TESTMPI
void TestMPI(int argc,char **argv);
#endif

void sigcatch(int signo)
{
char msg[80];
sprintf(msg,"Signal %d caughtRank %d\n",signo,Rank);
ReportError(msg,TRUE);
}

int
main(int argc,char **argv)
{
 Problem prob;

/* MPI test program */
#ifdef TESTMPI
 TestMPI(argc,argv);
 Exit(0);
 return(0);
#else /* TESTMPI */
```

```
/* Initialize the MPI message system and variables */
InitMPISystem(argc, argv);
signal(SIGINT, sigcatch);
signal(SIGQUIT,sigcatch);
signal(SIGFPE,sigcatch);
signal(SIGABRT,sigcatch);
signal(SIGHUP,sigcatch);
signal(SIGEGV,sigcatch);
signal(SIGSYS,sigcatch);
/* Initilize basic variables */
if(!InitProblem(&prob))
       Exit(0);
#ifdef NOTDONE

traceenable( "/home/baker/trace.out",1);

/* Run the required problem */
Run(&prob);

/* Clean up */
DeleteProblem(&prob);

#endif /* NOTDONE */
Debug("Exiting Normally\n");
Exit(0);
traceclose();
return(0);

#endif /* NOT TESTMPI */
}

void
Run(PProblem prob)
{
}
```

```
#ifdef TESTMPI
void
TestMPI(int argc, char **argv)
{
 int n,rank,i;
 MPI_Comm comm;
 float out,in;

 comm = MPI_COMM_WORLD;
/*
 MPI_Init(argc,argv);
 MPI_Comm_size(comm, &n);
 MPI_Comm_rank(comm, &rank);
*/
 InitMPISystem(argc,argv);
         /* like above but sets Rank,NProc, AllDest*/
 n=NProc;
 rank=Rank;

 Debug("PVM Initialized rank=%d\n",rank);
 traceenable( "trace.out",1);
 Debug(" traceenable returned\n");
 if(rank)tracenode(20,1,0);
 else tracenode(20,1,0);
 Debug(" tracenode returned rank=%d\n",rank);
 in = (float) rank+ 1.0;
 Debug(" before reduce MIN rank=%d\n",rank);
 MPI_Reduce(&in, &out, 1, MPI_FLOAT, MPI_MIN, 0, comm);
 Debug(" after reduce MIN rank=%d\n",rank);
 if(rank == 0)
         Debug("MIN of float ranks is %f\n", out);

 MPI_Reduce(&in, &out, 1, MPI_FLOAT, MPI_MAX, 0, comm);
 if(rank == 0)
```

```
      Debug("MAX of float ranks is %f\n", out);

MPI_Reduce(&in, &out, 1, MPI_FLOAT, MPI_SUM, 0, comm);
if(rank == 0)
      Debug("SUM of float ranks is %f\n", out);

MPI_Reduce(&in, &out, 1, MPI_FLOAT, MPI_PROD, 0, comm);
if(rank == 0)
      Debug("PROD of float ranks is %f\n", out);
Debug(" before BARRIER rank=%d\n",rank);
MPI_Barrier(comm);
Debug("Exiting psph\n");

traceexit();
Exit(0);
}


#endif
```

Figure 7.19: tracet.c, test driver for tracing.

Finally, file *tdump.c* converts the binary trace file into ASCII format for readability:

```
/* routines to implement a picl
-style tracing feature
  NOT compatible with ParaGraph!
  L.  Baker    DAGONET SOFTWARE 11/93


assumes an external  char *CurDir;
HOST = MASTER  in Master/Slave model (assumed)
caveat: recv has only 1023 bytes for msg! might have to
up this.
Also, potential problems if "host" does not generate traces
often to recover trace messages from other slave nodes.
```

```
*/

#define PICLCODE
#define DEBUG

/*#define TRUEPVM*/

/*#define TRUEMPI*/

#include <time.h>
#include <stdio.h>

char *CurDir="baker";/* dummy for now*/

/* below only for node zero. wasted space otherwise.
        Not much though*/

#define NAMESIZE 60
static char TraceFileName[NAMESIZE];
static FILE *TraceFileP=NULL;
static long int tracekt= 0l;

#define MaxCurDirS 20

typedef time_t Time; /* UNIX time: good to milliseconds */

typedef int MSGTYPE;
struct traceitem
        {
        Time  when;
        int what;
        int   who;/*rank*/
        char  where[MaxCurDirS];
        };

#define isize sizeof(struct traceitem)
```

```
static char event[17][11]={"SEND Start","END Send ",
        "START Recv","END Recv  ","Open Trace","Clse Trace",
        "FLUSH Strt","FLUSH EndT","LEVEL Chng",
        "START Trce","END Trce  ",
        "START Barr","END Barr  ","User Msg: ",
        "START Wait","END Wait  ",
        "NULL Msg  "};
FILE *in,*out;

main(int argc,char **argv)
{
/*convert a trace.out file into a file to be sorted and dumped */
int size;
struct traceitem data;
char str[21],*whats;
in=fopen("trace.out","rb");
out=fopen("trace.prc","w");
if(in==NULL||out==NULL)
        exit(0);
while(1)
        {
        size=fread(&data,isize,1,in);
        if(!size)break;
        strncpy(&str,&(data.where),20);
        str[21]='\000';
        whats =&( event[data.what-1][0]);
        fprintf(out,"%d %d %s %s\n",
                data.when,data.who,whats,&str);
        }
fclose(in);
fclose(out);
}
```

Figure 7.20: tdump.c.

Public Domain Packages

Chameleon

Chameleon is the system for message passing developed at Argonne National Laboratories (Gropp and Smith, 1993). As might be guessed from the name, Chameleon can present a number of user interfaces; currently, subsets of NX and PICL calls are supported by this "reverse compatibility" feature. It can employ a wide variety of message-passing systems for actual implementation, including P4, PVM, PICL, NX, EUI (IBM SP-2), and CMMD (Thinking Machines CM-5). Native Chameleon programs may be recognized by calls that look like PIbsend and PIbrecv. Chameleon serves as the basis for the MPICH system.

P4

P4 was an early message passing system, and one that may be considered superseded. See the paper by Butler and Lusk (1994).

PICL

PICL stands for Portable Instrumented Communications Library (Geist et al. 1990). It is obsolete and should be avoided. Its principal point of interest is that it provided extensive debugging diagnostics, including a tracing feature. Support for trace execution is limited in PVM and MPI, although it is generally promised to appear in future versions. PICL low-level primitive calls look like **recv0** or **probe0**, with higher-level calls such as **barrier0**, **bcast0**, and **gsum0**. PICL does not support nonblocking calls, with a potential loss of efficiency as a result.

PICL provides better diagnostic features than most other systems. There are nine calls: **traceenable**, **traceexit**, **traceflush**, tracehost, **tracelevel**, **tracemark**, **tracemsg**, **tracenode**, and **traceinfo**. The result will be a tracefile, which is then sorted by timestamp and used as input for the ParaGraph analysis program.

Proprietary Message Passing

MPL

MPL is the proprietary message-passing library of the IBM SP-2. MPL is largely superseded by the native MPI library. Although it is referenced as an option in our layered MPI code, we will not reproduce the corresponding support code here, as there is no real point to using MPL at this time.

NX

NX is the proprietary Intel Paragon message-passing system. It is of interest primarily because PVM would regularly crash the Intel Paragon, and MPI was not implemented for the Paragon at this time (in 1994). (Readers should check for the current situation at installations of interest if they intend to use a Paragon.) The code to support out MPI-layering for the Paragon, using the native NX system, is in file *pgon.c*, and is:

```
/*
Copyright 1994, 1995 Louis Baker, Bradley Smith, Anthony
Giancola. All rights reserved.
*/
/* MPI Implementation for Intel Paragon */

#include "all.h"

/* Some compilers require at least one external reference */
extern int NProc;

#ifdef PGON_MSG
static pid_t *pids; /* Task id array */
static int PGON_nproc,PGON_proc;
static long p_type;

#define PGON_PTYPE p_type
```

```
/* Initialize n copies of the named process */
int
PGON_Init(int n, int argc, char **argv)
{
 int i;
 int num;

 if((num=numnodes()) > 1)
       PGON_nproc = num; /* Already initialized */
 else
       PGON_nproc = n;

 if(n<=1 && num == 1)
       {
       PGON_proc = 0;
       return(MPI_SUCCESS);
       }

 if(num <= 1 && n > 1)
       {
#ifdef NOTDEF /* Doesn't work with IP switch */
       /* Initialize partition */
       if(nx_initve(NULL, (long)n, NULL, &argc, argv) <= 0)
              return(MPI_FAILURE);

       /* Fork them */
       pids = New(sizeof(pid_t) * n);
       if((i=nx_nfork(NULL, -1, 0, pids)) < 0)
              return(MPI_FAILURE);

       if(i > 0) /* Controlling process stays out of things */
              {
              nx_waitall();
              Exit(0);
              }
#else
```

```
        printf("Specify number of processes with '-sz' option as
in: myprogram -plk -sz 4\n");
        return(MPI_FAILURE);
#endif
        }

 PGON_proc = mynode();
#ifdef OLD
 setptype(PGON_PTYPE);
#endif
 p_type = myptype();

 return(MPI_SUCCESS);
}

int
PGON_Rank()
{
 return PGON_proc;
}

int
PGON_Nproc()
{
 return(PGON_nproc);
}

void
PGON_Abort(int errcode)
{
 int i;

 /* Kill everyone */
 kill(0, SIGTERM);

 /* Kill ourselves */
```

```
  Exit(0);
}


/* Overkill - but the paragon wants longs, not ints */
static long *Ldest;

/* Now capable of doing a multisend */
int
PGON_Send(void *buf, int count, MPI_Datatype data_type, int
*dest, int ndest, int tag)
{
 int i;

 if(!Ldest)
        Ldest = (long *) New(sizeof(long)*PGON_nproc);

 /* Copy to long array (probably overkill, but we
        want portability) */
for(i=0; i<ndest; i++)
        Ldest[i] = (long) dest[i];

 /* Begin multi-send */
 gsendx((long) tag, buf, (long) (count *
_MPI_SizeDataType(data_type)), Ldest, (long)ndest);

 return(MPI_SUCCESS);
}

int
PGON_Receive(void *buf, int count, int data_type, int source,
        int tag, MPI_Status *status)
{
 long info[8];

 if(source >= PGON_nproc || source < MPI_ANY_SOURCE)
        {
```

```
        UserMessage("PVM_Receive: Attempt to receive on bad
source=%d\n", source);
        return(MPI_FAILURE);
        }

 /* Blocking extended receive */
 crecvx((long) tag, buf, (long) (count *
_MPI_SizeDataType(data_type)), (long)source,
        (long) PGON_PTYPE, info);

 /* Grab message stats */
 status->count = (int) (info[1] / _MPI_SizeDataType(data_type));
 status->source = (int) info[2];
 status->tag = (int)info[0];

 return(MPI_SUCCESS);
}

int
PGON_Isend(void *buf, int count, MPI_Datatype data_type,
        int dest, int tag, MPI_Comm_request *request)
{

 request->msgid = isend(tag, buf, (count *
_MPI_SizeDataType(data_type)), dest, PGON_PTYPE);
 request->is_send = TRUE;
 request->status.tag = tag;
 request->status.source = dest;
 request->status.count = count;
 return(MPI_SUCCESS);
}

int
PGON_Irecv(void *buf, int count, MPI_Datatype data_type,
        int source, int tag, MPI_Comm_request *request)
{
```

```
  /* NOT IMPLEMENTED */
 return(MPI_FAILURE);
}

int
PGON_Wait(MPI_Comm_request *request, MPI_Status *status)
{
 msgwait(request->msgid);
 return(MPI_SUCCESS);
}

int
PGON_Test(MPI_Comm_request *request, MPI_Status *status)
{
 return(msgdone(request->msgid));
}

int
PGON_Probe(int source, int tag, int *flag, MPI_Status *status)
{
 long info[8];

 if(!iprobex((long) tag,(long)source, (long) -1, info))
       {
       *flag = FALSE;
       return(MPI_SUCCESS);
       }
 /* Count is inaccurate (in bytes) - but that's OK */
 status->count = (int) info[1];
 status->source = (int) info[2];
 status->tag = (int) info[0];
 *flag = TRUE;
 return(MPI_SUCCESS);
}

#endif /* PGON_MSG */
```

Figure 7.21: pgon.c.

CMMD

This is the proprietary message-passing system for the Cray T3D. We have used the native PVM implementation on the T3D. MPI support should be forthcoming from Cray Research, Inc.

References

Butler, R. M., and Lusk, E. W., "Monitors, Messages, and Clusters: The p4 parallel programming system," *Parallel Computing* , **20**, pp. 547-564 (1994).

Feitelson, D. G., Corbett, P. F., Baylor, S. J., Hsu, Y., "Parallel I/O Subsystems in Massively Parallel Supercomputing," *IEEE Parallel & Distributed Technology*, **3**(3), pp. 33-47, Fall 1995.

Geist, G. A., Heath, M. T., Peyton, B. W., Worley, P. H., "A Users' Guide to PICL A Portable Instrumented Communications Library," ORNL/TM-11616,August 1990. Available through netlib.

Geist, A., Beguelin, A., Dongarra, J., Jaing, W., Mancheck, R., Sundram,V., *PVM: Parallel Virtual Machine*, Cambridge, M. A.: MIT Press, 1994.

Gropp, W., Lusk, E., "Some Early Performance Results with MPI on the IBM SP1," available via anonymous ftp from ftp://aurora.cs.msstate.edu/pub/reports/Message-Passing.

Gropp, W., and Smith, B., "Users Manual for the Chameleon Parallel Programming Tools," ANL-93/23, 1993. Available through netlib.

Heath, M. T., Malony, A. D., Rover, D. T., "The Visual display of Parallel Performance Data," *IEEE Computer*, pp. 21-28, **28** (11) Nov. 1995.

Heath, M. T., Malony, A. D., Rover, D. T., "Parallel Performance Visualizaiton: From Practice to Theory," *IEEE Parallel and Distributed Technology*, pp. 44-60, **3** (4) Winter 1995.

Leighton, F. T., *Introduction to parallel algorithms and Architectfures: Arrays, Trees, Hypercubes*, San Mateo, C. A.: Morgan Kaufman, 1992.

Chapter 8

Performance Tuning and Optimization

Optimization

The most important factor controlling the efficiency (in terms of both time and memory) of your program is the choice of algorithm(s) employed. Other considerations amount to "fine-tuning." We will discuss both aspects here. To support optimization and debugging, we show how the code of the previous chapter may be modified to support tracing ('profiling') of parallel execution. The Winter 1995 issue *of IEEE Parallel and Distributed Technology* is devoted to the topic of "Performance Evaluation Tools," including visualization tools for profiling.

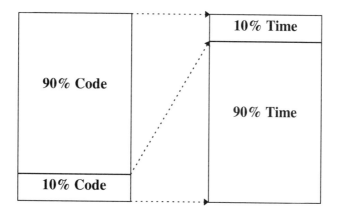

Figure 8.1: The 90-10 rule of thumb. 10% of the code typically accounts for 90% of the run time.

Jon Bentley, in his fine book *Programming Pearls* (Bentley 1986), discusses the experience document in Appel (1985). A speedup of a factor of 400 was achieved by optimizing a simulation code. Of this, a factor-of-

12 improvement was achieved by changing the algorithm to a more efficient method (with a new data structure). A number of changes achieved factor-of-2 improvements: Tuning the algorithm's parameters (increasing the time step), another algorithm change (to reconfigure the binary tree data structure each timestep for more efficient lookups), and replacing double-precision with single-precision computations. Profiling showed that 98% of the time was spent in one procedure; fine-tuning by hand in assembly language sped up the program by a factor of 2.5. Finally, moving to a machine with a floating-point accelerator gave another factor-of-two improvement. This example illustrates the significance of algorithm improvements in optimization. (Bentley's book has another chapter devoted to code tuning.) It also illustrates the value of profiling and of persistence.

Kernighan and Plauger (1974), another classic in the literature, provide three relevant maxims:

> "Don't diddle code to make it faster-find a better algorithm."

> "Instrument your programs. Measure before making 'efficiency' changes."

> "Let your compiler do the simple optimizations."

The first restates our point that algorithm changes are the most effective ways to speed up code. The second restates the value of profiling as a guide to determining where to make the optimization changes. Kernighan and Plauger remark that the "instrumentation" should be left in the code as it evolves. This way, profiling can later spot code that was "broken" in the sense of poor efficiency at a later date. "Regression testing" is the concept of re-running your test suite to be sure that an "improvement" has not broken the code, and that all the previous tests are still passed. This should be done for efficiency as well as program correctness. The ability of compilers to perform simple optimizations better than the user can in high-level languages will be discussed shortly.

Fundamental algorithm choices are complicated on parallel machines by the tradeoff between more intensive computational effort vs. more intensive data communications cost. Often, these choice can only be made by measuring the performance of the competitors. For this reason, profiling and tracing are important, and are discussed later in this chapter.

We have advocated developing the code first for a single processor, and then parallelizing and testing on multiple processors. Optimization should not wait until parallelization. Profile the serial code to determine the "hot spots," or places in the code where optimization will pay the greatest returns. Then parallelize and determine the "hot spots" or "bottlenecks" limiting parallel performance. Don't put the optimization effort where it will not substantially impact the overall performance.

There is an interesting convergence in computer hardware nowadays. Architectures of vector supercomputers, single microprocessors, and parallel machines are all developing similar features. This is not an accident, of course; it is merely the result of microprocessor designers incorporating whatever ideas they find to improve their products. The consequence is that optimization is similar in many ways for all machines.

Microprocessors are all either pipelined (such as the Pentium) or superpipelined (such as the Intel P6; see Rupley and Clyman 1995). The result is behavior similar to that of vector machines such as the Cray. The coding practices that used to "inhibit vectorization" on the Cray now cause pipeline stalls on the microprocessors. Interestingly, it becomes even more important to avoid such problems on the latest superpipelined processors, as the performance penalty is even more drastic; programming for the latest generation of microprocessors got harder, not easier.

Similarly, microprocessors are now all superscalar to some degree, that is, they posses functional units that can operate in parallel. The latest PA-RISC machine chip, the PA-8000 from Hewlett-Packard, has two floating-point multiplier/accumulators and two floating-point divide/square-root units, in addition to two integer arithmetic-logic units, two shift/merge units, and two load-store units (Pountain 1995). This appears to be an exceptional choice, however, as the general-purpose CPUs such as Intel's P6 appear to have chosen the direction of increasing clock speed (through superpipelining) instead of becoming increasingly superscalar. (Hewlett-Packard seems to give division more weight in design than other manufacturers. The allocation of two units for floating-point division, which have a latency of only 17 clock cycles compared to 39 for the Pentium, suggests they consider division and square-root extraction more common than others do.) Nevertheless, microprocessors all appear to implement "fine-grained" parallelism, implementing the ability to perform multiple operations, including floating-point math, simultaneously. The Cray XMP and YMP (but not the Cray 2) supported "chaining," which passed results directly from one computational unit to another, avoiding pipeline stalls that might have been caused by a unit having to wait for results from another. As a result, the performance of the Cray 2 was disappointing relative to that of its predecessors. Features such as "register renaming" on some microprocessors, and chaining on others, similarly avoid unnecessary pipeline stalls.

Cray supercomputer programmers will also recall issues involving memory- bank conflicts. The "stride" of memory access became an important issue. Code that accessed two data locations separated in their addresses by a power of two resulted in egregious performance, as these fetches could not be performed simultaneously. When a FORTRAN do loop of the form:

```
      Do 1 J=1,1000000,N
1     S(J)=S(J)*3.14159
```

was executed on the Cray-2 at the Air Force Phillips Laboratory at Kirtland AFB, NM, for a stride of N=1, the performance was 56 Mflops: it was 55 MFlops for N=3 and N=7,and 53 for N=5. However, for N=2 it was a mere 25 MFlops, fell to 15 MFlops for N=32, and was down to 3 MFlops for N=256. Caches typically fill "lines" of contiguous data. Consequently, if the stride is such that only one data item per line is of interest, the cache is being inefficiently used. Similarly, whether the cache is two-way or four-way set-associative or direct mapped influences its sensitivity to memory access patterns, as well is if the cache is unified or there are separate data and instruction caches. In fact, the RS/6000 processor in an SP-2 uses a four-way set associative data cache, usually 64K in size, with 512 lines of 128 bytes each. The instruction cache is smaller, and two-way set associative. On such an architecture, a stride that is a higher power of two will reduced the number of effective cache lines from 512 to as little as four. The user cannot control this, but he can check the effects and be ready to make whatever changes in code are required. The general rule is to try to keep data as close together as possible. The RS/6000 Optimization Guide (1992) recommends against using array dimensions of a power of two, and provides optimizations which include inserting dummy arrays (called "padding") within FORTRAN common blocks, and modifying array dimensions (e.g., changing 128 to 129) in order to prevent memory access conflicts.

Similar issues arise with the latest microprocessors, typically with multi-ported memories or with odd/even address banks. Therefore, it is often useful to learn about the idiosyncrasies of your particular hardware for best performance. Often the fixes are portable in the sense that they do not degrade performance on processors other than the target. If not, #ifdef...#else....#endif blocks may be used to isolate target-dependent code.

Also of interest is the hierarchy of memory in microprocessors. There is typically a relatively small cache (typically on the order of 16K if a unified cache, or two 8K caches for instructions and data) on the microprocessor, with a larger high-speed static RAM cache and then the DRAM memory itself. The Intel P6 is actually a multichip module, with a large cache chip mated with the microprocessor proper. The analogy with a parallel system, with a hierarchy of memory: fast, local memory and relatively slow-to-access memory on other nodes, is obvious. In parallel message-passing systems, the user may be able judiciously use spare bandwidth to import data from other processors before the data is needed. It is generally somewhat more difficult to fill a cache with data, as most implement cache management algorithms (often, the "least-recently used" method) that are beyond user control.

The moral of the foregoing is that it is important to optimize your scalar code for a parallel processor, as it will most likely be executing on an array of microprocessors that are sensitive to such optimization. The basic ideas of such optimization will work on the "fine-grained" level on individual processors as well as on the "coarse-grained" level of parallelization. Therefore, we will review such "serial" optimizations before discussing optimizations specific to parallel machines.

Astute readers will note that most pronouncements in this chapter are embedded within a collection of "weasel words." This is unfortunate but necessary, because with varying hardware and software, what is optimal for one may be terrible for another. The user who wants to obtain best performance will have to use trial and error for to determine what optimizations to apply to the code at hand.

Serial Optimization

Compilers differ widely in their ability to optimize. Therefore, it is probably a good idea to optimize by hand whatever can be done. Compilers typically offer a number of levels of optimization, controlled by "switches." It is usually a good idea to debug with minimal optimization and then turn on optimization gradually, noting when optimization "breaks" some code. Often the code can be rewritten to take advantage of the higher level of optimization, with a consequent gain in speed. Otherwise, *pragmas* may be used to protect the offending section of code from optimization, permitting the higher level of optimization to be used for the other sections of the code.

Compiler Optimizations

First of all, it is of interest to note what optimizations compilers can perform. These are of interest because the compiler will do a better job than hand-written user code; don't attempt these by using temporary variables. It is also of interest as it gives an indication of what code would be accelerated by increasing the optimization level permitted. Compilers are best at local optimization. Most code generators have "peephole" optimizers, which scan a relatively short section of generated code (either assembler language or P-code) and optimize that code. As many compiler systems use the same "back end" or code generator for a number of compilers, the optimization at this level is language-independent.

Common Subexpressions

Compilers, even those with simple peephole optimizers, are typically good at detecting and using common subexpressions. An example would be:

```
       a= (b+c);
       d=4.*(b+c);
```
There is no need for:

```
           register double temp;
           temp= (b+c);
           a=temp;
           d=4.*temp;
```
or

```
           d=4.*(a=(b+c));
```
Indeed, it is possible that these alternatives might inhibit optimization. Most likely, they will perform no differently.

Do not make it difficult or impossible for the compiler to recognize or use common subexpressions. For example, the code:

```
       a= d*(b*c);
       e= f*(c*d);
```
does not contain a usable common subexpression (c*d), as the first requires that b and c be multiplied before that product is in turn multiplied by d. Even without the parentheses, an optimizer might not recognize the common product in both expressions.

The famous distributive law of multiplication, (a+b)*c =a*c+b*c, can often be used to advantage. While the latter expression has two multiplications and one addition to the former's single addition and single multiplication, on modern microprocessors floating-point additions and multiplications are of the same cost; so if common subexpressions or another advantage might be gained, the latter expression can be more effective than the former. (On the other hand, when such is not the case, use the distributive law where possible to save a multiplication.)

Strip Mining

Strip mining is the term given to a machine-dependent optimization that depends on the characteristics of the cache memory or pipeline size. It breaks a simple loop into a nested loop, with the inner loop length optimized for memory access performance. Strip mining is sometimes referred to as the less-prosaic "blocking."

The loop

```
for(i=0;i<n;i++) a[i]=b[i]+c[i];
```

would become the more complicated:

```
#ifdef ARCH1
        #define increment 128
#elsif ARCH2
        #define increment 64
#endif
for(nstart=0,nstop=increment;nstop<n;nstart+=incremen
t,nstop+=increment)
        for(i=nstart;i<min(nstop,n);i++) a[i]=b[i]+c[i];
```

Here we assume that ARCH1 is an architecture for which 128 is the optimal value for increment, while the optimal value is 64 for ARCH2. If **n** is a multiple of increment, the test for completion of the inner loop may be simplified. Note also that we can, on a parallel machine, consider doing each of the inner loops on different machines, if the data communications costs make this parallelization attractive.

Integer-Real Conversions

Depending upon the hardware and software environment, the conversion between integers and floating-point numbers may be expensive. It may be desirable to keep a floating-point variable which mirrors an integer, e. g.,

```
int i; float im;
for(i=0,im=0.;...;i++, im+=1.0)
```

rather than code im=(float)i;. Certainly the latter might (depending upon compiler sophistication) invoke a library function, which would inhibit vectorization and be costly; but some compilers will do the conversion in-line, at moderate cost.

Float vs. Double, IEEE-754 vs non-IEEE-754 compliance

One some architectures, computing with floats (32-bit) is faster than computing with type double (64-bit or double precision in FORTRAN), but this is unusual. Memory bandwidth usage is doubled when double precision is used. On the other hand, alignment issues on some machines make it desirable to use doubles where possible. Also, as computations in C are normally of type double, there may be conversion costs in using type float.

Compliance with the IEEE-754 standard for floating-point has costs. One example is the RS/6000, which supports a multiply-add operation. This operation is not compatible with strict application of the IEEE-754 standard, which would require rounding the 80-bit operands between the multiplication and the addition. Omitting this rounding should give better accuracy than the standard requires, but might give different answers than those on a strictly compliant machine. On many machines, relaxed compliance can result in faster operation due to less time expended in the rounding step. Once again, experimentation is the only way to determine if relaxing IEEE-754 compliance is desirable.

Complex Arithmetic

Various tricks can be played with complex arithmetic; it is often more efficient to treat the real and complex parts separately. A well-known example is complex multiplication. The product of two complex numbers can be formed directly as $(a+bi)(c+di) = (ac-bd)+i(ad+bc)$, which requires 4 multiplications and two additions. Alternatively, we can form w=(a+b)(c+d) =ac+bd+bc+ad, x=ac, y=bd. The real part of the product is then x-y, and the imaginary part is w-x-y. We have used only three multiplications, with five addition/subtraction operations. If addition and multiplication cost the same, as they do on many architectures, this is a bad tradeoff, but on other architectures it results in a gain. Similar considerations apply to operations on matrices with complex elements or functions of complex arguments. Often, treating real and imaginary parts separately can result in improvement.

Note that, due to differences in round-off effects, results can differ depending on which method of computation is used.

Strength Reduction

A common optimization is to use a faster operation, e. g., replacing a division by a multiplication. For example, the code   x= a/5.; might be replaced by the compiler with x=a*.2;. Similarly, x=2.*y; might be rewritten as x= y+y;. On modern microprocessors, multiplication and addition are often equally rapid; as some have both floating-point addition and multiplication units, it might be faster to leave the multiplication as such if an addition could be done simultaneously on the other unit.

Many microprocessors, such as the P6 and PA-8000, support hardware square roots. Thus, it will be very much faster to perform x=sqrt(y); than x=pow(y., .5);. Extracting cube roots by Newton's method will typically be significantly faster than the general-purpose library routine, which must compute logarithms and antilogarithms (exponentials).

Once again, note the danger of altered answers.

Minimize Side-Effects

Particularly in code to be parallelized and vectorized, do not use overlapping data structures (unions in C, equivalenced arrays in Fortran, etc.). These will inhibit vectorization, confuse compilers, and make debugging a nightmare. Functions and procedures also should not have "side effects," such as modifying global variables, unless absolutely necessary for some reason. That also inhibits optimization, cache utilization, etc.

Vectorization and Caching

There is a rich literature on vectorization, from the heyday of supercomputing on Cray's and similar machines (e.g., Petersen 1983). These articles should be consulted for background. Petersen, gives a number of useful examples of vectorized code for Toeplitz system solvers, FFTs, and minimum path determination.

Short loops do not exploit the vector pipeline. Therefore, type to give the pipeline long vectors on which to operate. Typically, only inner loops vectorize if loops are nested. Therefore, the longest loop should be the innermost. If possible, it should be allowed to operate on a stride of one for best memory utilization efficiency. It is often cost-effective to do some preliminary data movement to form large vectors, which are then processed by vectorized loops.

Where possible, use simple subscripts (indices) involving constants and the loop index ("induction variable" in the terminology of vectorization). The more complex the indexing, the more likely a pipeline stall. If necessary, precompute the indices and put them into an array for use.

Depending on the hardware, loops with few or many operations may be preferred. With a limited cache size, it may be desirable to recode a loop with a number of operations as a number of simple loops. On the other hand, loop overhead will be minimized by incorporating a number of assignments, etc. within one loop. It may require some experimentation to determine the optimal configuration. On typical microprocessor-based parallel systems with hierarchical memory, it appears that the simpler loops perform better for reasonable vector lengths. This is discussed as follows.

Loop Unrolling

Loop Unrolling is a machine-dependent method for reducing the overhead in loop execution. Consider the code: **for(i=0;i<N;i++) x[i]= z[i]+y[i];**. Consider instead: **for(i=0;i<N;i+=2) {x[i]= z[i]+y[i]; x[i+1]=z[i+1]+y[i+1];}**. We assume that N is odd, so that an even number of assignments are made, in order that these two code fragments are equivalent. The second loop will be executed half as many times as the first, with half as many tests for completion. On the other hand, the code size is increased, and the caching may be less efficient. The virtue of loop unrolling is therefore dependent on the particular host environment, and unrolled loops may not perform any better on some machines.

Loop Reordering

This is simply the idea of choosing the innermost loop, either to operate on the longest vector, in order to exploit vectorization to the fullest, or to have unit stride to optimize memory reference efficiency. An example from Petersen (1983) is performing a convolution sum:

$$f_i = \sum_{k=1}^{m} a_k b_{i+k-1}$$

This may be coded as two nested loops, e. g.,

```
for(i=0;i<n-m+1;i++)
        f[i]=0.;
        for(k=0;k<m;k++)
                f[k] += a[k]*b[i+k];
```

Note that if **m** is substantially smaller than **n**, it may be desirable to re-order the loops

```
for(i=0;i<n-m+1;i++)f[i]=0.;
for(k=0;k<m;k++)
        for(i=0;i<n-m+1;i++)
                f[k] += a[k]*b[i+k];
```

to have longer vectors with which to keep the pipeline busy.

In converting code between C and FORTRAN, note that FORTRAN arrays are stored in "row major" order, with the first subscript incrementing first. C uses the opposite convention. Consequently, it may be desirable because of stride considerations to use different loop orderings.

Loop Collapsing

Loop collapsing refers to simplifying addressing arithmetic by treating arrays with multiple subscripts as singly subscripted arrays. This may not be absolutely portable, but is generally safe and effective. For example, the loop:

```
for(i=0;i<m;i++
        for(j=0;j<n;j++)
                a[i][j]=b[i][j]+2.;
```

could be implemented as:

```
mn= m*n;
        for(i=0;i<mn;i++)
                a[i]=b[i]+2.;
```

This, of course, makes assumptions about the contiguous storage of the a and b arrays, about their not overlapping, about the second limits of the arrays corresponding to the limit of the subscript index **n**, etc. With suitable care and testing, however, there should be a speedup on most systems.

Loop Fusion and Loop Distribution

Loop fusion refers to combining loops to reduce overhead. The two loops

```
for (i=0;i<n;i++) a[i]=b[i]+c[i];
for (i=0;i<n;i++) d[i]=a[i]+f[i];
```

could become

```
for (i=0;i<n;i++) {a[i]=b[i]+c[i]; d[i]=a[i]+f[i];}.
```

In the example shown, it is likely that the second loop would eliminate some overhead and a memory reference to one of the operands, and therefore would be somewhat faster than the implementation via two loops. As discussed below, Loop Fusion may be desirable in diminishing the effect of a data dependency.

Loop Distribution is the opposite of loop fusion, and involves splitting complicated loops into simpler ones. Loop distribution is desirable if loop code that did not fit into the instruction cache can be shortened so as to fit. This would eliminate the need to access slower memory for the instruction fetches.

As Loop Distribution and Loop Fusion are opposites, and as they are hardware-sensitive, there is no absolute general rule. Experiment with different options for different hardware environments. On most machines, if the vector length is significant, memory usage considerations should predominate over loop overhead, and loop distribution should be preferable.

Data Dependencies

There are a number of ways the sequence of computation can be important; when it is the case that calculations must be performed in a certain sequence, it is called a "data dependence." These will inhibit optimization, possibly cause pipeline stalls, and should be avoided if possible. In the sequence:

```
1:      a = b + c;
2:      d= a +2;
3:      e = a +3;
```

we find that the statements labeled as 2 and 3 must be performed after 1, but the ordering of 2 and 3 is irrelevant. This is called a *flow dependence* (Padua and Wolfe 1986). The sequence:

```
1:      a = b + c;
2:      d= a +2;
3:      a = e +3;
```

again requires 2 to follow 1, and 2 must precede 3 (which changes the value of a). This is called an *output dependence*. For

```
1:      a = b + c;
2:      b= d +2;
```

statement 2 must not precede statement 1, at least not in overwriting the value of b; this is called an *antidependence*. Finally, control dependence involves the effect conditional branches; e.g.,

```
1:      a=b+c;
        if( x!=0.) a +=2;
        else d=a;
```

which involves possible changes to the values of a and d depending upon which branch is actually taken. Often, the feature called *speculative execution* results in the machine computing both results, and discarding the results of the branch not taken. Many times, dependencies may be removed by judicious renaming of variables, or rearranging of loops; see Leiss (1995) for examples.

The most common cause of data dependence in scientific code is the use of recurrence relations, e.g., $a_i = a_{i-1}*b+c$, in computations. If a vector array is used for the *a* variable, the result of the calculation for the index value *i-1* must be known before the value for index *i* can be determined. The loop for this calculation cannot be parallelized or vectorized due to such a dependence. Such recurrences often occur in the use of Pade (rational) or continued-fraction approximations, for example. Often there is no alternative at reasonable computational cost. A somewhat more complex example, which provides an opportunity for some vectorization or parallelization, would be:

```
for(i=1;i<n;i++)
        {a[i]=a[i-1]+c[i]-f[i]*p; q[i]=a[i]*r;}
```

where some speed advantage would be usually be gained by recoding as:

```
for(i=1;i<n;i++)
        t[i]=c[i]-f[i]*p;
for(i=1;i<n;i++)
        a[i]=a[i-1]+t[i];
for(i=1;i<n;i++)
        q[i]=a[i]*r;
```

with two out of the three loops capable of vectorization or parallelization.

Another way to minimize the impact of data dependencies is to include other computations in the loop which can be performed while "waiting" for the dependent operand. This can sometimes be effected through Loop Fusion as discussed above.

Control dependencies can be minimized or eliminated in a number of ways. Often the loop can be simplified and conditionals can be pulled out of the loop. Arrays can be assigned values based on conditionals and then used in a loop that fully vectorizes as it does not contain conditionals. For example, the "antidependence" illustration above, a "dummy" variable **e** could be used to hold the **d+2** value, with a later loop assigning **e** to **b**.

Data dependencies should be minimized or eliminated if possible. There are a number of approaches and "tricks" which can be employed.

Often, in a loop, the dependence is caused by an endpoint. If so, split the endpoint out for special treatment, allowing the bulk of the computation to proceed efficiently.

One trick that is not generally applicable, but which can be useful in some rare circumstances, is "backward indexing," in which a loop index is decremented from its maximum value rather than incremented from its minimum value. This technique generally requires significant code rewriting (and thought) to have the same effect as the forward-indexed code.

Dependencies may be introduced by operators such as the += operation, depending on the use of machine registers. For example, the code

```
for(i=0;i<n;i++)
        for(j=0;j<m;j++)
                a[i] += b[i]*c[j]
```

produces a data dependency on the RS/6000 as the value of a[i] is added to the product and then stored back into a[i]. The *IBM Optimization Guide* (1992) recommends rewriting the code as:

```
a2=0.
for(i=0;i<n;i++){
        for(j=0;j<m;j+=2){
                a[i] += b[i]*c[j]
                a2[i]+=b[i+1]*c[j];
                }
        a[i]+=a2[i];
        }.
```

Reducing Number of Function Calls

Function calls inhibit optimization and vectorization. The P6 will implement hardware to predict not merely branches but subroutine returns. Nonetheless, it is a good idea to minimize the overhead of function and procedure calls. There are two ways to do this. If the procedure is small, consider in-lining the code. If not, consider moving the loop to within the subroutine, so that the code in the subroutine (function or procedure) may vectorize.

Parallel Optimization

We may assume now that the serial version of your code is as blazingly fast as possible. After getting the code running in parallel, your work is not finished. You want to make it run as rapidly as possible in parallel. This will entail a few additional possible optimizations, which take into account the architecture of your host and optimize the performance of the message passing.

Minimizing Communications

This has been discussed in chapter 4. The basic issue is how to distribute the data. As discussed by Gross et al. (1994), it may be desirable to structure the calculation so as to have the (partial) answer move to the data in systolic fashion, instead of the other way around, as is perhaps more intuitive and natural. The example they give is multiplying two matrices, $C=AB$. The "natural" way is to accumulate the values for each element of the product matrix C on a given processor, sending the rows and columns of the multiplier and multiplicand matrices A and B where needed. In the systolic approach, the partial sums for elements of the C matrix are sent to appropriate nodes to acquire the terms needed. The moral of the story seems to be that flexibility and originality in considering ways to organize computation and distribute data can be rewarded. Do not rush in to do things the "obvious" way. Time spent designing the computational approach before coding is generally not wasted. Gross et al. (1994) also present examples of LU and QR matrix decompositions and a Successive Overrelaxation (SOR) calculation employing systolic communication patterns. The advantages for the matrix multiplication and LU decompositions are most significant (factors of approximately three in MFlop rate for both), with smaller gains for SOR and QR problems.

Because computation typically involves tens of nanoseconds, whereas data transfers typically involve multiple microseconds, it may be desirable to compute quantities derived from basic variables redundantly on nodes where they are needed, passing only the basic variables. The waste in computational effort is more than made up by the reduced message passing.

Asynchronous Message Passing

Overlapping communication and message-passing is facilitated by asynchronous message passing. It is fairly common to have a program structure of the form:

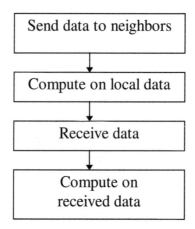

Figure 8.2: Overlapped communications and computation.

This improves program efficiency, as the send operation can to some degree overlap the computation. This occurs because the send operation may make use of DMA transfers, which can be done in parallel with computation and may require waiting for interrupt service, etc. to actually send the data. All this time will be wasted in busy waiting unless the computation is performed simultaneously.

There are limitations to this approach that should be noted. Obviously, sufficient buffer space must be available in order that all the received data can be accommodated while the computation is performed. Typically, system parameters have to be carefully specified, or else wasteful system traps are generated; on the Cray T3D, global buffer sizes need to be specified, and the job will fail if buffers fill before the messaged data is removed for processing.

Buffering Messages

Obviously, transferring large blocks of data takes time, and this slows computation. Even worse, time expended in such a manner only makes your Megaflop rate suffer. Hence, careful choice of methods for moving data, or avoiding data moves, can be useful. If the data is contiguous, the machine might be able to employ a DMA transfer. Generally, using memcpy() will be faster than using assignment statements. Finally, if possible, use of a pointer to specify a user-defined memory area as a "buffer" can be exploited in some message-passing situations.

Load Migration

Probably the most important way to speed up computation is to be sure that the load is well-balanced initially and remains reasonably well-balanced throughout the computation. On problems that involve simulating the evolution of a system with time, rebalancing the load, i.e., moving the boundaries between processor allocations of the problem, is often necessary.

Load balancing techniques are discussed in chapter 4. They rely on real-time estimation of performance, to be discussed below.

Optimize Communications Package

In chapter 5 we noted how the use of the "direct" mode of PVM could substantially improve performance over the "normal" mode in some circumstances. Opportunities like this should not be passed up. The user will probably not have to be concerned about such matters if their code is running on massively parallel machines at supercomputer centers, but running on a local network is another story.

Machine-Specific Optimizations

Understanding the Architecture

It should be obvious from the foregoing illustrations that is desirable to know basic machine characteristics such as cache organization and size. Machine and compiler peculiarities are of interest as well.

For example, consider the RS/6000 processor. It features a multiply-add instruction, which will more rapidly compute expressions of the form **a*b+c**. Where possible, computations should be organized to exploit this operation. One interesting "feature" of the RS/6000 (*Optimization and Tuning Guide*, 1992) is that if there is a data dependency between two successive floating-point operations and if one of the operands is zero, there is an additional delay. This can cause unexpected delays in computations where a large number of the data arc zero, such as if an array has been initialized to zero. It also can cause erroneous timing estimates if these are done using zeroed arrays instead of those with realistic entries. The moral here is to read the system documentation (or, better yet, talk to people who know!).

Many microprocessors employ branch prediction schemes, often beyond the control ("hinting") of the user. In such cases, it can be useful to know how the machine will guess and make this guess the correct one. Often, structured statements, such as the case statement in C, will work better than the if statement.

One interesting example concerns the use of temporary scalar variables to "hint" to the compiler. Consider matrix multiplication via two slightly different methods:

```
for(i=0;i<m;i++)
        for(j=0;j<m;j++){
            c[i][j]=0.;
            for(k=0;k<m;k++)
                    c[i][j] += a[i][k]*b[k][j];
            }
```

vs.

```
for(i=0;i<m;i++)
        for(j=0;j<m;j++){
            sum=0.;
            for(k=0;k<m;k++)
                    sum += a[i][k]*b[k][j];
            c[i][j]=sum;
            }
```

A manual produced by Convex computer (1986) for its architectures states that the former performs more efficiently than the latter, while the reverse is true on the RS/6000. This is of course a function of the compiler's optimizer, and could change without notice with a new release of the compiler.

Note that in the optimizations discussed here, results can change due to round-off error differences implicit in the different calculation sequences.

Understanding Networks

Optimization of a parallel program includes both optimizing the the running of the code on each node, and optimizing the communication. The latter requires some understanding of the behavior of the interconnection between nodes. As discussed previously, the Cray T3D has a number of unique features and foibles that make it highly desirable to familiarize oneself with its properties. The IBM SP-2 has its own quirks. A proprietary "high-performance" switch connects nodes to each other and to the network. The switch has a 500 nanosecond latency and a 40MB/s peak bidirectional bandwidth. Nodes may also communicate via Ethernet. Nodes are grouped on "frames" of sixteen nodes. One consequence is that program performance may be expected to change significantly between a case in which there are sixteen or fewer nodes on a single frame, and a case with nodes on different frames, as the latter involves switch or Ethernet communications. In its early days with 400 nodes, the MHPCC had fairly regular failures of the Network File System (NFS), which would cause the pvm daemons to die and your program to hang. This has improved with a number of system changes, but highlights the need to be informed of the situation at the computer site.

Profiling Parallel Programs

Timing Parallel Programs

Wall-clock information is needed in load-balancing and performance optimization, whether you "own the machine" or not. If you are the only user running, wall-clock time is virtually identical to user time; the latter does not include system time which in this case is exclusively devoted to servicing the single user. If you do not "own" the machine, other statistics based on "user" time are of interest as well.

The most important parallel statistic is the measure of idle time, i.e., the time spent waiting at synchronization barriers for the slowest processor to catch up. This can be measured in a number of ways, such as the maximum idle time of any of the processors, or the "standard deviation" (square root of the sum of the squares) of the idle times of all the processors. Such statistics are often used to determine if load balancing should be redone.

Such timings are "easy" if subtleties are ignored; simply record the (wall-clock) times before and after the barrier synchronization call in each program, subtract to obtain the difference, and send the results to the master/root for processing. Subtleties include problems if the time is too short for the wall-clock system time routine to adequately measure, but this is a problem we would like to have. Note that synchronization of the clocks on machines is not a problem for this measurement, as it would be for tracing programs, so long as each clock is self-consistent, as we are only interested in the difference in times on each node and not a comparison of absolute times between nodes. Tanenbaum (1994) discusses clock synchronization, but such problems are in the bailiwick of the system's programmers and if at all possible. Leave such problems to them. SNTP (Simple Network Time Protocol) is a standard system for performing this task. It uses a server node with clients requesting clock information as needed to synchronize to the server. It uses TCP/IP on UNIX systems, and should be generally available.

On (BSD) UNIX systems, we recommend using the **gettimeofday** function, e. g.,

```
#define <time.h>
#define <ctype.h>
#define <sys/time.h>
...
struct timeval
      {
      long tv_sec:
      long tv_usec:
      }tv;
struct timezone tz;
```

```
long time;
....
gettimeofday(&tv,&tz);

time= tv.tv_sec * 100L +((long)tv.tv_usec/10000L);
```

to get time in hundreths of a second. It may be desirable to subtract out the starting time in order to keep numbers in bounds and to have an elapsed time. The full time value returned is supposed to be the time since 00:00:00 GMT, Jan 1, 1970. Here **tv_usec** is the fractional component in microseconds. On System V UNIX, if gettimeofday is not to be found, use

```
#include <sys/types.h>
#include <sys/times.h>
struct tm{
      time_t tms_utime; /* user time*/
      time_t tms_stime;/*system time*/
      time_t tms_cutime; /* child user time */
      time_t tms_csttime; /* child system time */
      }
long times (struct tms *ptr)
```

which will return the number of clock ticks (the value of a clock tick being given in **<sys/param.h>**).

If **gettimeofday** is not available on your system, the function **long clock()** may serve.

Profiling message passing

Many systems provide trace information in some form; the question is what to do with it. Utter and Pancake (1991), for example, take the results of the IBM Parallel FORTRAN trace and provide a graphical interface as a debugging/performance-analysis tool.

In message passing parallel codes, there are two forms of communications costs. One is the actual message transmission time; the other is the time spent preparing the data for transmission. The former is of interest only insofar as processors have to wait for the data. The latter includes packing and unpacking data, format conversion (such as to and from the XDR format as employed by pvm), system requests, etc.

If computation and communication are overlapped, should one processor have to wait for data being sent from other machines, the computation is not slowed if this processor is not the last to arrive at a synchronization point (barrier). Consequently, time spend waiting for data is not generally of interest; time waiting at a barrier is. A large disparity between processors in wall-clock time for the arrival at a barrier is indicative of poor load balancing, and should be fixed. This can be examined during a run and the load rebalanced dynamically.

As in debugging, the usual approach to profiling is to profile large sections of code first, to find the likely location of hot spots and/or bottlenecks, and then to narrow the scope of the profiling. It is also to separately profile communications and computation to check for bottlenecks.

Serial and Parallel Profiling Tools

Obviously, if performance is of concern, you must profile your program. First you should profile and optimize the serial code.

Code for supporting performance tracing is given below.

Table 8.1:Procedures in trace.c	
InitTrace	Initialize tracing system
EndTrace	Terminate and display results
StartSendTrace	Begin timing send
StartRecvTrace	Begin timing receive
StopSendTrace	End timing send
StopRecvTrace	End timing receive

```
#include "all.h"

#ifdef TRACE
```

```
typedef struct tagTrace
        {
        long tsend,trecv,tstart;    /* Time in hundredths */
        int sendcount, recvcount;
        long bytes_send, bytes_recv;
#ifdef SYS_TRACE
        SysTimer ssys, rsys;
#endif
        } Trace;

typedef Trace *PTrace;
static PTrace traces;
static int MinTag, MaxTag;

/* Intialize the trace - tracing from mintag to maxtag */
void
InitTrace(int mintag, int maxtag)
{
 int i;
 traces = (PTrace) New((maxtag-mintag) * sizeof(Trace));
 MinTag = mintag;
 MaxTag = maxtag;
 for(i=0; i<(mintag-maxtag); i++)
        {
        traces[i].sendcount = traces[i].recvcount = 0;
        traces[i].tsend = traces[i].trecv = 0L;
        traces[i].bytes_send = traces[i].bytes_recv = 0L;
#ifdef SYS_TRACE
        InitSysTimer(&traces[i].ssys);
        InitSysTimer(&traces[i].rsys);
#endif
        }
}

 void
```

```
StartSendTrace(int tag, int nbytes, int ndest)
{
 int i;
 if(tag < MinTag || tag >= MaxTag)
        return;
 i = tag-MinTag;
 traces[i].tstart = GetCurTime();
 traces[i].bytes_send += nbytes*ndest;
 traces[i].sendcount += ndest;
#ifdef SYS_TRACE
 StartSysTimer(&traces[i].ssys);
#endif
}

void
StopSendTrace(int tag)
{
 int i;
 if(tag < MinTag || tag >= MaxTag)
        return;
 i = tag-MinTag;
 traces[i].tsend += (GetCurTime() -  traces[i].tstart);
#ifdef SYS_TRACE
 StopSysTimer(&traces[i].ssys);
#endif
}

void
StartRecvTrace(int tag)
{
 int i;
 if(tag < MinTag || tag >= MaxTag)
        return;
 i = tag-MinTag;
 traces[i].tstart = GetCurTime();
 traces[i].recvcount ++;
```

```
#ifdef SYS_TRACE
 StartSysTimer(&traces[i].rsys);
#endif
}

void
StopRecvTrace(int tag, int count)
{
 int i;
 if(tag < MinTag || tag >= MaxTag)
        return;
 i = tag-MinTag;
 traces[i].trecv += (GetCurTime() -  traces[i].tstart);
 traces[i].bytes_recv += count;
#ifdef SYS_TRACE
 StopSysTimer(&traces[i].rsys);
#endif
}

void
EndTrace()
{
 int i,k;
 int tsend=0, trecv=0;
 for(i=MinTag; i<MaxTag; i++)
        {
        k = i-MinTag;
        if(traces[k].sendcount > 0 || traces[k].recvcount > 0)
                {
                UserMessage("Trace for tag %d: trecv=%ld
sent=%d(%ld) recv=%d(%ld) tsend=%ld\n",
                        i, traces[k].trecv,
                        traces[k].sendcount, traces[k].bytes_send,
                        traces[k].recvcount, traces[k].bytes_recv,
                        traces[k].tsend);
                tsend += traces[k].sendcount;
```

```
                    trecv += traces[k].recvcount;
                    }
            }
    UserMessage("Total sends=%d received=%d\n", tsend, trecv);
    if(Rank == 0)
            {
            UserMessage("Exiting Trace\n");
            }
    }

#endif /* TRACE */
```

Figure 8.3: C code to trace parallel programs

These routines will time sends and receives.

Table 8.2: Timer routines	
InitSysTimer	Initialize timers
StartSysTimer	Begin timing
StopSysTimer	Stop timing
SPrintSysTime	Print results
NormalizeTime	Convert results to tenths of seconds

They use timer routines with header file:

```
/* various machines have different names for clock
 * ticks per second */
#ifndef CLK_TCK
#define CLK_TCK 60l
#endif
```

```
#ifndef CLOCKS_PER_SEC
#define CLOCKS_PER_SEC 1000000L
#endif

void InitSysTimer(PSysTimer t);
void StartSysTimer(PSysTimer s);
void StopSysTimer(PSysTimer s);
void SPrintSysTimer(char *s, PSysTimer tim, int fmt);
void NormalizeTime(clock_t *time);

/* Timer print formats */
#define ST_SYS_TIME 1
#define ST_USER_TIME 2
#endif /* TIMES */
```

and source code:

```
#ifdef TIMES
void
InitSysTimer(PSysTimer pt)
{
 pt->cur_tot.tms_utime = 0;
 pt->cur_tot.tms_stime = 0;
 pt->cur_tot.tms_cutime = 0;
 pt->cur_tot.tms_cstime = 0;
 pt->running = FALSE;
}

void
StartSysTimer(PSysTimer pt)
{
#ifdef DEBUG
 if(pt->running)
```

```
        Debug("WARNING - restarted running timer!\n");
#endif
 times(&pt->last_start);
 pt->running = TRUE;

}

void
StopSysTimer(PSysTimer pt)
{
 struct tms end;

 if(!pt->running)
        {
#ifdef DEBUG
        Debug("WARNING: StopSysTimer called on stopped
timer!\n");
#endif
        return;
        }
 pt->running = FALSE;
 times(&end);

 /* Running total of user and system times */
 pt->cur_tot.tms_utime += end.tms_utime - pt-
>last_start.tms_utime;
 pt->cur_tot.tms_stime += end.tms_stime - pt-
>last_start.tms_stime;
}

void
SPrintSysTimer(char *s, PSysTimer pt, int fmt)
{
        sprintf(s,"%f sec", (fmt == ST_SYS_TIME?
                ((float)pt->cur_tot.tms_stime/100.0) :
                ((float)pt->cur_tot.tms_utime/100.0) ) );
```

```
}

void
NormalizeTime(clock_t *t)
{
 long tim;
 /* Normalize times to 10ths of a second */
 tim = (long) *t;
 tim = (tim * 10L)/CLK_TCK;
 *t = (clock_t) tim;
}

#endif /* TIMES */
```

Figure 8.4: C Code for timing functions.

References

Anonymous, *Optimization and Tuning Guide for the XL FORTRAN and C Compilers*, IBM, 1992.

Anonymous, *Vectorization and Optimization Guidelines*, Convex Computer Corp., 1986.

Appel, A., "An Efficient Program for Many-Body Simulations," *SIAM J. Sci. Stat. Computing*, **6**(1),pp. 85-105, Jan. 1985.

Bentley, J., *Programming Pearls*, Reading, MA: Addison Wesely, 1986.

Gross, T., Hinrichs, S., O'Hallaron, D. R., Stricker, T., Hasegawa, A., "Communications Styles for Parallel Systems," *IEEE Computer*, **27** (12) pp. 34-43, Dec. 1994.

Kernighan, B. W., and Plauger, P. J., *The Elements of Programming Style*, N.Y.: McGraw-Hill, 1974.

Leiss, E. L., *Parallel and Vector Computing: A Practical Approach*, N.Y.: McGraw-Hill, 1995.

Padua, D. A., and Wolfe, M. J., "Advanced Compiler Optimizations for Supercomputers," *Communications ACM*, **29**, 1184-1201, Dec. 1986.

Petersen, W. P., "Vector Fortran for Numerical Problems on the Cray-1," *Comm. ACM*, **26**(11), pp. 1008-21, Nov. 1983.

Pountain, D., "HP's Speedy RISC;" *Byte*, pp. 176-177, July 1995.

Rupley, S., Clyman, J., "P6: The Next Step," *PC Magazine*, **14**(15),Sept. 12, 1995.

Tanenbaum, A. S., *Modern Operating Systems,* Englewood Cliffs, N. J.: Prentice Hall, 1994.

Utter, S., Pancake, C., "A Visualization System for Animating Parallel Fortran Traces," Cornell Theory Center, CTC91TR52, 3/1991.

Chapter 9

Putting it all Together - A Working Parallel Code

In this chapter we are finally going to assemble the concepts from the previous chapters to create a simple numerical application that will run in parallel. Creating a working parallel program can be a major undertaking. Mistakes made early in the development can cause serious problems later in the development as the original design is stretched to do things unimagined originally. The code presented in this chapter will be a SPMD program using the MPI message-passing system.

We will develop a parallel message passing application based on a Poisson elliptic solver. Though a simple method, solvers of this type are used in many applications to solve elliptic equations. In addition, we will demonstrate concepts that will be important for parallel developments of all types, including yours.

Problem Description

The WinMPI system was used to develop and debug the code. The problem is somewhat of a "toy" problem, as is the solver. Real-life solvers will be more complicated, but not by much, and the parallel aspects illustrated here are fairly representative.

The Poisson equation is of the general form: $\nabla^2 \phi = \rho$. It frequently occurs in electrostatics (where ρ is the charge density and ϕ is the electrostatic potential) or fluid mechanics problems (where phi is a velocity potential, stream function, or pressure). Often, it must be solved to determine initial conditions, as with electromagnetic PIC codes.

Consider a simple rectangular grid of points in the (x,y) plane, with lattice points specified by the integer pair (i,j). The Laplacian operator at the point (i,j) is given by the usual 5-point stencil:

$(u(i-1,j) +u(i+1,j)+u(i,j-1)+u(i,j-1)-4 u(i,j))/4.$

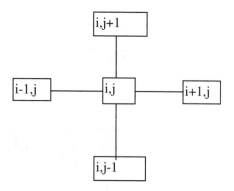

Figure 9-1: Laplacian finite-difference stencil.

Thus, if a function at (i,j) exceeds the average value in its neighborhood, the Laplacian is negative. The Laplacian measures the deviation of the value at a point from the local average, with a zero Laplacian leading to a smooth function as a solution.

We will impose simple Dirichlet boundary conditions, i.e., specify the required values of the potential function ϕ on the outer boundaries of the rectangular region. The charge density ρ will be taken to be zero everywhere. Neumann (derivative), periodic, or other boundary conditions could be used; the convergence will be slower, in general. Note that a value must be specified somewhere for a well-posed problem.

We will use the Gauss-Seidel iteration with an overrelaxation parameter to solve the problem. Such solvers are generally called Successive Overrelaxation (or SOR) methods. The term Gauss-Seidel implies that newly computed values are used as soon as they are available. This speeds convergence and improves the locality of memory reference. If we did not update the values until the next iteration cycle, we would have the more-slowly convergent Jacobi method. Thus the value at a point is updated by the use of the formula:

$u(i,j) \mathrel{+}= \omega*(rho(i,j)+u(i-1,j)+u(i+1,j)+u(i,j-1)+u(i,j+1)-4.*u(i,j))/4$

where ω is the acceleration parameter; generally, $1 \leq \omega \leq 2$.

A simple NEWS (North, East, West, South) array of processors will be used (Figure 9.2). Thus, each processor will be responsible for a rectangular region with four processors responsible for the regions on its sides and another 4 for the regions that are adjacent at the corners. Note that cells do not need to be squares, but rows and columns must mot vary in height and width, respectively. Due to the nature of the 5-point stencil, no communication is needed with the four "corner" processors.

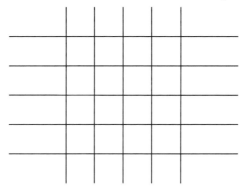

Figure 9-2: NEWS grid.

The boundary conditions imposed are *u=0* on the lower and leftmost boundaries, and linearly increasing along the other two. With the ten by ten grid used, the values range from 0 to 9 at the "north-east" or upper-right corner. This admits of a solution of the form *u=Axy*.

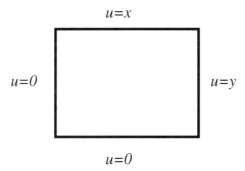

Figure 9.3: Boundary conditions.

Code

The program to solve the problem is:

```
/**********************************************************
SPMD  code for Poisson Solver.WinMPI message passing
system used.
**********************************************************/
/*#define WIN31*/
#include <stdio.h>
#include <stdlib.h>
/*below stmt for gcc compiler-non windows*/
/*
#define far
#define pascal
*/
#include "mpi.h"
#define DEBUG

#ifndef WIN31
#define Int int
#define LPPSTR char **
#endif

#define Index(i,j) [(j)+(i)*ny]
/*#define max(a,b) ((a)>(b)?(a):(b))*/
Int nproc,myid,nmax,ncol,nrow;
/*
   ncol,nrow= number of columns and rows of processors
nx,ny= number of grid lines on this processor
nmax= maximum of nx and ny
*/

struct neighborlist{
```

```
        Int procid,bindex;
        struct neighborlist *next;
        } *neighbors,*nn;/* send/recv to/from */

MPI_Status status;

/*double Iterate(Int nx,Int ny,float *u,float *b,float *rho,double
omega);*/

double Iterate(Int nx,Int ny,float *u,float *b,float *rho,double
omega)
{
Int i,j;
double om,resid,residg;
om=omega*.25;/* for 2-d*/
/*send interface data to neighbors*/
/* loop over neighbors, sending appropriate bndry of u array */
nn=neighbors;
while(nn){
        /*send to procid bindex(bindexs,...)*/
        switch(nn->bindex)
                {
                case 0: for(i=0;i<nx;i++)b Index(nn->bindex,i)=
                        u Index(i,0);
                        break;
                case 1: for(i=0;i<nx;i++)b Index(nn->bindex,i)=
                        u Index(i,ny-1);
                        break;
                case 2: for(i=0;i<ny;i++)b Index(nn->bindex,i)=
                        u Index(0,i);
                        break;
                case 3: for(i=0;i<ny;i++)b Index(nn->bindex,i)=
                        u Index(nx-1,i);
                        break;
                }
#ifdef DEBUG
```

```
if(!myid)printf(" root Sending\n");
#endif
        MPI_Send(&(bIndex(nn-bindex,0)),nmax,MPI_FLOAT,
                nn->procid,1,MPI_COMM_WORLD);
        nn=nn->next;
        }
/* interior nodes*/
residg=0.;
for(i=1;i<nx-1;i++)
        for(j=1;j<ny-1;j++)
                {
                resid= rho Index(i,j) + u Index(i+1,j)+u Index(i-1,j)
                            + u Index(i,j+1)+ u Index(i,j-1)-4.*
                                    u Index(i,j);
                /* immediate update= Gauss-Jordan */
                u Index(i,j) +=(float)( om *resid);
                residg+=resid*resid;
                }
/*receive interface data*/
/* put into b array */
nn=neighbors;
while(nn){
        /*recv from procid b Index(bindexs,0...<ny)*/
        /*BLOCKING recv*/
#ifdef DEBUG
        if(!myid)
                printf(" root at Recv\n");
#endif
        MPI_Recv(&(b Index(nn-bindex,0)),nmax,MPI_FLOAT,
                nn->procid,1,MPI_COMM_WORLD,&status);
        nn=nn->next;
#ifdef DEBUG
        if(!myid)
                printf(" root after Recv\n");
#endif
```

```
    }

/* apply interface NEWS 2-d grid assumed*/
j=0;
for(i=1;i<nx-1;i++)
        {
        resid= rho Index(i,j) + u Index(i+1,j)+u Index(i-1,j)
                    + u Index(i,j+1)+ bIndex(0,i)-4.*
                                    Index(i,j);
        /* immediate update= Gauss-Jordan */
        u Index(i,j) += (float)(om *resid);
        residg+=resid*resid;
        }
j=ny-1;
for(i=1;i<nx-1;i++)
        {
        resid= rho Index(i,j) + u Index(i+1,j)+u Index(i-1,j)
                + uIndex(i,j-1)+ bIndex(1,i)-4.* u Index(i,j);
        /* immediate update= Gauss-Jordan */
        u Index(i,j) += (float)(om *resid);
        residg+=resid*resid;
        }
i=0;
for(j=1;j<ny-1;j++)
        {
        resid= rho Index(i,j) + u Index(i+1,j)+u Index(i,j-1)
                + u Index(i,j+1)+ b Index(2,j)-4.* u Index(i,j);
        /* immediate update= Gauss-Jordan */
        u Index(i,j) += (float)(om *resid);
        residg+=resid*resid;
        }
i=nx-1;
for(j=1;j<ny-1;j++)
        {
        resid= rho Index(i,j) + u Index(i-1,j)+u Index(i,j-1)
                + u Index(i,j+1)+ b Index(3,j)-4.* u Index(i,j);
```

```
        /* immediate update= Gauss-Jordan */
        u Index(i,j) += (float)(om *resid);
        residg+=resid*resid;
         }
/* four corners: each with 2 b terms*/
        {
        resid= rho Index(0,0) + u Index(1,0)+b Index(0,0)
             + u Index(0,1)+ b Index(2,0)-4.* u Index(0,0);
         u Index(0,0) += (float)(om *resid);
         residg+=resid*resid;
        }

        {
        resid= rho Index(0,ny-1) + u Index(1,ny-1)+b Index(1,0)
             + u Index(0,ny-2)+ b Index(2,ny-1)-4.*
                     u Index(0,ny-1);
        u Index(0,ny-1) += (float)(om *resid);
        residg+=resid*resid;
        }
        {
        resid= rho Index(nx-1,0) + u Index(nx-2,0)+b
             Index(0,nx-1)
             + u Index(nx-1,1)+ b Index(3,0)-4.* u Index(nx-1,0);
        u Index(nx-1,0) += (float)(om *resid);
        residg+=resid*resid;
        }

        {
        resid= rho Index(nx-1,ny-1) + u Index(nx-2,ny-1)+
             b Index(1,nx-1)  + u Index(nx-1,ny-2)+
             b Index(3,ny-1)-4.* u Index(nx-1,ny-1);
        u Index(nx-1,ny-1) += (float)(om *resid);
        residg+=resid*resid;
        }
return residg;
}
```

```
#ifdef WIN31
int MPI_main (int argc, LPPSTR argv)
#else
int main (int argc, char *argv[])
#endif
/*
int MPI_main (int argc, LPPSTR argv)
*/
{
        double residual,localresid,abserr,
        /*relerr,*/ omega,start,fini;
        float *u,*b,*rho;
        Int iterno,nx,ny,nxtot,nytot,i,j,k,ibtm,jbtm,myrow,mycol;
        Int sendbuf[2],recbuf[2];
#ifdef WIN31
        LPPSTR far *argmnt;
#else
        char **argmnt[];
#endif
        /*init*/
#ifdef DEBUG
        if(!myid)
                printf(" before MPI calls\n");
#endif

        MPI_Init(&argc, &argv);
        MPI_Comm_rank(MPI_COMM_WORLD,&myid);
        MPI_Comm_size(MPI_COMM_WORLD,&nproc);
#ifdef DEBUG
        if(!myid)
                printf(" after MPI calls\n");
#endif
   /*define pblm */
```

```
nxtot=nytot=10;/*full grid size nytot>=nxtot*/
switch(nproc){
        case 1:
                nx=nxtot;
                ny=nytot;
                ncol=nrow=1;
                break;
        case 2:
                nx=nxtot/2;
                ny=nytot;
                ncol=2;
                nrow=1;
                break;
        case 4:
                nx=nxtot/2;
                ny=nytot/2;
                ncol=nrow=2;
                break;
        default:
                printf(" allowed proc number 1,2,4\n");
                exit(1);
        }
nmax= max(nx,ny);
abserr=1.e-6;
abserr=1.e-1;
/*relerr=1.;*/
omega=1.6; /*relaxation parameter. Should be >=1. */

/*printf(" enter omega,abserr\n");
scanf("%lf%lf",&omega,&abserr);
printf(" echo omega, abserr %lf %lf\n",omega, abserr);
*/
if(nproc==1)
        myid=0;
#ifdef DEBUG
if(!myid)
```

```
                    printf(" before MPI timer\n");
#endif

        if(!myid)
                start=MPI_Wtime();
#ifdef DEBUG
        if(!myid)
                printf(" after MPI timer\n");
#endif
        /*fill with 0 */
        u= (float *)malloc(sizeof(float)*((int)(nx*ny)));
        rho= (float *)malloc(sizeof(float)*((int)(nx*ny)));
        for(i=0;i<nx;i++)
                for(j=0;j<ny;j++)
                        {
                        u Index(i,j)= rho Index(i,j) =(float)0.0;
                        }
        b= (float *)malloc(sizeof(float)*4*(int)(ny)); /* fill with x*y*/
#ifdef DEBUG
        if(!myid)
                printf(" after malloc\n");
#endif
   if(!myid){
                start=MPI_Wtime();
#ifdef DEBUG
        if(!myid)
                printf(" after MPI_Wtime\n");
#endif
                /* assign processors their part of the problem */
                if(nproc==1)
                        {
                        ibtm=jbtm=0;
                        }
                else{
                        for(i=0;i<ncol;i++)
                                {
```

```
                        ibtm=i*nx;
                        for(j=0;j<nrow;j++)
                                {
                                if(!i&&!j)continue; /*self*/
                                jbtm=j*ny;
                                /* pack ibtm,jbtm into
                                        buffer and send*/
                                sendbuf[0]=ibtm;
                                sendbuf[1]=jbtm;

                MPI_Send(sendbuf,(Int)2,MPI_INT,(Int)(i+j*ncol),
                        (Int)0,MPI_COMM_WORLD);
#ifdef DEBUG
        if(!myid)
        printf(" prc=%ld i,jbtm=%ld %ld\n",i+j*ncol,ibtm,jbtm);
#endif

                                        }
                                }
                        }
        ibtm=jbtm=0;/*me*/
        }       /* root process*/
        else
        {
        /*receive my part of pblm: ibtm,jbtm*/

        MPI_Recv(recbuf,2,MPI_INT,0,0,MPI_COMM_WORLD,
                &status);
        /*ibtm, jbtm from root*/
        ibtm=recbuf[0];
        jbtm=recbuf[1];
        } /* slave*/
        neighbors=NULL;
        /* determine who my neighbors are and what
                portion of the b array  they send/recv */
        for(i=0;i<ncol;i++)
                for(j=0;j<nrow;j++){
```

```
                k=i+j*ncol;
                if(k==myid)
                        {
                        myrow=j;
                        mycol=i;
                        break;
                        }
        }
    for(i=0;i<ncol;i++)
        for(j=0;j<nrow;j++)
                {
                k=i+j*ncol;
                if(k==myid)continue; /*self*/
                if(i==mycol && abs(j-myrow)==1)
                        {
                        if(j>myrow)
                                {
                                /* other guy is to my north*/
                                nn= /*(struct *neighborlist)
                        */malloc(sizeof(struct neighborlist));
                                 nn->next=neighbors;
                                nn->procid=k;
                                nn->bindex=1;
                                neighbors=nn;
#ifdef DEBUG
if(!myid)printf(" root has neighbor to north\n");
#endif
                }
        else{
            /* other guy is to my btm(south) */
            nn= /*(struct *neighborlist)*/
            malloc(sizeof(struct neighborlist));
            nn->next=neighbors;
            nn->procid=k;
            nn->bindex=0;
            neighbors=nn;
```

```
#ifdef DEBUG
     if(!myid)
             printf(" root has neighbor to south\n");
#endif
             }
        }
      if(j==myrow && abs(i-mycol)==1)
             {
             if(i>mycol){
             /* other guy is to my right(east) */
             nn= /*(struct *neighborlist)*/
                    malloc(sizeof(struct neighborlist));
             nn->next=neighbors;
             nn->procid=k;
             nn->bindex=3;
             neighbors=nn;
#ifdef DEBUG
if(!myid)printf(" root has neighbor to east\n");
#endif
             }
           else
             {
             /* other guy is to my left(west) */
             nn= /*(struct *neighborlist)*/
                    malloc(sizeof(struct neighborlist));
             nn->next=neighbors;
             nn->procid=k;
             nn->bindex=2;
             neighbors=nn;
#ifdef DEBUG
     if(!myid)
             printf(" root has neighbor to west\n");
#endif
             }
        }
     }
```

```
        /*initialize*/
        for(i=0;i<nx;i++)
                {
                b Index(0,i)=(float)0.0;
                b Index(1,i)=(float) (i+ibtm);
                }
        for(j=0;j<ny;j++)
                {
                b Index(2,j)=(float)0.0;
                 b Index(3,j)=(float) (j+jbtm);
                }
        /*calculate*/
        if(!myid){
                iterno=0;
                do{
#ifdef DEBUG
        if(!myid)
                printf(" root calling Iterate\n");
#endif
                /*broadcast to all to iterate*/
                k=0;

                MPI_Bcast(&k,1,MPI_INT,0,MPI_COMM_WORLD);
                localresid=Iterate(nx,ny,u,b,rho,omega);
#ifdef DEBUG
        if(!myid)
                printf(" root returned Iterate\n");
#endif
                iterno++;
                if(nproc==1)residual=localresid;
                else
                {
                MPI_Reduce(&localresid,&residual,1,
                        MPI_DOUBLE,MPI_SUM,0,
                                MPI_COMM_WORLD);}
                printf(" iterno=%ld residual=%lf\n",
```

```
                          iterno,residual);
                  if((residual<abserr))
                  {
                  k=1;

                  MPI_Bcast(&k,1,MPI_INT,0,MPI_COMM_WORLD);
                  break;
                  }
          }while (1);
      }
  else
    {/*slave*/
      do{

          MPI_Bcast(&k,1,MPI_INT,0,MPI_COMM_WORLD);
                  if(k)break;/* done if k nonzero*/
                  localresid=Iterate(nx,ny,u,b,rho,omega);

          MPI_Reduce(&localresid,&residual,1,MPI_DOUBLE,
                MPI_SUM,0,MPI_COMM_WORLD);
          }while(1);
      }
  /* print solution*/
    if(!myid)
          {
          fini=MPI_Wtime();
          for(i=0;i<nx;i++)
                  for(j=0;j<ny;j++)
                          {
                          printf(" i=%ld,j=%ld u=%lf\n",i,j,
                                  u Index(i,j) );
                          }
                          for(k=1;k<nproc;k++)
                          {
                          MPI_Recv(u,(Int)(nx*ny),MPI_FLOAT,
                                  (Int)k,2,MPI_COMM_WORLD,&status);
```

```
                for(i=0;i<nx;i++)
                        for(j=0;j<ny;j++)
                        {
                        printf(" i=%ld,j=%ld u=%lf\n",
                        i+nx*(k%ncol),j+ny*(k/ncol),
                                u Index(i,j) );
                        }


                }
        printf(" number of iterations=%ld time=%lf\n",
                iterno,fini-start);
        }
  else{
        MPI_Send(u,nx*ny,MPI_FLOAT,0,2,
                MPI_COMM_WORLD);
        }
MPI_Finalize();
return 0;
}
```

Figure 9.4: MPI Code for Parallel SOR Poisson Solver.

The function **Iterate()** performs one iteration of the Laplacian operator.

The function **MPI_main** serves the role of the **main()** program in a typical MPI implementation; see Meyer (1994) for a detailed explanation.

The main program sets the parameters of the problem, and initializes the MPI system. It determines which portion of the problem domain will belong to each processor, and sends this information, in the form of the location (ibtm, jbtm) of the lower-left corner of the processor's responsibility, to each processor.

Each processor then determines who its neighbors are, and stores this information in a linked-list of the structure **neighborlist**. Each processor then initializes its own space; to zero. Boundary conditions (which may be irrelevant and overwritten with data from neighbors, as appropriate), are applied to the four sides of the rectangle as values specified in the **b[]** array.

The root or master proceeds by signaling each processor to do an iteration, using **MPI_Bcast**. All processors call their local function **Iterate()** to do so. This function overlaps computation and communication by sending the surface values from the **u** array to adjacent processors, then computing on interior values (which do not need to use the values in the **b** array). Only after that calculation is done do we wait at a **MPI_Recv** for the values to put in the **b** array, which are then used to compute the updated values at the surfaces of the u array. **Iterate()** then returns the sum of the squares of the error residuals. Obviously, overlapping communications and computation gains nothing on a single processor, as under WinMPI, but is of interest if the code is run in a true parallel environment.

The root **main()** then collects the sum of squares of all the residuals of all processors by means of the **MPI_Reduce** operation. If the error tolerance is exceeded, we perform another iteration. If the error tolerance is met, **MPI_Bcast()** is used to signal all processors to break out of the computational iteration loop. Results are printed out, with **MPI_Send** and **MPI_Recv** being used to gather the results. Note that it would have been possible to use a more "structured" collection with **MPI_Allgather()**. This would have required enough storage in the root processor to hold the entire array, which will not always be desirable.

The program employs "inner" and "outer" iterations. The inner iterations are those performed in each subdomain. The overall or outer iteration sequences over subdomains. Obviously, it does not pay to perform the inner iterations to full convergence at early times, as the boundary values imposed on the subdomain from the neighboring subdomains are very approximate. It is not our purpose here to optimize the convergence criterion as a function of iteration number to maximize efficiency.

We have used a coarse parallelization of the "outer" iterations by spatial decompsition. It would be possible to further subdivide and parallelize each inner iteration. For example, a red-black ordering or a cyclic reduction might be used to parallelize the SOR within one subdomain. Each subdomain could then be solved on multiple processors for additional speedup.

Discussion of Performance

Results for a 66-MHz 486 machine running Windows for Workgroups 3.11 are show in Table 9.1. Obviously, a single processor machine would show no speedup as the process count is increased, only a slowdown as overhead increases. It should be clear that Win MPI is a learning and development environment, not a production environment. Perhaps a Windows 95 version using threads instead of the DLL (dynamic link library) implementation will not show such a large penalty for message passing. In this context, it is perhaps worth noting that WinMPI exchanges data through the DLL, which would not work under Windows 95, so WinMPI will of necessity change implementation details.

Table 9.1: Performance of Poisson Solver under WinMPI		
Number of processes	Iterations used	Duration (sec)
1	17	.99
2	21	13.07
4	45	45.81

The convergence behavior of the solution is interesting. For a single processor, $\omega = 1.6$ is approximately optimal. More iterations are required as processors are added. The reason is that the Gauss-Seidel algorithm updates the u values as soon as new ones are available. In the case of a single process, this means all values. In the case of four processes, the interior "boundary values" passed from neighbors represent the previous values, and advantage is not taken of the fact that they can be updated on the other processor. If the Jacobi iteration were used, with the newly computed values for u being placed in another array, say $v(i,j)$, and the update $u=v$ being done only after all v values were computed, there would not be this sensitivity to the number of processes. More iterations would be required for convergence, however, for the Jacobi iteration.

We have previously remarked (chapter 4) how Schwarz iterations can be sensitive to details such as region overlap, sequence of computations, etc. Readers may be interested in exploring such issues on this simple problem. The optimal value for the acceleration parameter may change with partitioning schemes. More sophisticated methods use a sequence of acceleration parameters instead of a single value. The reader should consult standard works such as those by Varga (1962), Hageman and Young (1981), and Young (1968). It may be useful to vary the order in which points are updated, alternately sweeping up or down in an index. Partitioning into bands or stripes instead of square boxes might be tried, although it is likely inferior. The approach used here can easily be extended to three dimensions. See Birkhoff and Schoenstadt (1984) for a discussion of elliptic solvers, and in particular A. H. Sameh's article "A Fast Poisson Solver for Multiprocessors". A review covering Schwarz methods is Xu (1991).

Our simple illustrative problem did not include any dynamic parallelism. There was no need to rebalance the problem load, to move processor boundaries, or to alter the adjacency lists for processors. There are better iterative approaches to solving the Poisson equation, and if this must be done multiple times or for a very large array, an approach based on the conjugate gradient or other method should be considered. Aside from these considerations, the test problem illustrates SPMD programming with MPI.

The WinMPI system has its limitations, but on the whole it is an admirable and useful piece of work. It should be useful for preliminary debugging as well as helping users get their feet wet in parallel processing.

References

Birkhoff, G., Schoenstadt, A., *Elliptic Problem Solvers II*, N.Y.: Academic Press, 1984.

Hageman, L. A., Young, D. M., *Applied Iterative Methods*, N.Y.: Academic Press, 1981.

Meyer, J., *Message-Passing Interface for Microsoft Windows 3.1*, MS Thesis, University of Nebraska at Omaha, Dec. 1994.

Varga, R. S., *Matrix Iterative Analysis*, Englewood Cliffs, N. J.: Prentice-Hall, 1962.

Xu, J., "Iterative Methods by Space Decomposition and Subspace Correction," *SIAM Review*, **34**, pp. 581-613, 1991.

Young, D. M., *Iterative Solution of Large Linear Systems*, N.Y.: Academic Press, 1968.

Chapter 10

Suppliers: Good sources on parallel computing

Books

Babb II, R. G., *Programming Parallel Processors*, Reading, M. A.: Addison Wesley, 1992.

> This book had an interesting concept: It is a collection of chapters about a variety of machines, including the BBN Butterfly, Cray XMP, IBM 3090, and others. Most of the architectures discussed are now obsolete. It would have benefitted from the chapters having common structure, enabling a more direct comparison of the machines.

Chaudhuri, P., *Parallel Algoritms: Design and Analysis*, Englewood Cliffs, N. J.: Prentice Hall, 1992.

> Focuses on graph, sorting, and basic matrix algorithms, primarily for shared-memory (PRAM) architectures.

Codenotti, B., Leocini, M., *Introduction to Parallel Processing*, Reading, M. A.: Addison Wesley, 1992.

> Good coverage of architectures and the applications of algorithms to VLSI design.

JaJa, J., *An Introduction to Parallel Algorithms*, Reading, M. A.: Addison Wesley, 1992.

> A classic, but focused mostly on shared memory (PRAM) architectures.

Kronsjo, L., Shumsheruddin, D., *Advances in Parallel Algorithms*, N. Y.: J. Wiley, 1990.

> A collection of articles on a variety of applications of interest (discrete event simulation, matrix operations, neural network simulations, branch and bound optimization, genetic algorithms, dynamic

programming) and techniques (divide and conquer, packet routing on meshes, iterative algorithms), and theory (computational complexity and design of concurrent programs).

Kumar, V., Grama, A., Gupta, A.., Karypis, G., *Introduction to Parallel Computing*, Redwood City, CA: Benjamin, 1994.

This book has good coverage of both dense and sparse linear system solvers, discrete optimization and dynamic programming, the FFT, and general parallel issues.

Leighton, F. T., *Introduction to parallel algorithms and Architectures: Arrays, Trees, Hypercubes*, San Mateo, C. A.: Morgan Kaufman, 1992.

The title says it all: a book on parallel programming that goes beyond the PRAM shared-memory model to include discussion of distributed memory models of interest. Covers algorithms for problems invovling graphs, sorting, FFT, matrix operations, and arithmetic.

Leiss, E. L., *Parallel and Vector Computing: A Practical Approach*, N.Y.: McGraw-Hill, 1995.

Principally of interest for coverage of treatment of loop structures for best parallelization and vectorization. Contains an appendix discussing the parallelization of a Fortran code for seismic data analysis (3D DMO) for the CM-2 by altering the loop structure. The remainder of the book is oriented toward theoretical algorithm analysis, such as the optimal number of processors to use for various topologies to sort with maximum efficiency, etc.

Morse, H. S., *Practical Parallel Computing*, N. Y.: Academic Press, 1994.

Presents solutions to a toy problem (computation of student grade statistics) on SGI, Express, Paragon (using native NX library), C* (on Connection Machine), nCube, and Mas Par MP1.

Quinn, M.J., *Parallel Computing: Theory and Practice*, N. Y.: McGraw-Hill, 1994.

Theoretical analyses of matrix multiplcation, FFT, Jacobi iteration, sorting, searching, graph and combinatorial methods for parallel computers.

Internet software

Documentation:

PVM book by Geist et al. (see Chapter 5):
http://www.netlib.org/pvm3/book/pvm-book.html

the site: www-mitpress.mit.edu/mitp/recent-books/comp has geist.html as well as the Gropp et al. book on MPI.

MPI standard documentation in: info.mcs.anl.gov. Using netlib, one can send mail with the line "send mpi-report.ps from mpi" to get a postscript file.

MPI implementations:

MPICH: ftp://info.mcs.anl.gov/pub/mpi

CHIMP: ftp://ftp.epcc.ed.ac.uk/pub/chimp

LAM: ftp://tbag.losc.edu/pub/lam

MPI for Windows csftp.unomaha.edu in /pub/rewini/WinMPI. Based upon p4 by J. Meyer & H. El-Rewini of U of Nebraska at Omaha.

PADE: The Parallel Applications Development Environment. Based upon PVM. Developed by NIST and collaborators. ftp://gams.nist.gov/pub/pade

Papers on MPI experience: ftp://aurora.cs.msstae.edu/pub/reports/Message-Passing

Chaco load-balancing package. Bruce Hndrickson and Robert Leland of Sandia National Laboratories at bahendr@cs.sandia.gov or rwlelan@cs.sandia.gov.

TOP/DOMDEC load-balancing packagefrom Charbel Farhat and Horst Simon at NASA Ames Research Center: charbel@boulder.colorado.edu.

arc.unm.edu has a large number of packages usch as Sage, etc. available for anonymous ftp.

Sources for object-oriented languages:

CC++:

httpd://www/compbio.caltech.edu

cc++-bugs@compbio.caltech.edu

UC++:

N. B.Quin@qmw.ac.uk

ABC++:

billo@torolab2.vnet.ibm.edu

CHARM++:

httpd://charm.cs.uiuc.edu

charmbugs@cs.uiuc.edu

μC++:

usytem@plg.uwaterloo.ca

ESP:

problems@cryptic.mcc.com

Index

Disk Instructions

The diskette that accompanies this book contains program code for parallel programming applications. The files consist of C code and header files. These files can only be run in conjunction with a C/C++ compiler, such as the ones distributed by Borland and Microsoft. You will need such a compiler in order to use the files. The algorithms and applications of each file are explained in the text of the book.

See preceding page for disk instructions.

DISK WARRANTY

This software is protected by both United States copyright law and international copyright treaty provision. You must treat this software just like a book, except that you may copy it into a computer in order to be used and you may make archival copies of the software for the sole purpose of backing up our software and protecting your investment from loss.

By saying "just like a book," McGraw-Hill means, for example, that this software may be used by any number of people and may be freely moved from one computer location to another, so long as there is no possibility of its being used at one location or on one computer while it also is being used at another. Just as a book cannot be read by two different people in two different places at the same time, neither can the software be used by two different people in two different places at the same time (unless, of course, McGraw-Hill's copyright is being violated).

LIMITED WARRANTY

McGraw-Hill takes great care to provide you with top-quality software, thoroughly checked to prevent virus infections. McGraw-Hill warrants the physical diskette(s) contained herein to be free of defects in materials and workmanship for a period of sixty days from the purchase date. If McGraw-Hill receives written notification within the warranty period of defects in materials or workmanship, and such notification is determined by McGraw-Hill to be correct, McGraw-Hill will replace the defective diskette(s). Send requests to:

> McGraw-Hill
> Customer Services
> P.O. Box 545
> Blacklick, OH 43004-0545

The entire and exclusive liability and remedy for breach of this Limited Warranty shall be limited to replacement of defective diskette(s) and shall not include or extend to any claim for or right to cover any other damages, including but not limited to, loss of profit, data, or use of the software, or special, incidental, or consequential damages or other similar claims, even if McGraw-Hill has been specifically advised of the possibility of such damages. In no event will McGraw-Hill's liability for any damages to you or any other person ever exceed the lower of suggested list price or actual price paid for the license to use the software, regardless of any form of the claim.

McGRAW-HILL SPECIFICALLY DISCLAIMS ALL OTHER WARRANTIES, EXPRESS OR IMPLIED, INCLUDING, BUT NOT LIMITED TO, ANY IMPLIED WARRANTY OF MERCHANTABILITY OR FITNESS FOR A PARTICULAR PURPOSE.

Specifically, McGraw-Hill makes no representation or warranty that the software is fit for any particular purpose and any implied warranty of merchantability is limited to the sixty-day duration of the Limited Warranty covering the physical diskette(s) only (and not the software) and is otherwise expressly and specifically disclaimed.

This limited warranty gives you specific legal rights; you may have others which may vary from state to state. Some states do not allow the exclusion of incidental or consequential damages, or the limitation on how long an implied warranty lasts, so some of the above may not apply to you.